Schools Betrayed

Schools Betrayed

Roots of Failure in Inner-City Education

KATHRYN M. NECKERMAN

THE UNIVERSITY OF CHICAGO PRESS   CHICAGO AND LONDON

The University of Chicago Press, Chicago 60637
The University of Chicago Press, Ltd., London
© 2007 by The University of Chicago
All rights reserved. Published 2007
Paperback edition 2010
Printed in the United States of America
19 18 17 16 15 14 13 12 11 10   2 3 4 5 6

ISBN-13: 978-0-226-56960-4 (cloth)
ISBN-13: 978-0-226-56961-1 (paper)
ISBN-10: 0-226-56960-8 (cloth)
ISBN-10: 0-226-56961-6 (paper)

Library of Congress Cataloging-in-Publication Data

Neckerman, Kathryn M.
    Schools betrayed : roots of failure in inner-city education / Kathryn M. Neckerman.
        p.   cm.
    Includes bibliographic references and index.
    ISBN-13: 978-0-226-56960-4 (hardcover : alk. paper)
    ISBN-10: 0-226-56960-8 (hardcover : alk. paper)
    1. Education, Urban—Illinois—Chicago—History—20th century.   2. Racism in
education—Illinois—Chicago—History—20th Century.   3. Urban Schools—Illinois—
Chicago—History—20th century.   I. Title.
    LC5133.C4N43 2007
    370.9773'11—dc22

                                                                        2006101815

⊗ The paper used in this publication meets the minimum requirements of the American
National Standard for Information Sciences—Permanence of Paper for Printed Library
Materials, ANSI Z39.48-1992.

Contents

Preface

R ecent education reforms take aim at racial and class inequality in
public schools by demanding that they raise all children to a common standard of achievement. There is an admirable impulse here. For
too long, low-income and minority students have received a substandard
education. Fixing urban schools has become more critical now with recent changes in the job market. In our society, the educated stand on one
side of a widening economic gap, the uneducated on the other. At a time
when it is difficult to find a good job without a college degree, more than
half of inner-city youth do not even graduate from high school. Those
who do graduate are ill equipped to compete in the global economy.
Poor schooling condemns them to permanent economic marginality.

Yet when we demand that schools reach a common standard of
achievement, we are trying to do a new thing with an old institution. Urban schools were never designed to produce equality of achievement. If
there was a standard of equity, it was simply that school funding and resources should be distributed fairly—and even that standard was seldom
met. When an institution is created with one purpose in mind, it is not
easy to redirect it. Educators talk of reinventing urban schools: indeed,
in every city there are exciting experiments with governance change or
school choice or new curricula. But these innovations are usually short
lived, just as a tree branch, pulled aside, springs back to its old position
when released.

We have not taken seriously the staying power of institutions such as
the urban schools. An institution is more than a rulebook and an organization chart. It has stability. In part, this stability is political: an
institution creates constituencies who benefit from it and have a stake
in defending it. An institution's stability is also cognitive: beliefs and

expectations and patterns of behavior grow up around the institution, so much so that other arrangements become unthinkable. The institution recedes into the realm of the taken-for-granted; it becomes invisible. It takes history to make institutions visible again—to uncover the decisions, made early on, that foreclosed alternatives and made the expedient seem inevitable.

Schools Betrayed is a history of inner-city schooling. The narrative begins in 1900, before there was an inner city in the sense we know it now. Set in Chicago, the book follows the city's schools over the decades as school officials struggled with problems of politics, budgets, and personnel. It shows how their decisions reached into the classroom and why they were so damaging for inner-city teachers and students. Its most basic point is that the problems of inner-city schooling were not inevitable—they were the product of school policy choices made in the early twentieth century.

The history of inner-city schooling is, of course, also a history of race relations. The book shows how race came to matter in schools that had once been racially integrated. At the turn of the century, African Americans were a small and often overlooked minority in a city teeming with immigrant "races." By 1960, the end of the period under study, almost half the city's public school students were black, the schools were highly segregated and unequal, and the system as a whole was characterized by bitter racial division. The chilling thing about this history, as we will see, is how few of the schools' policies were explicitly biased against black students. Even race-neutral policies had racially disparate consequences when enacted in the context of racial inequality in city and schools.

Although I call it a history, the book is not a chronological narrative but rather a series of layered stories. The first several accounts describe conditions in the city; the rest of the book examines the schools themselves. An interdisciplinary history infused with social science, mostly sociology (my own home discipline), this work draws from a score of distinct areas of research. The disadvantage of writing across such a variety of subfields, of course, is exposing oneself as a rank amateur in each. The account of each field is necessarily selective, and specialists will all find things to fault. So be it. The book would be poorer without the insights of these varied fields.

With today's inner-city schools in such bad condition, one might ask why we should worry about their history. Certainly, history is no substitute for empirical study of present-day schooling and school reform.

In my view, history has two contributions to make here. First, it offers a tonic against the caricatures of the past that are often deployed in school reform debates. Too often, nostalgia gives a false resonance to reform proposals that may have little else to recommend them. The encounter with a richer and more complicated history makes these simple stories untenable—as the past takes on its own integrity and complexity, it is more difficult to appropriate it to serve today's ends. The second contribution, as suggested before, is to lay bare the institutional character of the inner-city schools. This work can help identify obstacles to change and show us where we may have neglected alternatives.

Acknowledgments

My first thanks are due to William Julius Wilson, who had an indelible effect on me, as on so many at Chicago during the 1980s, and who remains a beacon of scholarly integrity and engagement. Without his steady support throughout graduate school and beyond, this research could never have been carried out. The project got its start in a seminar taught by Mary Brinton, Thomas DiPrete, and David Grusky. Along with Brinton and Wilson, George Steinmetz provided valuable guidance on the dissertation that resulted. As the only historian on my committee, James Grossman brought to bear his extensive knowledge of Chicago, and made a key suggestion, although he didn't put it quite this way: do good sociology instead of bad history.

The Spencer Foundation provided crucial support with a Dissertation Fellowship, followed later by a National Academy of Education/Spencer Postdoctoral Fellowship. Along with funding, Spencer is wise enough to bestow connections to the community of education researchers, both junior and senior, and I gained a great deal from the stimulating meetings of Spencer fellows hosted by the National Academy of Education. At Columbia, the Department of Sociology offered practical support, and Monica Gisolfi, Jennifer Lee, Paolo Parigi, Kat Rakowsky, Colby Ristow (Chicago), and Mark Wilkins (Penn) all provided resourceful research assistance; Anthony Browne and Kathy Kaufman also worked with me on related papers. I am grateful as well to staff at the Chicago Historical Society (now the Chicago History Museum), the University of Chicago Special Collections, the Balch Institute for Ethnic Studies (now part of the Historical Society of Pennsylvania), and the Gottesman Libraries at Teachers College, Columbia University.

A number of people have read all or part of the manuscript at some point during its passage. I particularly want to thank Peter Bearman,

Prudence Carter, Elisabeth Clemens, Jack Dougherty, Herbert Gans, Mark Gould, Hiroshi Ishida, William McAllister, Suzanne Model, Kate Neckerman, and Christopher Weiss. Seminars at Brown University and the New York Sociologists of Education provided much-needed occasions to try out ideas. Robert Dreeben and Michael Katz read the manuscript for the University of Chicago Press and together applied the right mix of appreciation and goad. Of course, responsibility for errors remains mine alone.

At the Press, I have been fortunate enough to work with the astonishing Doug Mitchell. Doug "got" the book before I did; his enthusiasm carried me through the rough patches, and his tact and patience gave me the space to write the book I wanted to write. Sandra Hazel edited the manuscript with subtlety and precision, and Peter Cavagnaro wrested away a too-mystifying title. Many thanks also to Tim McGovern, Rob Hunt, Natalie Smith, and Joe Claude for their professionalism throughout the production process.

Through a long period of writing and not writing, colleagues, friends, and family put up with me, agreed that I was almost done when I wasn't, sympathized and brainstormed with me, and told me just to send the damn thing in. At Columbia, the Institute for Social and Economic Research and Policy has been a sustaining home base over the last six years; I thank everyone there who has made it such a vibrant community. Parents at my son's school became both support network and friends, and I feel very fortunate to have this connection. My family—from New York to Virginia to South Carolina to Arizona—kept me grounded, and my debt to them cannot be measured. My son, for whom this book has been a kind of shadow sibling, will now, at last, grow older than it is. He is glad. So am I.

Introduction

More than forty years ago, Kenneth Clark published his book *Dark Ghetto,* an account of life in New York City's Harlem neighborhood. In it he described in stark detail the deficits of Harlem's segregated schools. These schools had poor facilities and were short of books and supplies. Staff turnover was high, and many classes were taught by substitute or unlicensed teachers. Teachers had low expectations, believing that students' achievement was limited by low intelligence or cultural deprivation. Standardized test scores were low, and the longer students remained in school, the further below the norm their achievement fell. Poor morale, high dropout rates, and widespread discipline problems made matters worse. Clark, a psychologist, drew attention to the interpersonal dynamics in the schools. "The dominant and disturbing fact about the ghetto schools," he wrote, "is that the teachers and the students regard each other as adversaries. Under these conditions the teachers are reluctant to teach and the students retaliate and resist learning."[1]

What strikes the present-day reader is the familiarity of this portrait. With a few deft strokes, Clark described conditions that have troubled inner-city schools for more than four decades.[2] Of course, not all inner-city schools are this bleak—there are notable success stories—but these problems remain widespread and have come to seem characteristic of inner-city education. Their continuity despite several decades of public

scrutiny and school reform suggests that they have become entrenched—
or, to use a sociologist's term, institutionalized. Their staying power
comes from the rules, structures, beliefs, expectations, and practices of
the urban schools. To understand and remedy the problems of inner-city
schooling, both the material deprivation and the relational difficulties,
we need to understand the institution that generates these problems.

This book seeks to illuminate the roots of failure in inner-city education. At its most general level, this work challenges two fallacies. The
first is the view that the failure of inner-city schools was inevitable given
the concentration of economic and racial disadvantage in the inner city.
The second is the view that blames the problems of inner-city schools
on the faults of individuals—on incompetent or racist teachers, on dys-
functional families or unmotivated students. In response to both, I argue
that the problems of inner-city schooling are the legacy of school policy
choices made decades ago. This book traces these choices and their consequences over six decades, starting in the early twentieth century when
the inner-city ghettos were just beginning to form.[3] In this case study,
I focus on the schools of Chicago, which faced many of the same troubles
as the Harlem schools that Kenneth Clark profiled.

As we begin this foray into the past, we can consult the reports of
other recent travelers. Over the last twenty years, a number of historians
and social scientists have sought the historical roots of contemporary urban problems such as residential segregation, racial and class inequality,
and political division.[4] This work highlights a number of developments in
American cities that might have created problems for inner-city schools,
and are thus essential starting points for our inquiry.

The first of these developments is the economic and demographic
change that occurred in northern cities during the 1940s and 1950s. The
suburbs grew rapidly, drawing white and middle-class residents out of the
city. Manufacturing and other basic industries declined or relocated outside the central city. Black southerners, displaced by the mechanization
of cotton farming and drawn north by their hope of economic opportunity and political rights, crowded into growing ghettos. These developments are likely to have shaped urban schools. If the tax base declined
when industry and middle-class families left, school funding may also
have fallen. Given the city's changing demographic composition, big-city
schools may have faced growing numbers of poor and disadvantaged students at the same time their financial resources were dwindling.[5]

Also during this time, northern black workers were coming to terms
with racial discrimination. Black migrants were eager to escape the

racial oppression of the South, but northern cities had their own racial barriers, more subtle but no less real. The northern-born children of the Great Migration saw their parents' hopes of economic progress frustrated during the 1920s, and even more during the Great Depression. This cycle began again when a new wave of migrants came north during and after World War II. The problems of disadvantaged black workers deepened as industrial production was scaled back after 1945, and as middle-class black families moved out of ghetto neighborhoods. Inner-city youth lost touch with the men and women who could have linked them to the mainstream economy and given them hope of attaining success through conventional means. In this context, inner-city youth might reasonably have questioned whether education would help them get ahead economically.[6]

Over the same period, race relations were changing. Residential segregation intensified over time and became inscribed in the built environment of the city. As the ghetto grew, neighborhood racial transitions were often met by violence. This racial segregation and hostility may have fostered what anthropologists have termed an oppositional culture. This culture, in the work of John U. Ogbu and Signithia Fordham, frames academic effort as a betrayal of racial identity—as "acting white"—and discourages students from making a commitment to their education. In Ogbu's and Fordham's analysis, this cultural framework can be triggered by contact with racial prejudice and animosity. Thus, the racial segregation and hostility of the first half of the century might have fostered a cultural perspective detrimental to academic success.[7]

These three accounts, involving school funding and demographics, labor market discrimination, and oppositional culture, link the life of the city with the character of inner-city education. A fourth draws from histories of twentieth-century urban schooling. Of particular note is research concerning how schools responded to the rising enrollment of working-class and minority students. Specifics vary, but the thrust of the story is that academic standards fell over time, lowering the quality of education for all students, especially those who were poor, immigrant, or black. Some historians, for instance, write that working-class or minority students were channeled into lower-track or vocational classes. Others report that academic curricula were "dumbed down" and standards for promotion were diluted. Thus, the troubles of inner-city schools could reflect misguided or racist school policies that denied low-income and minority students a rigorous education and sent a message of low expectations.[8]

These swatches of history bring us successively closer to an understanding of inner-city schooling. What might be called the "urban decline" story describes key changes in the economy and demographics of the city, but doesn't explicitly link these trends to what happened in the classroom. The accounts of labor market discrimination and oppositional culture might explain the anger and disaffection that some inner-city youth displayed in school. Yet schooling is an interaction between students and the school; we miss half the story when we consider students only. The histories of curriculum, tracking, and other aspects of school policy take us a step further by describing school conditions to which students might have responded. When we delve into these histories, however, we learn more about "policy talk" than "institutional practice," to use David Tyack's terms. Elite discourse and broad policy directives may not be a reliable guide to what happened inside the school.[9]

This book begins with the premise that classroom relations, in particular the antagonism and distrust that Kenneth Clark observed, offer a key to the troubles of inner-city education. In an immediate sense, teacher and students act together to shape the character of classroom experience. Their interaction, however, is shaped by conditions outside the classroom. As we will see, classroom relations in inner-city schools began to sour because school policies undercut essential supports for the work that teacher and students did together. This history shows how those school policies came about, why they were particularly devastating in the inner-city schools, and how they reached into the classroom to taint teacher-student interaction.

Race, Classroom Dynamics, and Inner-City Schooling

Underlying the dynamics of inner-city schools are changes in two core dimensions of classroom life. The first is authority relations between teacher and students: the extent to which students trust the teacher and are willing to follow her direction. Authority and trust have a transparent connection to the antagonism between teachers and students that Clark and others have noted. The second is engagement in learning, in other words, the degree of attention and effort that students bring to their schoolwork. Authority and engagement are connected. Clearly, engagement suffers when discipline problems arise. Classroom conflict can be noisy and disruptive, distracting students and stealing instructional time. Engagement also cycles back to shape authority and trust. If students are interested in the schoolwork, they become self-motivated. The more the lesson pulls them, the less the teacher needs to push. Engaging work has a longer-term benefit as well: it creates a reservoir of goodwill and trust on which the teacher can draw in the future.

We often think of authority and engagement as reflecting the individual qualities of teacher and students. The teacher who commands respect through character or intellect is a stock figure in novel and memoir, along with other idealized types: the riveting lecturer, the compassionate advocate, the drill sergeant. Just as commonplace is the perception of difference among individual students. We readily apprehend that some students are well-behaved and industrious, others lazy or disruptive. Schools heighten these perceptions by exposing teachers to multiple students and students to multiple teachers. Yet these differences are real, and they matter.

But individual qualities are not the whole story. Authority and engagement also reflect decisions made outside the classroom, often outside the school, that limit what teachers and students can do together. Authority rests in part on the legitimacy of the school: on how well the school conforms to the institutionalized expectations of students and parents. Political battles over education may reverberate inside the classroom, raising doubts about the school's legitimacy and thereby weakening the teacher's authority. School policy also conditions engagement. Teachers work within parameters set at the school or district level, including the choice of curricula, the size and composition of classes, the temporal organization of schooling, and the character of teacher training. These parameters may either support or curtail teachers' efforts to interest and motivate their students.

Beginning in the 1930s, school policies changed in ways that undercut authority and engagement. These policy changes had their most negative impact on inner-city schools, either because the policies themselves were inequitable or because social and economic conditions made them particularly damaging for low-income black students. In Chicago, these changes in school policy and practice occurred at about the same time that a racial gap in school outcomes began to widen and that teachers began to complain of discipline problems in the city's predominantly black schools. In other words, the period between the 1930s and the early 1960s was when the characteristic problems of inner-city schooling began to appear.

Policy change took place in three domains. The first was a set of policies dealing with race. At the turn of the century, few black children attended segregated schools. By 1930, in part because of school officials' actions, racial segregation was nearly complete in elementary school and widespread in high school, and by 1940 the city's segregated black and white schools were demonstrably unequal. Activists in the black community, followed by liberal and left-wing white and interracial organizations, pressed school officials to redress this inequality. The district took a few steps to improve black schools and to promote racial tolerance among students and teachers. For the most part, however, school officials denied responsibility for, and did little to alter, conditions of racial segregation and inequality. Legal challenge to these conditions proved futile, and so long as black Chicagoans remained a marginalized minority, there were few political limits on the actions of school officials. But there were political costs as well as educational ones. Racial segregation and inequality violated the universalism expected of public agencies, as well as the schools' more specific responsibility for the well-being of children. For the black community, this history eroded the legitimacy of the public schools.

The second domain concerned vocational education. During the nineteenth century, Chicago's public schools did little to set students on a trajectory to the world of work. That role was taken by apprenticeships and private training schools, and by the informal networks that channeled so many workers to their jobs. This state of affairs changed after 1900, when the public schools created an elaborate array of vocational curricula and specialized technical schools, and tried to organize student motivation around these pathways into the labor market. These new programs were aimed especially at youth who were not college bound, who before had had little reason to stay in school. Even at the outset, because of racial discrimination in school and labor markets, these programs did not work well for black students. Then, beginning in the late 1930s, black students' opportunities for vocational education were limited further when the district began to create a two-tiered system of vocational education. Many black students, confined to the lower tier of this new system, were denied the present interest and future reward that high-quality technical and commercial training could offer. Their engagement in school suffered as a result.

The third domain was remedial education. Early in the century, Chicago's public schools did little to respond to low-achieving students, who were simply held back until they dropped out. As local educators began to view school failure as a problem, they experimented with measures to help low-achieving students catch up with their peers. By the late 1930s, however, their ambitious vision had been trumped by fiscal and political reality. Rather than promote learning among low-achieving students, the Chicago schools created channels so that these students could move through school with others of their own age. Black students were at high risk of school failure because of their poverty, and also because of racial inequality in the Chicago schools. The schools' failure to provide meaningful remedial education was costly for both achievement and motivation, denying many inner-city students the reward of growing mastery.

Plan of the Book

Schools Betrayed is a case study of the public schools of Chicago, a city chosen partly for its rich base of documentary evidence. The advantage of a case study as the form for this book's analysis is the depth and dimensionality of the portrait it allows. A single case can spotlight the teachers and bureaucrats who carried out (or thwarted) school policies, as well as the edifice of budgets and administration within which schooling occurred. To explore the practice underlying "policy talk," this fine-grained focus is essential. As with any case study, however, we must keep in mind that Chicago was distinctive in some ways. Although all northern cities saw the formation of racial ghettos, Chicago was very highly segregated, and its black community may have been more elaborate institutionally as a result. There were other differences as well. The city's Democratic political machine was unusually strong. Its schools were conservative pedagogically and reluctant to experiment. Chicago's diversified economy moderated the impact of industrial decline after World War II, when the city suffered less than single-industry towns such as Detroit.[10]

Yet at the same time, Chicago had a great deal in common with other northeastern and midwestern cities. There are parallels in the economic and demographic histories of these cities, and in the development of their public schools. Their leading educators were linked by professional organizations and networks, by journals and meetings; these school leaders faced similar problems with the same toolkit of ideas and solutions. Some unions and civil rights organizations were also linked across cities, sharing information and strategies. On different battlegrounds, these players fought similar battles. Moreover, there are striking similarities across cities in descriptions of inner-city education. Although details may vary, it seems unlikely that the historical account presented here applies only to Chicago.

The time period of the book, from 1900 to 1960, captures the years in which the distinctive features of inner-city schooling emerged. At the beginning of this period, Chicago's black community was small and scattered; there was no "inner city" in the sense we mean it now. By 1960 a large racial ghetto had formed, and Chicago's segregated black schools exhibited all the characteristic features that Kenneth Clark found in the schools of Harlem. Although the focus will be on the years between 1930 and 1960, we will go back to the turn of the century to find the roots of key school policies and practices.[11]

To highlight the role of race in the origins of inner-city schooling, the book compares the education of African-American children with that of white children, specifically southern and eastern European immigrant children. To sharpen the comparison, I focus on non-Jewish immigrants.[12] (Throughout the book, I refer to this group as "immigrants" or, when distinguishing by ethnicity, to "Italians," "Poles," and so on.) This comparison is telling because of what African Americans and immigrants had in common at the beginning of the century: their poverty, the timing of their entry into the city, their marginalized position in the labor market, and their outsider status within city and school. This initial similarity lets us focus on how race shaped their trajectories between 1900 and 1960. Of particular importance for these contrasting paths are racial prejudice and discrimination in Chicago by employers, labor unions, landlords, and school personnel; the deep poverty and racial oppression of the South; and the continuing in-migration of black southerners.

The book draws on a variety of evidence. One invaluable resource was the census microdata available from Integrated Public Use Microdata Samples. The IPUMS provides consistently coded samples of individual-level data from the federal decennial census between 1900 and 1960, with the exception of 1930.[13] I used these data to document changes in the racial/ethnic and socioeconomic characteristics of students, and also to examine patterns of labor market opportunity for black and immigrant workers. The samples available for Chicago alone were usually too small to provide reliable estimates, so the analyses reported here use a larger "city sample," which includes samples of the population from all central cities in metropolitan areas in the Northeast and Midwest. When the Chicago-only sample was large enough for analysis, comparison showed little difference between the results for Chicago and those for the city sample. Other quantitative evidence includes a 1925 survey of industrial workers in Chicago, and the budgets, enrollment figures, and graduation lists published in the annual Chicago Board of Education *Proceedings.*

Historians, political scientists, and sociologists have produced an extensive secondary literature on Chicago politics, communities, and schools, which proved a vital resource for this research. Mary Herrick's *The Chicago Schools,* a detailed history written by a sharp-eyed Chicago teacher, activist, and researcher, deserves special note. So does Michael Homel's *Down from Equality,* a carefully documented study of black education in Chicago during the interwar years. In addition, I drew on master's theses and doctoral dissertations written over the years by students at local universities. The Chicago Board of Education's annual reports were an important resource, as were surveys of the schools led by George Strayer in 1932 and by Robert Havighurst in 1964. A useful complement to the official reports was the *Chicago Schools Journal,* a magazine for local educators published by the Chicago Normal School beginning in 1906 under the title *Educational Bi-Monthly.* Newspaper sources include the *Chicago Defender,* the leading newspaper of Chicago's black community, and the Chicago Foreign Language Press Survey; the latter compiled translated excerpts from Chicago immigrant newspapers. Finally, I used materials archived at the University of Chicago's Regenstein Library Special Collections, the Chicago Historical Society, the Balch Institute in Philadelphia, and the library of Teachers College, Columbia University.

Even with these rich resources, there are gaps. The evidence about immigrant schooling was thin, particularly in the 1940s and 1950s. Many documentary sources did not identify the social class background of students and schools, making it difficult to know how school experiences differed by class. Evidence about classroom life was uneven: more information was available about some periods than others, and most of that from the perspective of teachers or administrators, not students. We can glean a surprising amount from this evidence, but inevitably there is some guesswork.

In its organization, the book moves from the outside in. It begins with the external environment of the schools, then considers school policies and practices, then enters the classroom. Chapter 1 examines the urban decline narrative, which relates the problems of inner-city schooling to changes after World War II in the economic and demographic conditions of northern cities. Chapter 2 describes patterns of racial discrimination in labor markets, comparing the experiences of black and immigrant workers to understand how discrimination might have shaped black students' disaffection with school. Chapter 3 compares orientations to education in black and immigrant communities, using the organization of status as a window into ethnic differences in the meaning of education. By themselves, I conclude, these accounts cannot explain the problems of inner-city schooling, but each provides an important layer of the story.

The book then examines school policy and practice. Chapter 4 considers how Chicago's public schools dealt with race, recounting the decisions that led to segregation, then to inequality, as well as efforts to promote intercultural education and improve race relations in a district splintered along racial lines. Chapter 5 tracks the rise of vocational education, showing how school officials preserved the economic value of these credentials by sacrificing open access to top-tier vocational training. Chapter 6 documents a lively period of experimentation as local educators sought ways to remediate school failure—an endeavor in which standardized tests played a dual and contradictory role. Finally, chapter 7 brings these strands of policy into the inner-city classroom, linking them to the dynamics of interaction between teachers and students.

The book closes with some reflections on the implications of this work for the history of urban education, and for public policy to address the problems of inner-city schools.

CHAPTER ONE

Urban Decline

This chapter considers the simplest explanation for the troubles of inner-city schooling: less money and more needy students. Based on well-known economic and demographic changes of the period after World War II, this explanation posits that school resources declined because the tax base eroded as industry and middle-class families moved out of the city. At the same time, the schools faced an influx of disadvantaged students because economic conditions deteriorated and impoverished southern black migrants moved into the city, while the more affluent families moved out. If true, this account would still leave us with questions: why, for instance, did the problems of inner-city schooling take the specific form they did? However, at least for Chicago through 1960, trends in school funding and student disadvantage do not match popular conceptions of the postwar period. This chapter first examines trends in school resources, relating these trends to the economic history of the city and to institutional change in the schools. The following sections examine demographic change among students.[1]

Urban History and School Funding

To place Chicago's trajectory in context, it is useful to begin with a quick sketch of the city's history. Chicago was incorporated in 1833, and very

early on became a regional center for trade and transportation. Within a
few decades, a canal to the Mississippi River was completed, multiple rail-
road lines were routed into the city, and a major harbor and extensive wa-
terways were under construction. The Chicago Board of Trade, founded
only fifteen years after the city itself, reflected the city's rapid emergence
as a clearinghouse for agricultural products. In the late nineteenth century, with this infrastructure in place, the young city began to annex
nearby townships, more than quadrupling its area within a few decades.
At the time, much of this land was sparsely settled, but with its industrial
base and its advantageous location on transportation routes, the city was
poised for growth. City officials promoted new investment in manufacturing with a series of industrial districts, including the Central Manufacturing District, set up in 1890. Industry and population grew in tandem as
immigrants flooded into the new factory neighborhoods. Between 1870
and 1930, the city added a million residents every two decades, an arc
that continued until the start of the Great Depression in 1929 (fig. 1.1).[2]

The economic boom caused by World War II revived the city's economy. Like other cities, however, Chicago suffered some postwar decline
in the manufacturing and transportation sectors that had been its engine
of growth. Technological advancement, urban renewal policies, and the
growth of the suburbs shifted economic activity away from the inner city.
Older factories and transportation facilities near the downtown were
abandoned. Canals and rail yards, now obsolete, were replaced with
trucking facilities on the outskirts of the city. Most of Chicago's fabled
meatpacking plants closed during the 1950s. New expressways displaced

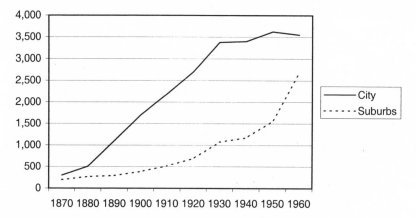

FIGURE 1.1 Population of Chicago city and suburbs (in thousands). Source: Chicago Community Fact Book Consortium, *Local Community Fact Book*.

the smaller factories near the city center; three thousand jobs were lost in the city's garment district alone. Overall, the city lost more than 132,000 manufacturing jobs between 1947 and 1958, while surrounding suburbs gained slightly. With the shift of more affluent residents to the suburbs, the city's flagship department stores lost much of their business to the new suburban shopping centers, sparking concern about urban blight in the downtown district.[3]

However, we should not exaggerate the economic downturn of the postwar period. With its diversified economy, Chicago was less vulnerable to structural economic change than were single-industry towns such as Detroit. The city retained its central position in trade and transportation networks. By 1950, it was a hub for truck and air traffic; its Midway Airport was the busiest in the world until it yielded that position to O'Hare International Airport, another Chicago facility. Moreover, Chicago's residents grew more prosperous during the postwar period. With union gains and a rise in the minimum wage, real earnings more than doubled and rates of home ownership increased. City government shared in this prosperity. Local property tax revenue rose by more than 70 percent in real terms between 1948 and 1960.[4]

Just as important, school resources did not depend on the city's economic fortunes alone. The district's capacity to support education also reflected school enrollment, city politics, and state aid to local school districts. Over the first few decades of the century, school budgets were strained by rapid growth in enrollment (see fig. 1.2), which between 1900 and 1935 grew by an average of more than 5,700 students—the equivalent

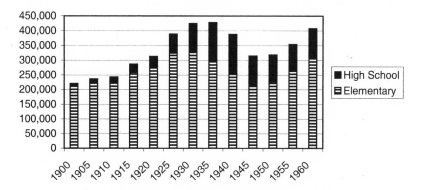

FIGURE 1.2 October daily average membership in the Chicago Public Schools. Source: Chicago Board of Education, annual *Proceedings* volumes. Note: Junior high students in 1925 and 1930 are allocated based on grade to elementary (grades 7 and 8) or high school (grade 9).

of six or seven schools—each year. Not surprisingly, the Chicago Board of Education's annual reports were filled with blueprints, construction plans, and anxious calculations. To house students while new schools were being built, the school board rented space in commercial buildings, set up portable classrooms, and ran existing schools on double shifts. The burden of rising enrollment was compounded by the growing share of high school students, who were more costly to educate. The proportion of high school students in the overall student population rose from 4.5 percent in 1900 to 30.1 percent in 1935.[5]

One reason enrollment grew so rapidly was the expansion in the city's population, discussed above. Another factor was a rise in enrollment rates, or the proportion of school-aged children who were enrolled. Compulsory education in Chicago dates from 1883, but enforcement was lax at first; in 1888 there were only three truant officers for the entire city. After 1900, however, the state passed new laws restricting child labor and expanding the ages of compulsory school attendance. The city also strengthened enforcement, employing 40 truant officers by 1908. For children whose age fell within the compulsory-attendance range of seven through thirteen years, school enrollment became nearly universal by 1910 (see fig. 1.3). These measures also affected youth above the compulsory age of fourteen years in that the schools began to require regular attendance (130 days within the school year) and completion of fifth grade (then sixth, then eighth) before students would be eligible for a work

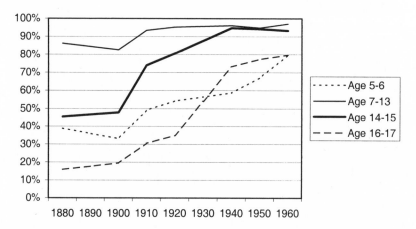

FIGURE 1.3 School enrollment rates by age. Source: IPUMS city sample. Note: Figures for 1890 and 1930 are interpolated.

permit.[6] At the same time, younger adolescents were being squeezed out of the labor market. Technological developments such as the telephone eliminated many jobs for young workers. Most apprenticeships became restricted to youth aged sixteen years and over. Credentials requirements rose for other jobs, particularly among clerical occupations. And during the Great Depression, even older adolescents stayed in school because it was so difficult for them to find work.[7]

To pay for educating its growing enrollment, the Board of Education had revenues from several sources. The district received rent from land it had been deeded in 1833, when the city was incorporated. This rental income amounted to little, however; the city fathers had squandered most of the land immediately by selling it at fire-sale prices. Some tenants of the remaining property—valuable land in the downtown business district—were granted ninety-nine-year leases at a fixed nominal rent, which with inflation soon became absurdly low. The schools also received revenue from the state government, but this, too, was minimal. Between 1871 and 1907, the State of Illinois gave Chicago's public schools a fixed allocation of $1 million a year—$1.5 million after 1907—which by the 1920s provided only about 6 percent of the total budget. In 1927, the state began to allocate funds based on average daily attendance. Its flat grant of $9 per student brought Chicago about $3.8 million in 1930. Adjusted for inflation, and for the changing composition of enrollment, state aid per pupil was actually slightly lower in 1930 than in 1900.[8]

During the early twentieth century, the Board of Education drew about 90 percent of its revenue from the local property tax. Thus, the resources available for education were contingent on the city's property assessment and tax collection practices. Assessments were highly political; ward committeemen were rumored to lower assessments as favors to constituents. Some businesses, including the large utility companies, avoided paying taxes altogether. Once revenues had been collected, some were diverted by unscrupulous school officials and board members. The most notorious administration was that of Mayor William Hale Thompson, who reportedly told the school board upon his re-election in 1919, "We're at the feed box now—and we're going to feed." During this time, according to Mary Herrick, "non-existent companies got huge contracts. School principals were directed by calls from Board members to order unwanted, unneeded equipment at quadrupled prices. Furniture was taken from schools to Board members' summer homes." Few officeholders were quite as shameless as Thompson, but corruption was common.[9]

The district's budgetary woes came to a head in the early 1930s, the result of unwise borrowing and some spectacular bad luck. The school board could legally borrow up to 75 percent of the property taxes that were expected to be collected in the following year. But Superintendent William McAndrew, who served from 1924 to 1927, began to borrow two years in advance, and the board's debt mounted quickly. The situation was manageable as long as the expected taxes were actually collected. The district hit a snag, however, when the county's 1927 assessment was challenged in court. Clearly, something was wrong: assessed valuation in the city had risen by only $320 million since 1915, although building permits were filed for nearly $900 million worth of construction in 1921–24 alone. An independent evaluation found virtually identical properties which differed in their assessed value by a factor of 10. On average, the county's assessments were only 31 percent of the independently assessed value. The State Tax Commission called for a new valuation, which was completed in April 1930. By the time tax bills were finally mailed, the stock market had crashed and the city was in fiscal chaos. In 1933, the Board of Education imposed desperate cost-cutting measures: shortening the school year, laying off 1,400 teachers, paying others in scrip, assigning elementary principals to two schools instead of one, closing the junior college and junior high schools, and eliminating household arts, manual training, and physical education in elementary schools. Despite these cuts, the district's debt and interest charges continued to rise. In 1935, debt service was $20 million, or 28 percent of the schools' total budget.[10]

As Julia Wrigley has described, the response to this fiscal crisis highlights the influence of politics on school funding. The ascendancy of the Democratic political machine in 1931 rested on support from both business and labor. With a Board of Education appointed by the mayor, the school administration was closely tied to the machine; this was particularly so during the 1930s and early 1940s under James McCahey, president of the school board from 1933 to 1946, and William H. Johnson, superintendent from 1936 to 1946. The schools' retrenchment plan, developed in 1933 by the school board and the mayor, reflected the interests of both business and labor. Business approved the stringent cuts in school spending, while the Chicago Federation of Labor supported the plan because it spared the jobs of school janitors, well-paid patronage employees who were affiliated with the union. During the 1930s, Chicago spent only 67 percent of its budget on instruction, compared with 78 percent in other large cities.[11]

The budgetary pressures on the district began to abate after 1935, and the financial picture improved significantly in the postwar period. Reflecting the decline in fertility during the 1930s, enrollment fell by 25 percent between 1935 and 1945, reducing costs accordingly. Although the postwar "baby boom" brought enrollment up again in the 1950s, the number of students remained below its Depression-era peak. The city's financial condition also improved. Although Chicago lost some of its industrial base after World War II, its property tax revenues continued to rise over the 1950s. State aid rose as well. The state's aid formula favored small downstate districts, and spending on education remained modest; nationally, Illinois ranked near the bottom in state education funding relative to wealth. However, the per-pupil allocation increased to $47 per year by 1955, with a supplement for high schools of $2 per student.[12]

School governance also improved. Johnson, a notoriously corrupt superintendent, was ousted in 1946 along with all but two members of the Board of Education. He was succeeded by Herold Hunt (1947–53) and then by Benjamin Willis (1953–67), both credited with running a relatively clean administration. Hunt's arrival coincided with a change in school governance that reform groups had urged for decades: the appointment of a general superintendent with authority over all aspects of the district administration. This new structure replaced a tripartite system in which the superintendent of schools shared authority with a board attorney and a business manager. With this change in governance structure, the public could be more confident that dollars spent on the Chicago schools would get to the classroom.[13]

Together, these developments led to a sizable increase in per-pupil spending for education in Chicago. Figure 1.4 shows budgeted expenditures per pupil for education in 1960 dollars. (These figures exclude capital costs, debt service, and a few small categories of spending.) Per-pupil spending for education changed little between 1900 and 1920. The district kept up with rising enrollment but did not increase resources for education. Spending rose in the 1920s, then dipped during the Depression. After 1935, school expenditures rose substantially, doubling by 1960.

This increase in funding was reflected in teacher salaries, the largest component of the school budget. Figure 1.5 shows the minimum and maximum salary levels for elementary school teachers, again in 1960 dollars. Between 1900 and 1920, salaries barely kept pace with inflation. A new salary schedule in the early 1920s was the last raise the teachers

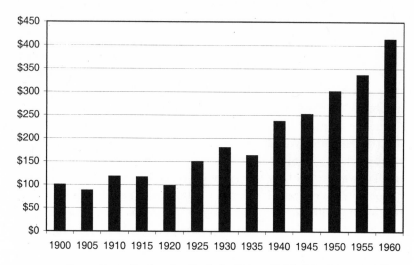

FIGURE 1.4 Per-pupil spending for education in the Chicago Public Schools in 1960 dollars. Source: Chicago Board of Education, annual *Proceedings* volumes.

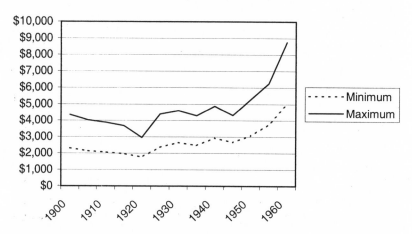

FIGURE 1.5 Minimum and maximum salaries for Chicago elementary school teachers, in 1960 dollars. Source: Chicago Board of Education, annual *Proceedings* volumes and Herrick, *Chicago Schools*, 404.

would receive for nearly two decades. During the 1930s, the Board of Education imposed temporary salary cuts, although the impact on teachers' pay was offset by price deflation. These cuts were fully reversed by 1943, and pay scales were raised in the late 1940s—although many young teachers remained so poor they were eligible for public housing. The biggest change in teacher salaries came during the 1950s, when a growing

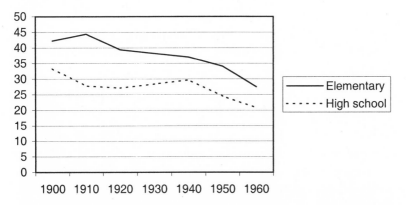

FIGURE 1.6 Students per teacher in the Chicago Public Schools, 1900–1960. Source: Calculated from Herrick, *Chicago Schools,* 403, 406. Note: Figures for 1930 are interpolated. Herrick's figures for 1930 include junior high school teachers with the elementary teachers, but the ninth grade junior high school students are included with the high school students; thus, her figures for 1930 yield class sizes that are too small for elementary and too large for high schools.

teacher shortage, compounded by competition from the rapidly growing suburban districts and pressure from the Chicago Teachers Union, spurred the board to raise salaries several times.[14]

School officials also lowered class size. Turn-of-the-century classes were quite large, with as many as sixty students per teacher in the elementary grades. Teachers' organizations—the Chicago Federation of Teachers and later the Chicago Teachers Union—lobbied regularly for smaller classes. Their pressure was reinforced by the North Central Association of Schools and Colleges, which accredited the city's high schools. In 1908, the association refused to certify two Chicago high schools because of their large classes. The warnings continued, and in 1936 a North Central Association report described half of Chicago's high school teachers as "heavily overloaded." Superintendents Hunt and Willis both lowered class size significantly. Figure 1.6 shows the ratio of students to teachers in the elementary and secondary grades.[15]

The period after World War II presented some financial challenges, including a sharp rise in enrollment as the baby boom generation began to reach school age. As neighborhoods developed far from the city center, new schools had to be built, requiring multiple bond issues and earning Superintendent Willis the nickname "Big Ben the Builder." Yet whatever problems the Chicago Public Schools faced during the postwar period, they were minor compared to those caused earlier by mismanagement and corruption and by the economic shock of the Great Depression. While Chicago's downtown grew shabbier and its factories began to close, the postwar period did not mean significant financial privation for the schools.

Chicago's Students

The urban decline story is not just about school funding; it also highlights changes in the socioeconomic and racial/ethnic mix of students after World War II. In part, this explanation rests on shifts in the composition of city populations during this time. Since its founding, Chicago had been a city of immigrants. During the nineteenth century, most immigrants were from Ireland, Germany, or other western or northern European countries. The city's ethnic profile changed quickly after the turn of the century, however. By 1920, one-third of all Chicagoans were first- or second-generation immigrants from southern or eastern Europe; within a few years, Poles overtook Germans as the largest ethnic group in the city. Students from southern and eastern European backgrounds became a significant presence in the schools (see fig. 1.7), though their prominence declined after 1940. World War I and then the Immigration Act of 1924 cut off emigration from Poland, Italy, and other countries in the region. Consequently, by 1960, only 30 percent of Chicago's population was foreign-born or had foreign-born parents. (Third-generation immigrants, not counted here, remained a large presence in the city.)

At the same time, the proportion of black students was rising. African Americans had lived in the city since its founding, but remained a very small fraction of the population until World War I. When the war began, local factories increased production just as emigration from Europe began to drop. The resulting labor shortage spurred the African-American Great Migration to northern cities. In just a few years, the black community in Chicago doubled in size. Black in-migration continued during the 1920s, slowed somewhat in the 1930s, then surged again during World War II to meet the wartime labor demand. After the war, the mechanization of southern cotton production displaced millions of tenant farmers and sharecroppers and sustained black migration out of the region. Between 1940 and 1960, Chicago's black population grew from 278,000 to 813,000. During the same period, many white Chicagoans moved to the suburbs, which grew rapidly under the impetus of federal subsidies for highway and home construction.[16] As figure 1.7 shows, the proportion of black students in the city rose steeply after 1940.

Proportion of immigrant students

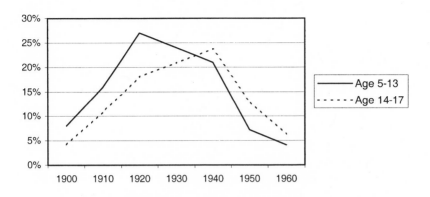

Proportion of black students

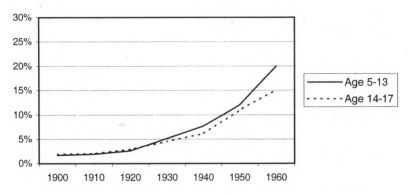

FIGURE 1.7 Ethnic composition of students in city sample. Source: IPUMS city sample. Note: Includes only those enrolled in school. Figures for 1930 are interpolated.

If we considered public schools only, the rise in black enrollment would be even more striking. Figure 1.7 represents *all* students—not just those in the public schools but also a large and growing fraction of students attending private schools. In Chicago, the share of elementary school students enrolled in Roman Catholic schools rose from 19 percent in 1900 to 37 percent in 1960. The Catholic high schools grew more slowly, but by 1930 these secondary schools enrolled about half of the high-school-bound graduates of parochial schools—about 13 percent of all high school students—and the numbers continued to climb.[17] Almost all of these students were white. Most parish schools simply did not enroll black students; the city's small African-American Catholic population worshipped in a series of segregated parishes and missions. In 1945, Chicago's Cardinal Stritch instructed all archdiocesan schools to admit black children. Informal racial exclusion continued, however, and black enrollment in Catholic schools rose only slowly. In the city sample in 1960, only 5 percent of black students aged seven through thirteen years were enrolled in any private school, compared with 35 percent of white students. The growing private school enrollment amplified the rise in black representation in the city's public schools, as the estimates in figure 1.8 show. In 1960, the estimated proportion of black students in Chicago's public elementary schools was about 40 percent, compared with 28 percent among *all* elementary school students.[18]

Despite this significant change in racial and ethnic composition, there is little sign of a rise in poverty among Chicago students after World War II. Most social indicators related to poverty improved between 1940 and 1960 (table 1.1). Mother's education, parents' white-collar employment, and home ownership rose over time. Parents' occupation scores, an IPUMS index based on the earnings associated with each occupation, were stable over the period. Standards of living also improved in ways the census did not measure, such as housing quality, sanitation, and public and private social insurance.[19] A few indicators changed in ways less favorable to education—there were declines in the proportion of children born in northern states and of those with a parent in the labor force—but these declines were modest. Even if we could consider the

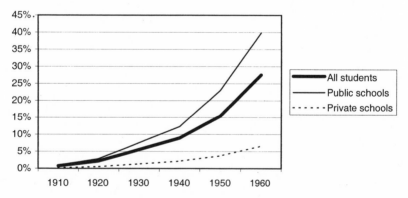

FIGURE 1.8 Estimated proportion of black students in public and private elementary schools, Chicago, 1910–60. Source: Calculated from IPUMS census data and enrollment information from Herrick, *Chicago Schools,* 403, and Sanders, *Education of an Urban Minority,* 5. Note: Figures for 1930 are interpolated.

TABLE I.I: **Family characteristics of students aged 5–17 years, city sample, 1920–60**

	1920	1940	1960
Mother is high school graduate	—	17.4	45.2
Parent in white-collar occupation	27.7	28.3	32.2
Own home	35.9	30.0	52.4
Number of siblings	2.8	2.2	2.2
Mother's occupation score (mean)	19.5	20.7	21.5
Father's occupation score (mean)	28.9	28.4	29.5
In two-parent family	85.2	83.6	83.1
Born in northern U.S. state	91.8	95.4	90.0
At least one parent in the labor force	98.7	96.7	98.2

Source: IPUMS city sample.
Note: Includes only those enrolled in school. Figures on parent occupation and labor force status exclude children not living with at least one parent.

socioeconomic status of public school students only, as we did for race in figure 1.8, it is unlikely we would find that socioeconomic status fell over time.[20]

The Racial Gap in Education

Among Chicago students, the important change in the postwar period was not a rise in poverty but a widening education gap between black and immigrant students. On measures including school enrollment, grade retention, and high school graduation rates, immigrant students began to have better school outcomes than black students. The gap is not explained by trends in southern migration; it also appears when we consider only children born in the North. Southern-born black children were more disadvantaged socioeconomically than northern-born children, but the differences were small (table 1.2). Moreover, the proportion of southern-born black students rose only modestly after 1940: from 15.3 percent in 1940 to 22.3 percent in 1950, then to 16.9 percent in 1960. Clearly, the growing racial gap reflects conditions in northern cities and schools. To highlight these developments, the rest of this chapter will focus primarily on northern-born students. (See appendix A for comparable information on southern-born and all students in northern cities.)

The racial gap begins with enrollment. In the early part of the century, black students had a small advantage in school enrollment above the compulsory age, especially among older youth. By age sixteen, most immigrant teenagers had dropped out of school to work. Facing discrim-

TABLE 1.2: **Family characteristics of northern black students by region of birth, 1960**

	North	South	All
Mother is high school graduate	32.5	23.2	30.4
Parent in white-collar occupation	15.0	8.7	13.6
Own home	34.1	22.5	31.5
Number of siblings	2.9	2.9	2.9
Mother's occupation score (mean)	18.0	16.8	17.8
Father's occupation score (mean)	24.3	23.6	24.2
In two-parent family	62.7	62.1	62.5
At least one parent in the labor force	96.8	96.8	96.8
In same house as five years ago	45.0	33.1	42.6
In poverty	46.4	49.9	47.2

Source: IPUMS city sample.

Note: Includes only those enrolled in school. Figures on parent occupation and labor force status exclude children not living with at least one parent.

ination, black youth did not find work so easily, so more remained in school. The black advantage in enrollment disappeared by 1940; from that year onward, immigrants were more likely to be in school (fig. 1.9).

A racial difference also appears in the proportion of students who were "over age," or older than the normative age for their grade, due either to a late start or to nonpromotion. Grade retention was very common in the early twentieth century. In Chicago, some 20 percent of students failed their first semester of first grade. Poverty was often the underlying reason: low-income students were more likely to miss school because of illness, inadequate shoes or clothing, or the need to work to help their families.[21] In 1909, nearly two-thirds of all "Negro and Indian" children in Chicago were over age, with similar figures for southern and eastern European immigrants (see table 1.3). (These figures include all students in the city regardless of place of birth.) By 1920, figures from the Chicago Commission on Race Relations show higher proportions of over-age students in mostly black schools than in mostly immigrant schools—75 percent versus 49 percent. (Again, these figures include all children regardless of where they were born.) There was no difference in failure rates, however. About 9 percent of students in black schools were not promoted, compared with 10 percent of students in immigrant schools. The difference in the share of over-age students is likely to reflect the World War I–era influx of southern migrant children, who were often demoted a grade or two when they arrived in Chicago.[22]

Beginning with the 1940 census, we can estimate the proportion of over-age students by comparing a student's age with his or her highest

Ages 14-15

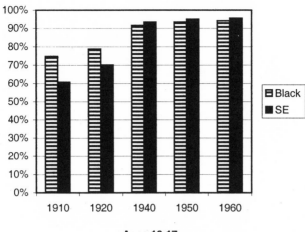

Ages 16-17

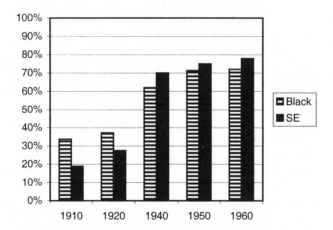

FIGURE 1.9 School enrollment rates, northern-born youth. Source: IPUMS city sample.
Note: *SE* denotes southern or eastern European.

grade completed. Those with a difference of more than 6 are counted as
over age. (Inevitably, some students will be misclassified, but there is no
reason to think this misclassification differed over time or across group.)
Considering northern-born students only, in 1940 there was little difference between black and immigrant students in the proportion over age

TABLE 1.3:   **Percentage of Chicago students aged 10–12 years who were over age for their grade, by race and birthplace of father, 1909**

Native-born father	
Black and Indian	63.9
White	36.0
Foreign-born father	
Bohemian and Moravian	48.9
Italian (northern)	65.6
Italian (southern)	72.1
Lithuanian	66.7
Magyar	51.4
Polish	74.2
Slovak	65.6
Slovenian	33.8

Source: U.S. Immigration Commission, *The Children of Immigrants in Schools* (Washington, DC, 1911), 2:548.
Note: The tables in the original source do not distinguish between first- and second-generation (foreign- and native-born) students. A separate tabulation of Chicago public school students showed that 63 percent of students with foreign-born, non-English-speaking fathers were born in Chicago; the remainder were born elsewhere, including abroad; see p. 549 of *The Children of Immigrants in Schools,* cited above.

for their grade. After 1940, however, the difference widened considerably (see fig. 1.10).

The U.S. Census did not report educational attainment before 1940, but we can approximate high school graduation rates for earlier times using data on the school attainment of older cohorts of people. Figure 1.11 shows estimated graduation rates for black and immigrant adults who were born (and probably educated) in northern states. At first there was little black/immigrant difference in graduation rates, except that black women had a small advantage over immigrant women. For those who reached adolescence during the late 1930s and early 1940s, it was immigrants who were more likely to receive a diploma. This gap widened over time. For students who entered high school after the end of World War II, the black/immigrant difference in graduation rates was about 20 percentage points.[23] These estimates for high school graduation are consistent with the figures for enrollment and grade retention. All indicate a gap between black and immigrant students that widened after 1940.

Black/immigrant differences in academic achievement also may have widened, although the evidence is quite sparse and must be interpreted cautiously. In small studies conducted by education researchers during the 1920s and 1930s, black and immigrant children scored below white children with native-born parents, but seem to have differed little from

1940

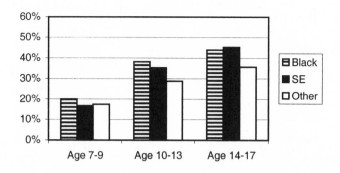

1950

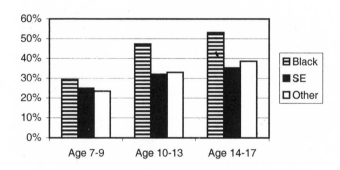

1960

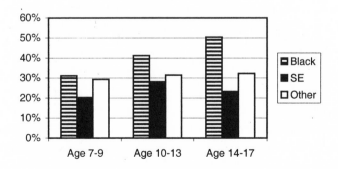

FIGURE 1.10 Proportion of all students over age for their grade, northern-born students only. Source: IPUMS city sample. Note: *SE* denotes southern or eastern European.

Men

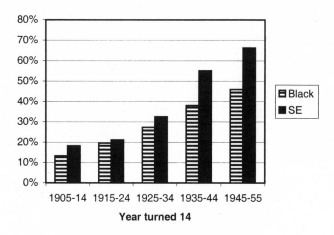

Year turned 14

Women

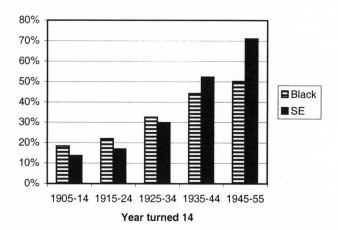

Year turned 14

FIGURE I.II High school graduation rates by year turned 14 years old, northern-born adults only. Source: IPUMS city sample. Note: *SE* denotes southern or eastern European.

each other. Chicago researcher Henry Burton tested sixth-grade students on civics information; black students averaged a score of 36.9, compared with Italians' average of 30.9. Fanny Segalla studied the writing vocabularies of high school students at a predominantly black school and a heavily eastern European school in Chicago and found little difference between the schools in vocabulary size. More systematic evidence comes

from the Board of Education, which in 1926 printed average achievement test scores for the city's junior high schools, including Phillips
(predominantly black) and Farragut (in a heavily southern and eastern
European neighborhood). The Phillips students averaged scores of 6.2
in English and 6.5 in math, compared with Farragut students' average of
7.1 in English and 6.9 in math. The difference in the average test scores
was almost a grade level in English and four months in math. In comparing these averages, keep in mind that Farragut, like most "immigrant"
schools, included a number of students from northern and western European backgrounds, who tended to score better on standardized tests.[24]

Figures for the early 1960s are not comparable with the earlier data,
but they do indicate a sizable racial gap in achievement. Robert Havighurst's 1964 study of the Chicago Public Schools reports social class,
racial composition, and school outcomes for the high schools. About
one-third of all ninth-grade English classes in predominantly black high
schools were taught at the "Basic English" level, intended for students
who were three or more years below grade level, compared with fewer
than 5 percent in predominantly white schools. Although these figures
do not distinguish schools by immigrant composition, low-income white
schools are likely to have a higher concentration of southern and eastern European immigrants. In these schools, fewer than 10 percent of the
English classes were taught at the Basic level, compared with 40 percent
of the classes in low-income black schools.[25]

Socioeconomic Inequality and the Racial Gap in Schooling

If the black/immigrant difference in school outcomes began to widen
in the 1930s, it could reflect the growing socioeconomic differences between these two groups. In 1959, only 11 percent of immigrant students
in elementary school were poor, compared with 48 percent of black children. Moreover, by some measures there was a divergence in the family characteristics of black and immigrant children. Between 1920 and
1960, the home environments of immigrant children improved more
than those of black children on a number of indicators, including family structure, family size, home ownership, parents' education, parents'
labor force status, and parents' occupation.[26]

The racial gap in schooling, however, appears even when we take account of socioeconomic differences. Figure 1.12 shows estimates of the
percentage point difference in the proportion of sixteen- to seventeen-

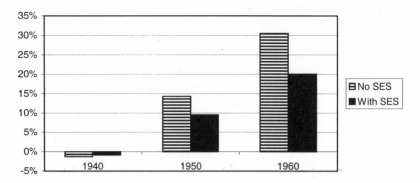

FIGURE 1.12 Immigrant-black difference in predicted proportion enrolled in school at expected grade, ages 16–17, northern-born youth only. Source: IPUMS city sample. Note: *SES* denotes socioeconomic status.

year-olds who were enrolled in school at the expected grade—in other words, youth who were right where they should be educationally. Racial differences increased between 1940 and 1960. This gap becomes smaller but doesn't disappear when we control statistically for black/immigrant differences in socioeconomic status.[27] Of course, the simple measures available from the census do not capture all economic or demographic differences between black and immigrant children. The census measures family conditions at a single point in time, while school outcomes reflect influences throughout the child's life. Family disruption or poverty when a child is young may have an effect on schooling that persists even after the family's status improves. Given the widespread poverty in the black population, many black children are likely to have experienced poverty at some point during childhood, which may have had long-term consequences for schooling. The evidence at hand, however, provides no indication that the widening racial gap is simply a matter of poverty or family characteristics.

Conclusion

The urban decline thesis cannot by itself account for the problems of inner-city schooling that emerged in northern city schools in the 1940s and 1950s. In Chicago, at least, per-pupil funding for education rose, not fell, during this time, while most indicators of students' socioeconomic status were stable or even improved. This does not mean that school resources or student demographics were irrelevant. These trends form an essential foundation for understanding the path taken by the Chicago Public Schools. However, they do not by themselves constitute an explanation for the problems of inner-city schools.

This chapter also leaves us with some key information about differences in black and immigrant schooling. A racial gap in education began to appear in 1940 and widened during the 1940s and 1950s. This pattern is not fully explained by southern migration or widening socioeconomic differences between black and immigrant students. This racial gap confirms anecdotal reports that the problems of inner-city schooling began to appear during the 1940s and 1950s. These findings also focus our attention on conditions related to race itself, such as discrimination or differential treatment by the schools, rather than socioeconomic disadvantage. The next chapter considers one such condition: racial discrimination in labor markets.

CHAPTER TWO

Labor Markets

This chapter examines the role of labor markets in the problems of inner-city schooling. Given the long history of racial discrimination, African-American youth might reasonably have been skeptical about the economic value of education. Stanley Lieberson and others have identified the 1930s as a time when racial disadvantage in the labor market may have increased.[1] Direct evidence regarding perceptions of the labor market is very limited. What we can do, however, is track the labor market experiences of black and immigrant workers over time. Perceptions of the labor market are likely to have been grounded in the experiences of family, friends, and neighbors. Thus, we can gain some indirect insight into how black and immigrant youth saw the economic value of schooling by observing labor market opportunity and employment patterns of black and immigrant Chicagoans over time.

This chapter begins with a discussion of opportunity and discrimination in white-collar employment, the sector in which education has traditionally been the most important. Next, we consider opportunity in blue-collar and service occupations. The third section examines quantitative evidence of the economic value of education for black and immigrant workers, and the final one addresses economic alternatives in the face of labor market discrimination.

White-Collar Labor Markets

White-collar work is the employment field in which education is the most explicitly rewarded. When someone pursues an education with hopes of an economic payoff, it is usually with a white-collar position in mind. But white-collar employment is not a single labor market: it comprises multiple markets, each with a distinct profile. These markets vary in the importance of education and in the extent of racial and ethnic discrimination. To understand black and immigrant opportunities in white-collar work, we should consider each separately. I distinguish four sectors within the white-collar field: private-sector employment, public-sector or government employment, self-employment such as small business, and the independent professions of medicine, dentistry, law, and the clergy. (This last sector includes self-employed professionals as well as those employed in government or in private firms.) The importance of these sectors for black and immigrant workers changed over time, partly because the sectors themselves expanded or contracted, but also because patterns of discrimination changed, as did the educational profiles of these two populations. Table 2.1 compares these sectors on key attributes, and the discussion below considers each in turn.

Private-Sector Employment

Private-sector employees were the most vulnerable of all workers to racial and ethnic discrimination. The hiring practices of private firms were subject to little scrutiny except that of public opinion. Antidiscrimination legislation, when it began to be passed in the 1940s and 1950s, was weak. Over time, credentials, skills tests, and other merit-based criteria became increasingly important, but personnel decisions continued to reflect ethnic and racial bias.

TABLE 2.1: **White-collar labor markets**

Sector	Vulnerability to discrimination	Credentials requirements	Employment trend, 1900–1960
Private	More	Low to high	Expanding
Public	Less	Medium to high	Expanding
Entrepreneur	Less	Low	Contracting
Independent professions	Less	High	Contracting

As oral history accounts illustrate, immigrants faced some discrimination in the private sector. For instance, a college-educated Polish man said of his work in sales, "My work record was excellent. My territory was tops and when promotions came somebody else got it. See. And that only worked once. The second time it happened I walked out, I was through." An Italian man reported, "When I started working at Sherman Williams Company in 1941 there was prejudice against the Italians and some of the other nationalities too—other ethnic groups by the Anglo-Saxons." Class and cultural differences also made some immigrants feel unwelcome in the white-collar workplace. A young Italian man worked as an office boy in a downtown business, later recalling, "At first I wanted to run away from all this. It was impossible, I thought, for me to participate in this new world. I was self-conscious of my meager and clumsy vocabulary, which included a liberal number of 'dees and does,' 'dis and dat' and the other typical jargon of the streets . . . I was nervous when speaking in the presence of the self-composed, complacent office manager and always uneasy in the presence of the officers of the firm."[2]

Ethnic barriers were not severe, however, and could sometimes be avoided with a little subterfuge. According to a Polish woman in Chicago, "Quite a few people, very proud Polish people who were using other names, they got along beautifully . . . they found it was much easier for them to get a job." A Chicago-born Italian woman described what happened when she sought a clerical job during the Depression:

> There was one interview that I was sent on and I felt that I had all the qualifications and I didn't get the job . . . So I asked the employment agency person that I was in contact with why did she think that I didn't get the job and she told me the next time you fill out your application don't say that you're Italian. You know, they would ask you what your nationality was, and what your religion was, and she said write down that you're French . . . So the next time I went on an interview I said that I was French. And I got the job . . . Another girl was hired at the same time and her name was Florence Berish, I'll never forget it. Really a fine young lady. So we got to have lunch together because we were hired at the same time. One day I said come on Florence level with me you're not French. She said, no I'm Jewish. She said, you're not French either are you? I said no, I'm Italian. But here we were, we both put French on our applications, we both got our jobs.

A survey of Chicago employers taken a few years later found that only 3.0 percent of clerical job openings specified no Italians and 1.5 percent no Poles. As figure 2.1 shows, when we consider high school graduates only, in 1940 and later, immigrants and other white women differed little in rates of private-sector white-collar employment.[3]

Discrimination may have persisted longer among men, but appears to have diminished after World War II. Chicago-born Leonard Giuliano began his career at Sears as a stock boy, and he described the management of Sears as solidly Irish in the early 1940s. After the war, however, two Jews and two Italians, including himself, were promoted to managerial positions, and "the nationality barrier continually kept breaking down, kept breaking down, because they found out that they had some pollocks [sic] that could do one hell of a job, and they found out they had some pretty smart Jews in the company." As he told it, awareness of ethnic differences didn't disappear but was no longer the basis of conflict or exclusion: "sure, the guy'd call me a dago or wop, but it was a loving term, just like, you know, I might call someone a pollock [sic], but I like them or the Swedes, 'Hey, you damn Swede, get over there.' You know, because we're all on the same team." Among male high school graduates, the gap in private-sector white-collar employment between immigrants and other white workers narrowed significantly between 1940 and 1960.[4]

African-American workers, by contrast, faced a rigid color line. For the most part, they were not hired into private-sector white-collar positions regardless of their qualifications. In 1897, for instance, two black men graduated from Chicago's new engineering college, the Armour Institute, with degrees in electrical engineering, but even with their exceptional credentials no one would employ them. Like so many other black college graduates, the two left the city to teach in southern schools. In 1901, an observer noted that black employment in white-collar positions was "so rare that [it is] generally announced in the Negro newspapers." As figure 2.1 shows, black workers had very low levels of representation in private-sector white-collar work. The few exceptions included employees in black-owned businesses or nonprofit agencies as well as those who passed for white.[5] The color line was breached temporarily during World War I, when a few employers, facing a labor shortage, recruited black workers into clerical positions. To handle a seasonal rush, two Chicago mail-order houses set up segregated offices and employed black female clerks, with one firm hiring 650 women in 1918 and more than a thousand in 1919. These temporary employees were better educated than their white counterparts; 75 percent had graduated from high school, and 12 percent had attended college. Both employers were pleased with the

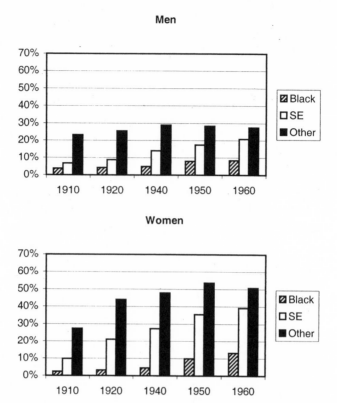

FIGURE 2.1 Percentage of all workers in private-sector white-collar employment. Source: IPUMS city sample. Note: *SE* denotes southern or eastern European.

young women's job performance. Said one, "The Negro girl is equal to the Italian or Bohemian in working ability and superior for executive work, such as instructing or supervising." Despite their good record, few were retained after the labor shortage had passed: "The white girls object."[6]

Spurred by the frustration of a vocal segment of the community, local civil rights organizations began to fight for white-collar jobs. The Chicago Urban League visited employers and tried to persuade them to break the color barrier, sometimes a painfully slow process. In the mid-1930s, it took months of calls and meetings before a downtown department store hired a black man with a master's degree from the University of Illinois—to work as an elevator operator. Soon afterward, the same store recruited a black woman with a college degree for a job as a matron. She might, they said, be promoted later to stock girl. Some black

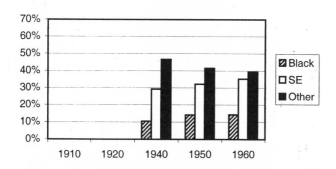

Men, high school graduates only

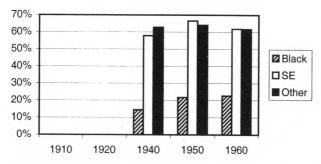

Women, high school graduates only

FIGURE 2.1 (*Continued*)

organizations were more confrontational than the Urban League. On the eve of the Depression, the *Whip,* one of Chicago's black newspapers, mobilized black churches and community groups to boycott local firms that refused to hire black employees. The *Whip*'s first target was an insurance company that hired only white collectors, but the campaign soon shifted to cashier and sales clerk positions at Woolworth's and other large retailers with stores in the city's Black Belt. In the late 1930s, the Negro Labor Relations League mounted a new series of boycotts, targeting technical and supervisory jobs such as motion picture projectionists and newspaper branch managers. In Chicago and elsewhere, this "Spend your money where you can work" campaign had an effect. Although racial exclusion remained the norm, a 1940 report concluded that "the Negroes' gain in white collar jobs has been substantial."[7]

After the Depression, the federal government began to take action against racial discrimination in employment. In 1941, after labor organizer A. Philip Randolph threatened a massive march on Washington, D.C., President Roosevelt agreed to require federal contractors to adhere to nondiscriminatory hiring guidelines. Workers who experienced discrimination could appeal to the Fair Employment Practices Committee. Although the FEPC was disbanded at the end of the war, the nondiscrimination requirement for government contractors was renewed and strengthened in 1953, and a number of northern states also banned racial discrimination in private-sector employment. (Illinois did so in 1961.) Under pressure from the federal government and local civil rights organizations, some large Chicago firms quietly integrated their white-collar workforces. By 1956, Edwin Berry, executive director of the Chicago Urban League, spoke of a "new era" in which black workers were employed "on jobs running the gamut of professional, industrial and commercial pursuits which would have been considered beyond comprehension as recently as 1945."[8]

Racial discrimination was far from gone, however. As late as 1960, Chicago employment bureaus reported that 98 percent of their white-collar job orders specified no black applicants. Among black workers, rates of private-sector white-collar employment rose only a little between 1940 and 1960. The experience of Chicagoan Albert Miller represents what many black jobseekers may have faced during that time, when racial discrimination remained widespread but was becoming more covert. Miller learned through friends that an encyclopedia publisher was hiring a political science editor, and he telephoned about the position. Miller had degrees in political science and sociology, and some training in psychology as well; the personnel manager was delighted with his qualifications and told him to come in the next morning to "talk salary." "You do have an open employment policy? You do employ Negroes?" Miller asked. Certainly, he was told, although none in editorial positions at the moment. Upon learning that Miller was black, the personnel manager told him, "I personally am not racially prejudiced. I've worked, lived with Negroes . . . but all the people working under you would be white (a pause which [Miller] thought was longer than it probably was), so I had better check. Incidentally, you had better call before coming for the interview in the morning." Miller called the next three days, but in vain. "No one," he wrote later, "had the slightest idea of where the personnel manager could be found."[9]

Public-Sector Employment

For black workers, the most important alternative to private-sector employment was the public sector, and specifically the civil service. Although public-sector work was less lucrative, civil service rules tempered the impact of racial discrimination. Hiring procedures varied by the type of position and level of government, but civil service positions were generally filled by examination. In the federal civil service, for instance, the top three scorers would be interviewed for the open position. The law also provided for a formal process of merit-based promotion and protection against arbitrary dismissal. Public agencies hired black workers into white-collar and supervisory positions at a time when such opportunities were very rare in the private sector. Civil service opportunities expanded as Chicago became more segregated and more public schools and city agencies were opened in black neighborhoods.[10]

For black Chicagoans, the U.S. Postal Service was the largest single public employer. The city's first black postal worker passed the exam and was hired in 1883, just after the Pendleton Act established the federal civil service. In 1930, when blacks comprised less than 7 percent of the Chicago population, 16 percent of the city's mail carriers and 28 percent of its postal clerks were African American. The black community had many channels of information about these positions. A black teacher told of passing out Postal Service applications to her high school class. The *Chicago Defender* carried advertisements for refresher courses for civil service examinations. The National Alliance of Postal Employees, an independent association, advocated for the rights of black Postal Service employees.[11]

Public-sector work was not without disadvantages. Although it was not as severe as in the private sector, racial discrimination still occurred. A young black woman employed in the Chicago Post Office described how she got her job:

> I took the examination and was called down in a group of five, three white girls, a Negro man, and myself. The three white girls were taken on. I then went to see the alderman who was a family friend. He wrote a letter and sent the Senator a wire. I was called and hired within a week.

Those who were hired might still face a hostile workplace. As a library assistant reported, "The other girls on the staff were very prejudiced against colored people. They would not speak to me except on library business and did everything they could to make me leave."[12] Moreover, many public-sector jobs were low skilled and monotonous, falling far short of the ambition of their incumbents. The magazine *Opportunity* remarked in 1923 that postal work was the "Siberia" of black college graduates unable to find more fulfilling work. So it remained into the 1960s. "According to legend," an observer noted in 1965 in a discussion of the black community, "the Chicago Post Office employs enough college-trained postal clerks to start a university of its own." Asked what work they hoped their children would do, very few black parents selected the Postal Service.[13]

It was the scarcity of other white-collar opportunities that made the civil service so vital. As figure 2.2 shows, public-sector employment represented a large share of total white-collar employment for black workers in Chicago and other northern cities. In contrast, government employment was less important for southern and eastern European immigrants. Those who were not from English-speaking backgrounds were often screened out by the civil service examinations. When the historian Edward Kantowicz reviewed the city's civil service rosters, he found few Polish names on the list. Over time, second-generation immigrants made inroads into civil service employment. However, because immigrants faced less private-sector discrimination than African Americans, civil service remained less critical to their mobility strategies.[14]

Self-Employment

Self-employment allowed immigrant and black workers to avoid employer discrimination and turn their race or ethnicity into an asset. Many customers were more comfortable with proprietors who shared their culture and were a part of the local community. Among immigrant men in the early 1900s, half of all white-collar workers were self-employed. Most ran small shops such as grocery stores, restaurants, and taverns, or worked as real estate or insurance agents. Rates of self-employment fell over time as ethnic prejudice diminished and second-generation immigrants entered the labor market. In addition, small entrepreneurs were pushed out by competition from grocery store chains and other large firms. The decline of small business was further hastened by assimilation. As immigrants learned English and became Americanized, they no longer sought out shopkeepers who spoke their native language and carried Old World products.[15]

To a more limited extent, self-employment was an avenue of opportunity for black men and women. Many of their businesses were small and undercapitalized; in a 1901 survey of black proprietors, more than one in five were wood and coal dealers, buying in bulk to sell door to door by the armload or bucket. "Black capitalism" had some ideological appeal, and black churches and fraternities joined the Colored Merchants' Association in the effort to "corral the Negroes' wayward dollars, astray in white pastures." As the ghetto expanded, a few of its banks, insurance companies, and newspapers grew to prominence. By and large, however, black entrepreneurs fought a losing battle against the economic power of the chain stores.[16]

Independent Professions

Like self-employment, the independent professions of law, medicine, dentistry, and the clergy offered a chance to avoid some of the discrimination that private-sector employees faced. Professionals were an important element of the elite in both black and immigrant communities. They drew support and prestige from associations such as the Polish Medical and Dental Association, the (Italian) Justinian Society of Advocates, and the (African-American) National Medical Association and Cook County Bar Association. The professions were especially important for black men during the early years of the century, accounting for one out of every seven white-collar workers. Surveys of black students indicate a keen interest in medicine and law.[17]

Although the independent professions offered prestige, there were disadvantages as well. Many black doctors and lawyers were professionally isolated. Young attorneys lacked sponsorship from older lawyers in the early stages of their careers: "The white lawyer is taken into a firm when he comes out of law school and is protected and assisted in getting started. The Negro lawyer is thrown immediately out on his own." Chicago's black-run Provident Hospital provided staff appointments for black physicians, but few other hospitals granted them admitting privileges; by the 1950s, this discrimination had become such an embarrassment that the Chicago City Council passed a resolution denouncing it. Given these institutional barriers, as well as the high poverty rates among black patients and clients, professional status was no guarantee of financial security. During the Depression, jokes circulated about dentists who slept in their examination chairs because they couldn't afford an apartment. A

Black men

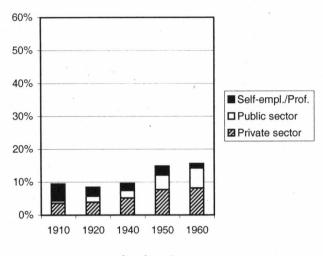

Immigrant men

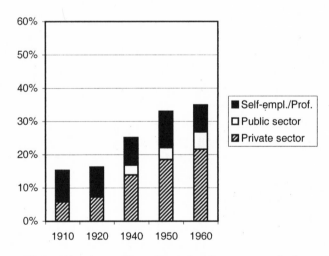

FIGURE 2.2 Black and immigrant white-collar workers by sector, 1910–60. Source: IPUMS city sample.

black lawyer recalled, "When I'd get behind in rent I'd go out and earn some money by laying bricks."[18]

For African Americans, opportunity in the independent professions became more limited in the early twentieth century. Black applicants faced rising discrimination in white-operated professional schools,

Black women

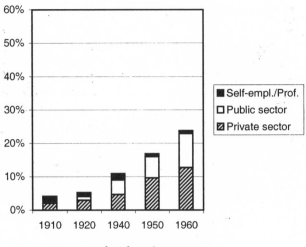

Immigrant women

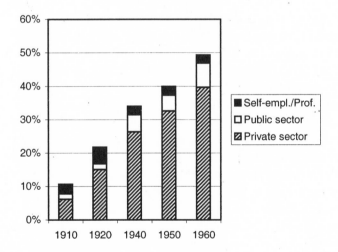

FIGURE 2.2 (*Continued*)

particularly in medicine, where new requirements for clinical training would have brought black medical students into contact with white patients. By 1940, Northwestern University and Rush Medical College had reportedly stopped accepting black students; the University of Chicago and the University of Illinois "admit[ted] a few under pressure," and a few attended Chicago's Loyola University. By the mid-1930s, the two historically black medical schools, Howard (in Washington, D.C.) and Meharry (in Tennessee), were training almost all of the black physicians. The constriction of opportunity in the independent professions was undoubtedly a source of frustration within the black community because of the high status of professionals and the limited alternative routes of economic mobility.[19]

Racial Discrimination and the White-Collar Labor Market

Patterns of labor market discrimination had mixed implications for black students' view of education. Black workers faced severe discrimination in the white-collar employment sector, and this discrimination abated only a little between 1900 and 1960. Moreover, immigrant workers moved more quickly into white-collar occupations than black workers did (see fig. 2.3, panel A). These figures do not take into account the changing composition of the black and immigrant populations, however. With time, the second generation succeeded their immigrant parents. These second-generation workers were native English speakers, educated in American schools, and familiar with American culture, all qualities conducive to success in the white-collar labor market. On the other hand, through 1960 a large fraction of black workers came from the South, and thus were disadvantaged by Jim Crow schools and by bias against southern speech styles and regional culture. And if we consider the workers most likely to be deemed eligible for white-collar jobs, it is less clear that white-collar employment rates diverged for black and immigrant workers. Panel B of figure 2.3 shows the percentage point gap in white-collar employment between northern-born black and second-generation immigrant workers between 1910 and 1960. Although the gap grew a little between 1940 and 1960, the immigrant advantage was as high in the earlier years as it was after 1940. Panel C shows the same information for high school graduates between 1940 and 1960 (information on education was not available before 1940). The immigrant advantage was sizable, but no larger in 1960 than it was twenty years earlier.

Moreover, within the white-collar labor market, racial discrimination had the ironic consequence of making education more salient. Black workers pursued paths to white-collar employment in which education provided some protection against discrimination, first in the independent professions, then the civil service. Immigrant workers, on the other

Panel A: All workers

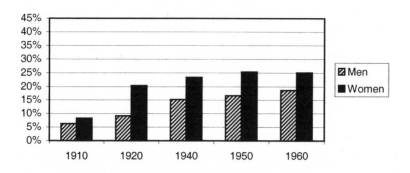

Panel B: Northern-born workers only

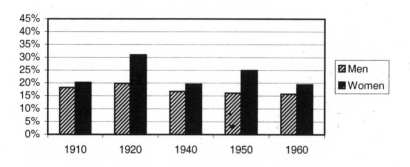

Panel C: High school graduates only

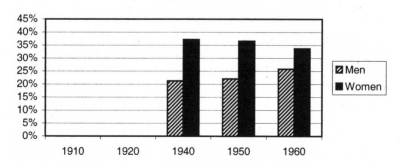

FIGURE 2.3 Percentage-point gap in white-collar employment between immigrant and black workers. Source: IPUMS city sample.

hand, entered the white-collar labor market through self-employment, a pathway in which education mattered little, then moved readily into the private sector as discrimination diminished. For them, education was less critical to white-collar opportunity.

Manual Labor

The other piece of the discrimination puzzle is manual labor, including blue-collar and service positions. When we consider the rewards of education, we do not ordinarily think about manual work, because school credentials were less important for these occupations.[20] Yet manual work is important for exactly this reason. The more attractive it was, in terms of pay, stability, and working conditions, the smaller would be the economic incentive for schooling. Racial discrimination was present in the blue-collar and service labor markets, just as it was among white-collar workers, creating a very different profile of opportunities for black and immigrant workers.

The history of manual labor over the first half of the twentieth century is a story of improving pay and working conditions for a substantial share of positions. At the turn of the century, most manual jobs were poorly paid and unstable, with unpleasant and sometimes hazardous working conditions. There were few skilled positions, and only about one in twenty workers were unionized. Most manual workers, whether in factories, shops, hotels, or private households, were readily interchangeable, had little bargaining power, and were paid at or near the level of "common labor."

Over the next several decades, conditions improved in parts of the manual labor market. During the 1920s, some jobs improved in pay, benefits, stability, and working conditions as employers sought to dampen labor unrest and curb turnover. During the "welfare capitalism" movement of that time, some employers enhanced their blue-collar jobs by adding benefits such as pensions, life insurance, accident and health insurance, and mortgage assistance. By 1929, 15 percent of large firms offered health and accident insurance, and 30 percent offered mutual benefit associations. At the same time, internal labor markets became more widespread; employers delineated promotion ladders within the firm and set up seniority rules protecting workers against arbitrary dismissal. Although many firms dropped these benefits with the onset of the Great Depression, workers regained them during the labor struggles of the 1930s and 1940s.[21] By 1940, one-third of all manufacturing workers were represented by unions. Over the next twenty years, through the collective bargaining process, these unions gained significant increases in wages and benefits.[22]

However, these improvements were uneven. They were concentrated among large firms and in manufacturing and utilities, and were often limited to skilled workers or those with long tenure. The lower tier of manual workers comprised most service workers—in private households as well as commercial settings—and also included a growing number of contract and day laborers. Temporary employment services expanded after World War II. In 1948 there was only one temporary industrial labor firm in Chicago; by 1961 there were twenty-eight.[23]

Newcomers like black migrants and southern and eastern European immigrants rarely got the good manual jobs. Newly arrived immigrant men were sent to do "gang work" for railroads, lumber camps, or farms; women worked in hotels, restaurants, or private households. Black men and women most often were employed in domestic and personal service, in either private households or commercial establishments such as hotels and Pullman dining cars. A survey in Chicago conducted around 1910 found that one out of eight black men worked in a saloon or poolroom. Among black female manual workers, more than 80 percent were domestics in private households.[24]

Yet even among these newcomers, immigrants had an edge. One reason was the long history of racial exclusion in both union and nonunion manufacturing work. Most AFL-affiliated trade unions refused to accept black members, even those who had worked in skilled trades in the South. In nonunion factories as well, black workers were excluded by employer prejudice and white workers' resistance. In contrast, southern and eastern European immigrants were heavily represented in manufacturing, albeit mostly in unskilled and semiskilled positions. By 1920, about half of all immigrant manual workers—both men and women— held blue-collar jobs in manufacturing (see fig. 2.4).[25]

Once they were in, immigrants helped their kin and neighbors find factory employment. Informal recruitment through personal networks— usually patterned along ethnic lines—was common, particularly for more desirable blue-collar jobs. For instance, an Italian immigrant described how he found his first job in Chicago: "I met an Italian by the name of Ben Mirabelli who was superintendent of a gas plant on the west side. He

Men

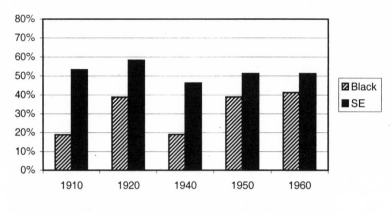

Women

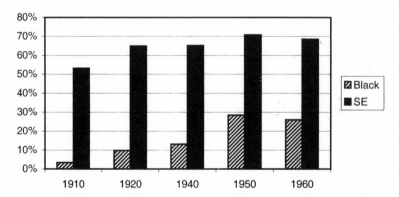

FIGURE 2.4 Percentage of manual workers in manufacturing. Source: IPUMS city sample.
Note: *SE* denotes southern or eastern European.

didn't have anything for me then but said that he would help me when he could. I laid around for a few more days looking for work but then I got word from Ben that I should put on my over-alls and come out to go to work as a pumper's helper."[26]

Black men's opportunities expanded when wartime labor shortages spurred employers to change their hiring practices. During World War I, meatpackers, steel plants, and other manufacturers hired sizable numbers of black men for the first time. Many of these newly-hired workers retained their positions after the war, although they lost ground again during the Depression. Black women gained much less. Most who entered new lines of work did so in hotels, restaurants, and commercial laundries, although a few made inroads into manufacturing employment, including meatpacking.[27]

Black workers who gained a foothold in manufacturing remained at a disadvantage relative to immigrants. Hostile supervisors dismissed them arbitrarily or gave them less overtime and less lucrative piecework. A personnel manager in a packinghouse reported during the 1920s that "I have to let many colored women go on account of a certain forelady. She says they are lazy and saucy. I know that they are better workers than the white girls who preceded them in that department. But this forewoman doesn't like colored girls." In her study of Chicago's meatpacking industry during the 1920s, Alma Herbst found little sign of racial animosity among the workers, but black applicants were less likely to be hired, and black workers more likely to be laid off or discharged. In addition, black factory workers were concentrated in lower-paying firms. In a 1925 survey of industrial workers, 42 percent of the black respondents worked at Swift, which paid the lowest wage of any factory studied; average weekly wages were $23.30 for black workers, compared with $25.65 for southern and eastern European immigrants.[28]

During World War II, more firms crossed the color line, prompted by the wartime labor shortage and also by the FEPC and local civil rights organizations. In 1941, the Chicago Urban League approached more than three hundred employers and petitioned them to change their hiring practices. Almost a third did so, hiring more than five thousand black workers into skilled or semiskilled positions. The CIO's interracial organizing strategy also boosted black opportunity in blue-collar work. As figure 2.4 shows, the proportion of black men and women in manufacturing employment jumped between 1940 and 1950. For those who remained in service employment, wages and working conditions improved due to organizing by the Brotherhood of Sleeping Car Porters and many smaller unions, such as the Laundry Workers International. Finally, reflecting the expansion of opportunities for black women, the rate of private household employment dropped sharply during the 1940s. In 1940, 55 percent of *all* black women workers worked as domestics, while only ten years later the rate was 30 percent.[29]

Racial differences remained, however, in skilled and supervisory employment. Given their seniority and their ethnic and kin connections, immigrants were well positioned to move into these positions. As turnover slowed, the resulting stability promoted solidarity among the incumbent workers, making them more resistant to the entry of racial or ethnic "outsiders."[30] Discrimination persisted even in CIO-organized plants, as we can see from a 1954 ethnography of a Chicago meatpacking plant. The anthropologist Erdman Palmore encountered it on his first day, when he was waiting in line at the employment office. Someone pulled him aside and invited him to apply for the position of oiler, a relatively easy and well-paid job. The man told him, "We have to do this on the side because we don't have niggers on this job, it's a white job." Palmore also learned that white workers resisted blacks' bids for promotion by imposing arbitrary tests of skill or withholding informal training. An informant told him, "I knew a mechanic (Negro), I guess he was a good one, and he applied for a job in the mechanical division. Well, they sent him up to see the foreman and the foreman asked him 'How many threads are there on a bolt?' . . . Now if it was anybody else they wouldn't ask him such a thing." White workers also resisted racial integration by withholding informal training. A black man who began working in a skilled department "found out later that they usually give a man a week of going around with another man to learn the job. Well, when I came in I only went around with a man for five hours and the next day I was expected to do the job all by myself. That was to trip me up so they could get me out."[31] As figure 2.5 shows, black men remained less likely than immigrant men to hold skilled positions.

The effect of discriminatory barriers was compounded after World

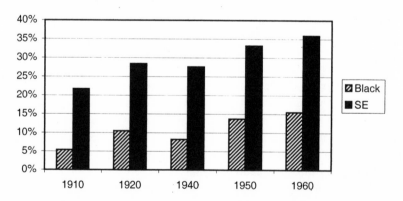

FIGURE 2.5 Proportion of male manual workers in skilled occupations. Source: IPUMS city sample. Note: *SE* denotes southern or eastern European.

War II by technological changes in manufacturing and by the relocation of industry from city to suburb. These trends lowered demand for low-skilled manual workers in the city. Black men were more vulnerable to these shifts because they had less seniority and could less easily relocate to follow the jobs. Plant closings in the stockyards hit black Chicago-ans particularly hard; in 1950, one out of three packinghouse workers was black. The Chicago Urban League studied the city's labor market around 1960, and found that when poorly educated black men changed jobs, the change was usually involuntary—the result of a layoff—and usu-ally led to a drop in income.[32] Black men fortunate enough to be steadily employed benefited from the advances made in the unionized sector, but growing numbers of black men were unstably employed or had dropped out of the labor force.[33]

The Economic Value of Education

As the last two sections have described, black workers faced extensive discrimination in both white-collar and manual work, although oppor-tunity expanded in both sectors for blacks—as for immigrants—between 1900 and 1960. Now we examine the consequences of these patterns for the economic value of education. We might assume that racial discrimina-tion lowers this value for minority workers. The effect of discrimination, however, depends on how it is patterned in the labor market. Figure 2.6 provides an illustration. It shows four simplified scenarios for the rela-tionship between education and earnings. The upper line in each graph, labeled A, is for workers who do not face discrimination. For these workers, the line always slopes upward: the more education they have, the higher their earnings. The lower line in each scenario, labeled B, is for workers who face discrimination. The pattern of discrimination dif-fers, however. In scenarios 1 and 2, education has no relation to earnings for the B workers—those with more education earn the same as those with less—and so the economic value of education is nil. In the first sce-nario, B workers with little education face no discrimination in earnings, but those with more education do. In the second, all the B workers face discrimination, although discrimination is more severe for those with more education. In the third scenario, B workers face discrimination at all educational levels, but education still "pays off" in higher earn-ings. In fact, education is as valuable here for the B workers as for the

Scenario 1

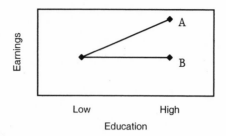

Scenario 2

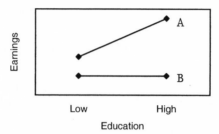

Scenario 3

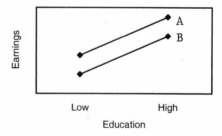

Scenario 4

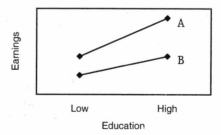

FIGURE 2.6 Scenarios for the relationship between education and earnings.

A workers, as the slope of the two lines is the same; education raises their earnings by the same amount. Finally, in scenario 4, the slope of the line is lower for B workers than for A workers. Here, education is economically valuable, but less so than it would be in the absence of discrimination.

Which of these scenarios best characterizes the situation of black and immigrant workers? To find out, we can examine census data for the years from 1940 to 1960. (Before 1940, the U.S. Census did not collect information on education and earnings.) The usual way of estimating the economic value of education is to compare workers with varying amounts of education, taking account of other characteristics that might affect their economic outcomes. Using what is available from the census, the results are adjusted for age, age squared, southern and foreign birth, marital status, number of children, state of residence, and school enrollment. There may be other differences among workers that are associated with both education and earnings; ideally, we would control statistically for these characteristics as well, but we are limited to the data collected in the census.

On average, individuals with more education earned more, had higher status occupations, were less often unemployed, and worked more steadily during the year. The question is whether the apparent benefit of education differed for black and immigrant workers. Consider annual earnings. Figure 2.7 shows predicted earnings—based on the census analyses—for black, immigrant, and other (white) men at different educational levels.[34] The lines usually slope upward, because people with more education tended to earn more. The effects of racial discrimination are clear. Estimated earnings for black workers were substantially lower than earnings for immigrants or other workers. However, among both immigrant and black men, those with more education tended to earn more, and overall there were no statistically significant differences in the effect of education on earnings. Immigrant men may have gained more from high school completion while black men gained more from college, but on average each additional year of schooling raised earnings for black men as much as it did for immigrant men. This situation best resembles scenario 3 in figure 2.6.

Comparable estimates for women are in figure 2.8, although we must interpret these results cautiously, because many women were not in the labor force. In 1940, there was no difference between immigrant and black women in the economic value of schooling, but in 1950 and 1960, black women gained *more* from schooling than immigrant women did.

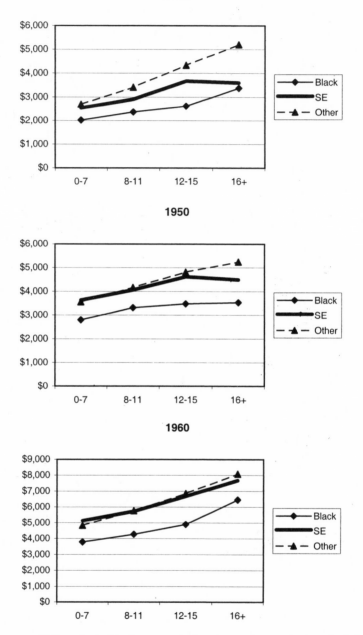

FIGURE 2.7 Estimated earnings by years of education, men, 1940–60, in 1960 dollars. Source: IPUMS city sample. Note: *SE* denotes southern or eastern European.

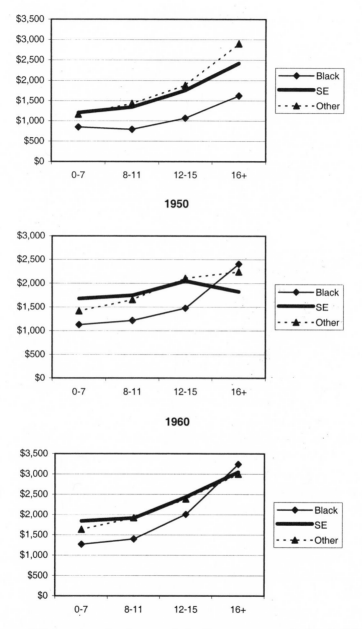

FIGURE 2.8 Estimated earnings by years of education, women, 1940–60, in 1960 dollars. Source: IPUMS city sample. Note: *SE* denotes southern or eastern European.

TABLE 2.2:   **Difference in effects of education for black and immigrant workers**

	Men			Women		
Economic outcome	1940	1950	1960	1940	1950	1960
Annual earnings	=	=	=	=	B > I	B > I
Occupation score	I > B	I > B	I > B	B > I	B > I	B > I
White-collar occupation	B > I	=	=	=	=	=
Occupational status	I > B	I > B	I > B	=	I > B	I > B
Unemployment	=	=	I > B	=	=	I > B
Labor force	=	=	I > B	=	B > I	B > I
Weeks worked	=	B > I	B > I	I > B	=	=
Full-time employment	=	=	=	=	=	B > I

Source: IPUMS city sample.

= Effect of education on outcome for black and immigrant workers does not differ significantly at the $p < .05$ level.

B > I Effect of education on outcome is significantly stronger for black workers at $p < .05$.

I > B Effect of education on outcome is significantly stronger for immigrant workers at $p < .05$.

Note: The statistical significance of the black-immigrant difference in the effects of education is affected by sample size. The IPUMS city sample is larger in 1950 and 1960 than in 1940. When the 1950 and 1960 samples are reduced to the size of the 1940 sample, several of the differences become non-significant at the .05 level: for men, weeks worked in 1950, and unemployment, labor force, and weeks worked in 1960; for women, earnings, occupation score, and labor force in 1950, and earnings, unemployment, and full-time employment in 1960. (Most remain significant at the .10 level.) Also for women in 1960, the difference in the effect of education on weeks worked becomes significant, favoring black women.

This is not because black women's prospects in white-collar work were so good, but because their alternatives outside that sector were so bad. As late as 1960, almost half of employed black women worked in service occupations, and one in five were domestic servants in private households. Education mattered because it gave black women a chance of escaping domestic service and similar low-paid lines of work.

When we consider other economic outcomes, the results are varied. Table 2.2 summarizes the results of statistical tests comparing the association between education and various economic outcomes for black and immigrant workers. In most comparisons there was no statistically significant difference in the effect of education. For men overall, immigrants seemed to have a small edge, while for women, at least by 1960, blacks did. Education consistently had a stronger effect on the occupation measures for immigrant men than black men. Results for labor force attachment, unemployment, and stability of work were mixed. Black women were less likely than immigrant women to move into higher-status occupations through education, but by 1960 they were more likely to benefit in other ways. Overall, however, there is no consistent pattern of racial difference. The economic returns to education—the extent to which education improved the chance for a better job, steadier employment, or higher earnings—was similar for black and immigrant workers.

Labor Market Discrimination and Economic Alternatives

The quantitative analysis just above describes similarities in the value of education for black and immigrant workers, yet the historical material that precedes it highlights the sharp differences in black and immigrant work experiences. These contrasting accounts can be reconciled if we distinguish between two aspects of opportunity: the economic value of education and the range of economic alternatives. Researchers have given little attention to the range of economic alternatives, yet this aspect of opportunity can be important. In economists' terms, it allows a better match between person and job, a better fit of talent and disposition to occupation. If one line of work proves unprofitable or unbearable, one can try another. A range of alternatives also allows for second chances, and thus buffers people against the twists and turns of fate. Someone who can't complete college, for instance, can find other ways to earn a living.

Immigrants had a wider range of economic alternatives. As they learned English and gained more education, they could enter the white-collar workforce through small business or through public- or private-sector employment. Given their extensive kin and ethnic connections to the skilled trades and unionized manufacturing work, those who were indifferent to school might make a decent living in the blue-collar world. Home ownership represented a third economic alternative. Immigrants had higher rates of home ownership than native-born Chicagoans, and many bought into the market at the start of a rapid rise in housing values. Some sold at a profit; others bought two-flats or apartment buildings, which generated rental income. Working-class families struggled to make ends meet while keeping up their mortgage payments, but their struggles underline the point that buying a home was a form of investment that was open even to those of very limited means.[35]

Black Chicagoans had fewer options. Discriminatory barriers confined black workers to a few channels within the white-collar labor market, chiefly in civil service and the professions. Most avenues of mobility in manual labor were also blocked. In home ownership as well, black opportunities were more limited. At the turn of the century, black Chicagoans were concentrated in neighborhoods of inexpensive wood-frame cottages, but as the ghetto expanded southward, it encompassed more large apartment buildings—better quality housing, to be sure, but prohibitively expensive. In 1930, only about 10 percent of the housing units in the Black Belt were single-family homes, and another third were in relatively affordable two- or three-flat buildings. After 1945, the ghetto expanded into some neighborhoods of single-family housing, giving middle-class black families an opportunity to invest in property. In many inner-city neighborhoods, however, the private-housing stock was razed and replaced with public housing. In addition, "redlining" prevented most blacks from getting access to federal mortgage programs and hurt them as well in obtaining private bank loans.[36]

Given this paucity of alternatives, education loomed large in African-American economic strategies. From early in the century, observers noted the motivation that black students felt to attend high school and college. A 1924 survey found that black students were more likely than immigrant students to aspire to high school, college, and the professions: "If possible, the younger colored children go on to high school, as they realize they must be better equipped educationally than white boys or girls in order to compete in getting a position. Parents are ready to make real sacrifices in order to give their children a chance." Aspirations for college and the professions remained high through the 1950s despite discrimination. As a middle-class black Chicagoan remembered, "There were a lot of our parents who were college trained, but the degrees were buried in the post office because they simply could not be hired. They were not accepted. But they had high standards for us because they wanted us to have a better life than they did. And they did everything within their power to provide us with the wherewithal—education, whatever—to have that better life." At the same time, not surprisingly, discrimination created some ambivalence about education as an economic strategy. As a Chicago Urban League report noted during the 1950s, "Negroes in America have been long depressed, and job opportunities have been limited on a color basis . . . This is reflected in a serious way in the Negro youths' psychological frame of reference about self and future and in turn results in a negative attitude toward school (preparation) and about future job opportunities (incentive). Thus the incentive threshold is low." For disadvantaged black students, the continuing salience of education—the aspirations to attend college when there was little prospect of doing so—did not reflect real hope. Instead, it signaled the lack of any better alternatives.[37]

Conclusion

Compared with immigrant workers, black workers faced more severe, more pervasive, and more persistent discrimination in the labor market. Black workers were excluded from most white-collar and skilled positions, especially those in the private sector. Educated black workers earned less than immigrant or other white workers with the same level of education. Although the color line shifted over time, under pressure from civil rights groups, the federal government, and the changing labor force itself, racial discrimination remained common in 1960. The surprising paradox, however, is that education was economically valuable for black workers, much as it was for immigrants. The reason is the very pervasiveness of racial discrimination. While black workers had limited opportunities within the white-collar labor market, they were also blocked from well-paid skilled or unionized blue-collar jobs. With all its flaws, education remained one of the only ways off the bottom rung of the labor market. This possibility of economic mobility through education, however, was more real for some black Chicagoans than for others. For disadvantaged black youth, those who were struggling academically and unlikely to finish high school, let alone go on for further schooling, aspirations to college and white-collar employment had little chance of fulfillment. Such aspirations were telling evidence of the narrow range of economic alternatives for black Chicagoans.

If race itself was implicated in the education gap described in chapter 1, then we must look for ways that black and immigrant experiences were different. Accordingly, this chapter focused on the labor market; the next considers the communities that black and immigrant workers went home to. These communities were quite distinct in their internal organization and their relationship to the larger city. Chapter 3 asks whether the social significance of education might have differed in black and immigrant communities. We find a curious parallel between the labor market patterns described above and the role that education played in the status order of black and immigrant communities.

CHAPTER THREE

Communities and Cultures

E ducation bestowed income; it could also bestow status. Its social significance had particular import for both black and immigrant Chicagoans because of their marginalized position within the city. It resonated most for black and immigrant elites, who promoted education as a means of group uplift. Yet the response to their message depended on the contours of their respective communities. As this chapter describes, the meaning of education turned on contrasts in elites' roles in these communities, in the internal organization of black and immigrant neighborhoods, and in the capacity of these communities to protect their members against white/American surveillance and stigmatization. Consequently, despite the similarity in elite views, education took on a different social significance for the black and immigrant working classes.

This chapter engages cultural explanations for the rise of inner-city schooling. It extends an influential account that links minority orientations to schooling to the group's relation to the dominant society. Over time, according to this account, immigrants were accepted into the mainstream of American society, while African Americans remained excluded. Although immigrants faced prejudice, it was not severe and it gradually diminished. Eventually, they became acculturated to the American status system and began to value education as a marker of prestige. By contrast, African Americans faced barriers to assimilation that only intensified over time. In reaction, an oppositional black culture emerged. This culture defined an authentic black identity in terms of its rejection of the white status system and of attributes, including education, which white culture denied to blacks.[1]

With this contrast between communities as a starting point, I explore how the process of their incorporation into the city shaped the meaning of education for each. The interpretation developed here retains a concern with minority group relations to the dominant white culture, but also builds in a consideration of class relations and social organization within the black and immigrant communities. We begin with a discussion of the ethnic elites and their campaigns for education, followed by an examination of working-class communities, first among immigrants, then among African Americans.

Elites

The African-American and immigrant communities each contained a small and cohesive elite comprising professionals, politicians, businessmen, journalists, and cultural and religious leaders. These elites were knitted together through civic and social organizations. In the black community, the Chicago Urban League, the National Association for the Advancement of Colored People, the fraternities and sororities, and the most prestigious churches and social clubs linked members of the elite. In the immigrant communities, the fraternal societies, Roman Catholic organizations, ethnic and nationalist societies, and ethnic trade and professional associations played a similar role. The black and immigrant elites were poised between the white American "mainstream"— itself a congeries of groups jostling for position—and the poor and working-class members of their own communities. Perhaps more than the working class, elites were conscious of white American racial and ethnic prejudices; many had been to college and participated in politics or in professional and civic organizations, where they had first-hand encounters with ethnic insult and exclusion. During the early twentieth century, elite anxiety about white American prejudice was heightened by the influx of disadvantaged migrants from Europe or the rural South; they feared these newcomers would reinforce stereotypes and impede group progress.[2]

Both black and immigrant elites sought to counter prejudice by spotlighting the most educated and cultured elements of their communities.

In 1927, for instance, Chicago's *Herald and Examiner* invited immigrant elites to profile their national groups. Judge Francis Borrelli highlighted the classical heritage of Dante and Galileo and the accomplishments of Chicago's Italian-American doctors and lawyers. He added:

> True, certain remnants of the immigrant community are still visible. The center of those remnants is at Taylor and Halsted sts.—the old-time heart of Little Italy. There one may still see a few foreign-looking women with shawls thrown over their heads, shuffling through the old-world street marts that abound in the district and give it a European atmosphere. But that picture is quickly fading. It is being erased by education. And the old immigrant community has bec[o]me merely a transient stage in the development of real Americans of the highest caliber.

African-American elites also seized opportunities to display the education and cultivation of their class. In the early 1920s, black students in an interracial club at the University of Chicago found that the white students "had no idea of the lifestyle or the life of the black persons who had achieved and who had lovely homes." To rectify this, they invited white students to visit prominent black Chicagoans such as the banker Jesse Binga. Similarly, in the 1930s a group of professional men held dinners at downtown hotels in order to "get white people who do not know us to come out and see us." A story for the *Chicago Daily News* indicates the effect: "In dress, deportment, evidence of culture and refinement, the Negroes at this gathering, regardless of the degree of pigmentation in their skins . . . were indistinguishable from their white guests. The speaking was on a considerably higher plane than obtains at most white banquets."[3]

Elites also tried to bring the behavior of the working class into conformity with middle-class American standards. The foreign-language press urged working-class immigrants to practice thrift, sobriety, and public decorum, and to protect the reputation of their nationality. The Lithuanian newspaper *Lietuva* complained that immigrants stayed up late, drinking and singing loudly, and added, "It is not necessary to mention here what an unfavorable impression this creates in the minds of the non-Lithuanian residents of the community." The Polish newspaper *Dziennik Zwiazkowy* exhorted its community about the delinquency of youth: "Let [Polish parents] visit the German colonies. Will they find there vagrants in the streets? On the contrary, the youth display their bringing up with grace and politeness. . . . Why does our youth, which is better fitted than the German, or any other, waste itself? Because of this the parents suffer, their poor example slanders their people, and as a whole the entire Polish population is blamed for this condition."[4]

Although the immigrant elites pressed for conformity with American middle-class norms, they did not want their working-class countrymen to sacrifice their ethnic identity. Indeed, many immigrant elites themselves remained active in ethnic organizations. The profiles in the Polish-American and Italian-American *Who's Who* volumes show that many immigrant doctors were retained by ethnic fraternal organizations, journalists wrote for the foreign-language press, and artistic and literary figures performed the music and theater of their home country and translated its literature into English. Elites also fretted over "denationalization" and organized private schools and cultural societies to preserve their national language and heritage. Many were staunch nationalists who supported and identified with struggles for sovereignty in Europe. They wanted their countrymen to shed customs associated with the peasantry and lower class, but to retain a sense of national identity and pride.[5]

Likewise, the black elite pressed the working-class members of their community to conform to middle-class expectations. The Chicago Urban League, founded in 1915, instructed southern migrants about appropriate behavior in public settings and at work; a card distributed to new arrivals cautioned, "Do not carry on loud conversations in street cars and public places"; "Do not loaf. Get a job at once"; and "Be industrious, sober, efficient, and prompt." Black elites enjoined new migrants not to appear in public in clothing that evoked the servitude of the South: overalls for men, and for women "dust caps, bungalow aprons, house clothing and bedroom shoes." During the early 1920s, black social workers urged newly arrived workers to adhere to standards of proper behavior and work discipline. During World War II, when southern migration surged again, prominent black Chicagoans organized a chapter of the national "Hold Your Jobs" committee to press for reliable work habits and decorous public behavior. This appeal was typical:

Negro workers in war industries have been severely criticized for their conduct. Reporting late to work, wearing grotesque clothes, using obscene and boisterous language are some of the specific charges made against them . . . Every colored worker, therefore, must be constantly on guard to see that by his conduct, he does not retard the march toward the objectives and aims for which his race is struggling.

Like their immigrant counterparts, black elites tried to activate concern about the reputation of their group.[6]

As they promoted assimilation, elites campaigned specifically for education, taking steps to promote an ethnic "intelligentsia." The foreign-language press emphasized the contributions that the educated could make to the immigrant community. The *Denni Hlasel,* for instance, urged Czech youth to train as schoolteachers, noting the "repercussions upon the opinions of our foreign elements, and also upon our American public whose opinions we value most." New elite-supported organizations gave financial and moral support to college students. The *Matice Vyssiho Vzdelani* made loans to Czech college students who had "the sentiments of a Bohemian." Similar groups included the Lithuanian *Ausra* and the Polish University Club. Italian students at the University of Illinois formed their own fraternity, and their compatriots held banquets every year to fete Italian college graduates.[7]

Advocacy of mass education became part of this campaign. Beginning in the 1910s, the immigrant press directed appeals at the working class. The *Denni Hlasel* spoke "particular[ly] to our immigrants whose past has been anything but rosy. To say, 'I am a laborer, unskilled worker, and the same lot should be good enough for my child,' is not only entirely wrong but also quite a confession of inferiority." The newspapers highlighted the economic payoff to schooling. For instance, *Dziennik Zwiazkowy* noted the high salaries that women doctors, chemists, and teachers could earn, adding,

> Tuition fees in the Chicago schools are practically nonexistent with the exception of the universities. Even books are given without charge if one tries to arrange it so. But even so, what do these small costs, as well as the loss of the wage the child would earn, signify in view of the fact that a qualified teacher or chemist earns from seventy-five to a hundred dollars per month in her first year?

The newspapers also played on immigrants' concerns about American opinion. *L'Italia* complained that truancy among Italian children "lower[s] our social position in Chicago." Because of Poles' limited schooling, opined the *Dziennik Zwiazkowy,* "we become the laughing stock of others, our abilities are scoffed at, and we are dubbed as the retarders of education." Moreover, as the editor of *Polonia* wrote, "In comparison to the Jewish immigration that is later and smaller than ours in the United States, how does our immigration stand in a high education? Let us be frank and admit that it is very poor."[8]

Immigrant elites did not speak with one voice about education, however. Several immigrant groups were marked by a schism between religious and secular factions. Among Poles, this divide was embodied in the distinction between the Polish Roman Catholic Union and the Polish National Alliance, which maintained parallel structures of fraternal lodges. Early in the century, their newspapers, the PRCU's *Narod Polski* and *Dziennik Zjednoczenia* and the PNA's *Zgoda* and *Dziennik Zwiazkowy,* carried on a vituperative battle about education. The secular newspapers vigorously promoted academic education; they also criticized the quality of the parochial schools, and cautioned that Catholic schools run by non-Polish religious could undermine nationalist sentiments. The church-affiliated newspapers, on the other hand, framed the aims of education first as moral, then as practical, and disparaged academic and literary pursuits. The *Narod Polski,* a PRCU newspaper, mocked, "A young lady of 15 summers, may know all about the capes of Africa and can name historical events in chronological order; but she does not know how to prevent her washing from getting yellow; how to economize on fuel, or how to detect an inferior quality of butter."[9] Despite these differences, however, secular and religious factions agreed on the importance of some kind of education for working-class children.

There were close parallels to these differences in the African-American community. Like their immigrant counterparts, black elites disagreed among themselves about whether the race should promote an academic education, as W. E. B. Du Bois advocated, or a vocational one, as Booker T. Washington espoused. In Chicago, however, this division did not run deep, and members of the black elite found many ways to promote the development of their own intelligentsia. Black fraternities, sororities, and other associations advocated higher education. The Washington Intercollegiate Club, a black social club, held events for college men and women and gave students small amounts of financial aid. Like the immigrant press, the *Chicago Defender* lauded graduates of local high schools and colleges, reporting enthusiastically on their graduation parties and career plans.[10]

Mass education was prominent in black elites' vision of racial progress. Among the Urban League's dicta to new arrivals was "Do not keep your children out of school." The Intercollegiate Club scolded, "The

number[s] of truants are altogether too many. More co-operation must
be given social agencies. The parents should not be so indifferent. Some
means should be provided to take care of the many delinquents aside
from reformatories." The *Defender* reinforced this pro-school message.
"Bud Billiken," the mascot of the *Defender*'s children's page, exhorted
children to attend school regularly and study industriously. "Don't forget, if you want to be a 100 percent Billiken just return to school" was a
typical September reminder.[11]

Not coincidentally, elite appeals for education echoed the intensifying pressure from social workers, truant officers, and Progressive Era
reformers. These advocates sought to protect children from delinquency,
vice, drink, gambling, and other threats by keeping them in school or
other protected venues, such as municipal playgrounds or settlement
houses. Even when adolescents found work, these advocates claimed,
these young workers earned little and jeopardized their health while
sacrificing the education that could lead to better jobs in adulthood.
Social workers often blamed selfish parents for denying immigrant youth
the benefits of schooling, framing these decisions as a reflection of Old
World or peasant customs. In this discourse, a child's school attendance
became another part of a package of behaviors, including thrift, sobriety, and diligence at work, that garnered approval from representatives
of charity, relief, and social welfare agencies.[12] Given this context, it
is not surprising that black and immigrant elites concerned about the
social standing of their group would become advocates for education.
But these elites did not simply echo the message of Progressive Era reformers. They invoked ethnic pride, linking education to the reputation
and collective interests of their group, and sought to use their authority
and status as leverage to sway others in the community.

Immigrant Communities

Although African-American and immigrant elites both promoted education, the working classes did not always follow this advice, any more
than they followed the advice of social workers from outside their own
communities. To understand the differences between black and immigrant orientations to education, we need to consider the context of
social relations in both communities. These communities differed in
three ways. First, the immigrant elites could readily assimilate, which

diminished their contact with the working class. Black elites, on the other hand, remained within the ghetto as advocates for education. Second, the social structure of immigrant working-class communities, because of its localism and residential stability, supported a status order which emphasized conformity to behavioral norms. By contrast, the black working class was embedded in a more fluid community in which education was a more salient marker of status. Finally, working-class immigrants found alternative routes to status through the growing power and legitimacy of institutions with which they were closely identified, such as labor unions, the Democratic machine, and the Roman Catholic Church. For the black working class, such alternative routes were largely blocked, leaving the onus on education as the way to gain status within the city. The remainder of the chapter develops these contrasts through an examination first of the immigrant community, then the African-American.

Class Relations

Although turn-of-the-century immigrant communities were class integrated, those residents who could afford it eventually moved away from the congested and deteriorating neighborhoods near the city center. When working-class and middle-class immigrants moved out, they typically moved in opposite directions. Middle-class immigrants tended to settle in neighborhoods north or northwest of downtown, where new subdivisions were being built. Some looked simply for better housing, while others sought to distance themselves from the poor. As a Polish woman said, "I kept moving further out, further out because I wanted to better myself and I wanted to get away from that environment . . . I didn't want to wear a babushcka always." Working-class immigrants, on the other hand, settled in the new industrial neighborhoods clustered around factories in the southern and western districts of the city, including the steel mill neighborhoods in South Chicago and the meatpacking plants on the Near Southwest Side.[13]

These residential shifts separated the working classes from upper- and middle-class immigrants. When the Balch Institute's Italians in Chicago oral history project inquired about local leaders, working-class Italian Americans tended to describe those who by occupation were located in the community—Catholic priests, ward and precinct politicians, shopkeepers—rather than those from the secular and upwardly mobile middle class. As Frank Bertucci recalled, "We all were in the economical similar to it you know? We had no outstanding. No one we could point the finger to. That's our fairy godfather. Well maybe you could do that with the priest if you want to. But he wasn't earning." Around 1940, *Who's Who* volumes were produced for Polish Americans and Italian Americans; in samples of the Chicago-area notables, only a few lived in the heavily working-class southern and southwestern neighborhoods of the city.[14]

This residential separation strained relations between elite and working class. A 1928 statement by an association of Polish priests expressed resentment at the withdrawal of elite members of the community:

> Our intelligentsia, who grew up in our Polish parishes, where they got rich, are now leaving our parishes more and more. They have climbed to a high political level, still they desire from their country men, some backing up. They leave us, not paying much attention to the rearing of their children in Polish traditions and teaching them the language of their fathers; they don't marry in Polish churches; they bring up their children in non-Polish churches; they support non-Polish parishes and leave all the difficulties of up-keeping these basic traditions of our fathers to the poorest of our people.

When elites tried to sustain their ties to the working-class communities, their social and geographic distance made this difficult. The two leading Polish fraternal organizations—the PNA and PRCU—tried to unite Chicago's Polish neighborhoods with citywide newspapers that printed news from all the parishes. However, as Edward Kantowicz describes, "Poles in outlying areas sometimes felt that the leaders in Polish Downtown either ignored them or else put on airs in considering the *Stanislawowo* [the parish of 'Polish Downtown'] the intellectual and spiritual heart of Polonia's capital. In South Chicago, particularly, such resentment rankled."[15]

Moreover, in their effort to appeal to their middle-class American audience, immigrant elites chose a framing of their ethnic identity likely to alienate working-class immigrants: they highlighted their shared artistic and literary heritage but muted peasant and working-class customs. Their version of immigrant culture evoked Old World status hierarchies that elevated education, refinement, and gentility and disparaged manual labor. Working-class immigrants, by contrast, rejected this status hierarchy in favor of an egalitarian and democratic ideal. To the chagrin of the intelligentsia, their proletarian countrymen had little interest in the artistic, literary, and linguistic heritage of their forefathers.

Writing about Chicago's Italian community, for instance, a well-educated Italian-American man fretted that "not one individual (of the older group) could name one Roman poet or writer."[16]

Within the working-class immigrant communities, people did not gain status from displays of education and high culture—quite the contrary. Educated Polish Americans reportedly spoke a less refined version of Polish so as not to appear to be affecting superiority. "Many, especially of the younger people growing up here, [felt] that it was putting on airs to speak a cultivated Polish, that 'regular guys spoke plain and rough.'" The *Dziennik Zwiazkowy*, the newspaper of the Polish secular nationalist organization, complained that parish schoolboys "think it humiliating to bow to any one on the street . . . intentionally assuming rude manners and postures in order not to appear different and so expose themselves to the ridicule of their school friends, who have not the slightest notion of polished behavior or of the accepted rules of social conduct." Those who displayed erudition were quickly cut down to size. An Italian-American man commented that his friend "who majored in literature at Chicago University has a philosophical trend. His father wanted him to be a druggist instead of anything else. Many times I go to the drug store to 'chat' with this person. Our discussions run along philosophy, literature, and sociology. We analyze such things as 'hedonism,' the 'Mexican Invasion,' and 'Cultural life of our neighborhood.' The doctors who accidentally come in to ask about calls listen to us only to turn away saying, 'You fellows are nuts.'"[17]

Status in the Working-Class Community

The social structure of working-class immigrant communities shaped the salience of education by supporting a status order that emphasized conformity to shared behavioral norms. Studies of "social capital" suggest that a community can better monitor behavior when its members are linked in stable and densely connected social networks.[18] Immigrant neighborhoods tended to be residentially stable, and social and economic life was organized by neighborhood. Many immigrants worked near their homes, and their walk to work took them through the neighborhood; they saw their neighbors on the job and at the end of the day in nearby taverns.[19] The Roman Catholic or Greek Orthodox parish reinforced the localism of social life. The parish church was the focus of numerous societies and activities—the choir, sodalities, annual feasts and

processions, and the activities of the parochial school—that brought parishioners together and gave them a sense of shared identity. These over-
lapping memberships in family, parish, fraternal organization, precinct,
workplace, and union sustained dense local ties even as ethnic identity
declined in importance.[20]

Because of the stability of the community and the density of its social
ties, immigrants could gain status from personal qualities readily moni-
tored by their neighbors. This community structure fostered a status order based on conformity to codes of behavior that blended religious pre-
cept, ethnic and working-class custom, and economic reciprocity. This is
not to say that status markers such as education or material success did
not matter. Because of the community's social organization, however,
other attributes could confer status within the local area. As an observer
of the Polish community wrote, "To stand at the top of social life here, it
does not require any education."[21]

Status in the City

Although elites emphasized education as a means to counter ethnic
prejudice, the immigrant working class found alternative ways to gain
status within the larger social arena of the city. The early twentieth century saw the elevation within Chicago of three institutions with which
immigrants were closely identified: labor unions, the Democratic Party,
and the Roman Catholic Church. Immigrant workers had been staunch
unionists from the turn of the century, with a class consciousness forged
in Europe and sharpened by early twentieth-century labor struggles in
Chicago. Southern and eastern European workers were the backbone
of labor-organizing campaigns in the garment, meatpacking, and steel
industries. Most early campaigns went down to defeat, but in the 1930s
this struggle was finally redeemed with the rise of industrial unionism.
The Wagner Act and other New Deal legislation had symbolic as well
as practical resonance, legitimating unions as vehicles for redressing
the grievances of a generation. With half of the immigrant workers employed in manufacturing, and many of them organized, the strength of
the industrial unions gave immigrants a claim to status that had nothing
to do with education.[22]

At the same time, the ascendancy of the city's Democratic machine
began to make a place for immigrants at the table of local politics. The
1931 mayoral victory of Anton Cermak, a Czech, brought this machine

to power. After Cermak's death in 1933, the Irish mayors who followed were careful to dispense patronage jobs and other kinds of material and symbolic benefits to the immigrant communities, which remained reliable sources of Democratic votes. The Democratic machine also championed the views and interests of immigrants, for instance by opposing Prohibition. This representation gave southern and eastern European immigrants some standing in the political life of the city.[23]

Finally, during the early twentieth century the Roman Catholic Church moved from margin to mainstream in the life of the city. Before the turn of the century, immigrants in Chicago had faced anti-Catholic animosity and bias. As the number of Catholics grew with migration from southern and eastern Europe, the Roman Catholic Church began to gain recognition and influence in the city. At the same time, these immigrants became less marginal within the church hierarchy. Religious and lay leaders from southern and eastern European backgrounds gradually moved into positions in the Archdiocese of Chicago. Immigrant neighborhoods organized ethnic or "national" parishes where their native language was spoken and their culture reflected during worship. Increasingly, the immigrants could recruit teachers from their own religious orders: the Lithuanians from the Sisters of St. Casimir, the Poles from the Felician Sisters and other Polish teaching sisterhoods, and the Czechs from the Bohemian Benedictines.[24]

This collective mobility through union, precinct, and church raised the status of immigrants in the city. But group status also reflects encounters that stigmatize by placing people in a subordinate or dishonorable role. American stereotypes associated immigrants with poverty, slum residence, social disorganization, and attendant problems such as domestic discord, juvenile delinquency, and drunkenness. These stereotypes were activated and reinforced when immigrants sought assistance from American charities or relief agencies, or faced inquiries from the police, truant officers, or social workers. But as blue-collar work became more stable and wages increased, fewer immigrants resorted to public aid or charity. The immigrant communities also began to establish their own ethnic or religious charitable organizations, such as Catholic Charities (founded in 1918), which provided alternatives to charity and relief organizations run by "outsiders" to the community. By the mid-1920s, blacks had overtaken Poles as the most numerous minority group receiving assistance from both public relief and United Charities. Moreover, as neighborhood institutions grew, they buffered youth from the juvenile justice system; minor delinquencies were handled within the community. Later on, the Chicago Area Project had the same effect. Finally, immigrant employment in domestic service became less common after the turn of the century, relieving immigrants of this subservient role.[25]

As Matthew Frye Jacobson has written, prejudice against southern and eastern European immigrants diminished over time. At the turn of the century, it was commonplace to speak of Italians or Slavs as a different race; the eugenics movement of the 1920s gave these conceptions a scientific language. Only two decades later, this view appeared more retrograde. This is not to say that ethnic prejudice was put to rest. Old stereotypes resurfaced after World War II, for instance, when immigrants opposing racial integration were criticized as backward and illiberal. Overall, however, prejudice had diminished, and working-class immigrants were affiliated with, even central to, institutions that had power and standing in the larger community. For them, education was not the only way to counter prejudice and gain status.[26]

The African-American Community

Among African Americans, by contrast, class relations, community social structure, and relations with whites all combined to make education salient for the working class. Elites deployed education to mark status distinctions within the community; class tensions generated some ambivalence about education. But given the continuing presence and visibility of the elite in the black community, and the absence of an alternative route to status, education retained a significance it did not have for the immigrant working class.

Class Relations

While immigrant elites could move out of their old neighborhoods and integrate into mainstream society, black elites and working classes remained in uncomfortable but meaningful proximity. Class relations in the black community were shaped by the intensifying racial segregation of the early twentieth century. After the turn of the century, few black elites lived outside black neighborhoods. At the same time, the growth of the ghetto created opportunities for the black businessmen, professionals, and politicians who served this community.[27] Stratified though it was, the black community also promoted contact between the classes. Within the South Side Black Belt, middle-class blocks and apartment buildings were interspersed with working- and lower-class areas. Government agencies and social service organizations such as the Urban League, the Young Men's Christian Association, and the Colored Big Brothers brought poor blacks in contact with more advantaged members of their community. Some churches and community organizations had a mixed-class membership. St. Clair Drake and Horace Cayton, in their classic 1945 study of Chicago's black community, reported that one-third of lower-class churchgoers attended churches in which middle- and upper-class blacks predominated.[28]

Although private socializing tended to be segregated by class, the elite exercised an indirect influence on the middle class and even the working class through status competition within the community. As Drake and Cayton wrote,

> People change their status by acquiring money and education, and then changing their "set." The dynamics of social mobility in Bronzeville [Chicago's black community] can only be understood by observing individuals actually shifting from clique to clique, church to church, and club to club in the struggle to get ahead. The people who are "in" control this upward mobility by setting the standards and holding the line against those who don't make the grade.

According to these authors, there were perhaps a thousand social clubs in the Black Belt during the 1930s, rising to two thousand by 1945. These clubs were arrayed in an intricate hierarchy. Club members bid for status by inviting or being invited to events sponsored by higher-prestige clubs. The *Defender,* by then the most widely circulating black newspaper, publicized and fueled this competition. Its social columns reported extensively on the activities of the clubs, and club members anxiously sought this mention, just as they sought recognition from higher-prestige clubs.[29]

The social clubs disseminated elite and middle-class prescriptions for behavior. According to Drake and Cayton, their influence extended even into the lower class:

> Recent migrants who form clubs in imitation of the pattern they see displayed in the *Defender,* and rising lower-class people who have never belonged to a "good club," sometimes form groups which display a mixture of lower-class

and middle-class behavior. Over a period of time, however, as they begin to compete for prestige by attending the pay dances of other clubs, and through interclub visiting, as well as the desire to get bids to formals, they are likely to knock off the rough edges. The drift toward conformity is in the direction of middle-classness.

At the clubs' large "pay dances," standards for behavior were much stricter than at the commercial dance halls: "[Attendees] are all 'on their behavior' when attending a club affair. If somebody gets into a scrap, they know they are blacklisted from then on. So they keep on their P's and Qs."[30]

This class juxtaposition could mean ambivalence and social friction. Among the black elite were men and women who had succeeded against the odds but were denied full recognition for their achievements. As they moved within the larger society, they were reminded of their second-class status by a stream of petty insults and constraints and by steep obstacles to professional advancement. They could not escape these restrictions, but they could accentuate their status by distancing themselves from the less fortunate within their own community. As a black professional told researcher Ethel Ramey Harris, "[Cheap taverns] are not fit places for me, my children, my associates. I never go to a public beach. I never go to dances unless they are formal. I can't see the point of spending ten or twelve years in a university only to throw that education away in two or three minutes." At the same time, elite disapproval and distancing was tempered by an acknowledgement of shared fate and by an understanding of the harsh conditions that circumscribed the lives of the poor. In a 1943 editorial, the *Defender* scolded the lower classes for their rough demeanor, and in the same breath chided the "better-class, better-paid, and better-groomed elements" for their censorious "good conduct" campaigns, asking, "Can we expect good conduct from any man, no matter his color, when he feels he is society's outcast, when he is forced to live in primitive slum ghettos, when he must do the filthiest, most degraded work to earn a living, when he can never feel sure about his tomorrow?"[31]

Working-class blacks were also ambivalent, recognizing elites' accomplishments but resenting their distancing from the less well-off. This resentment was expressed with an elaborate lexicon: Drake and Cayton wrote that working-class blacks "are always referring to the more affluent and successful as 'dicties,' 'stuck-ups,' 'muckti-mucks,' 'high-toned folks,' 'tony people.' The 'strainers' and 'strivers' are well-recognized social types, people whose whole lives are dominated by the drive to get ahead." In a mixed-class housing project during the mid-1950s, a war of words erupted between students from working-class and middle-class families. A middle-class high school student reported,

> Most of the people think we feel that we are better than they are. Frankly I think I am. They started calling us names like "hanctie" and "high-minded" when my mother started working for the PTA. She was trying to get some of the mothers to take an interest in the school. She must have made some of them mad. They have been calling her Miss Ann ever since. Their kids started calling me "mariney" and "white folks." They call every body in my crowd those names. It doesn't bother us now. We never called them any names except low class. But that's what they are—doing all of those low class things.[32]

Cross-class interactions were complicated by these resentments. A study of black lawyers, for instance, noted black clients' sensitivity to their attorney's manner with them: "The families were more inclined to excuse [a] lack of personal concern in the [white] attorney than in the Negro lawyer. The lower-class family is especially alert to any signs of condescension or 'airs' on the part of the Negro lawyer." While the upper class used a rhetoric of distancing, the working class employed one of leveling. In the mid-1930s, as a truant officer described, a mother tried to intercede when her son was harshly disciplined by a black teacher: "The teacher, however, was not to be conciliated, which led to a rather sharp interchange of words between her and the mother, ending with the mother's remark, 'You may think that because you're a teacher, you're better than I am, but I want you to know that your hide is just as black as mine and I can go any place that you can.'"[33]

This orientation has some resemblance to that of the immigrant working classes. In their community as well, refined diction or displays of education could be read, and resented, as distancing. The difference was that black elites remained active and visible within the community, setting the tone in the community's status hierarchy. While their advocacy of education might be resented, it was not so readily ignored.

Status in the Working-Class Community

Another contrast with immigrants appears when we consider sources of status within the community. The localism of immigrant communities was conducive to monitoring of behavior. Although the black community as well had a vibrant social life, it was organized differently. Although a few middle-class enclaves were residentially stable, for the most part residential mobility was more common among African Americans than immigrants, a reflection of their economic marginality and the inflated rents of the ghetto. In a 1925 survey of Chicago industrial workers, 20 percent of black families had moved the previous year, compared with 3 percent of immigrant families. Many black households included extended kin or lodgers who were even more transient. As Drake and Cayton wrote of Chicago's West Side during the 1930s: "Usually there was a nucleus maintaining the home while an ever-shifting circle was coming and going."[34]

Moreover, social relations were not territorially organized to the extent they were in the immigrant communities. To be sure, working-class black neighborhoods had communal places—taverns, salons, barbershops—where residents could find esteem based on character rather than education or economic success. But many of their activities took people outside the confines of their immediate neighborhoods. Most black workers commuted to jobs outside the Black Belt. Most churches were Protestant and did not have geographically defined parishes: on Sundays, neighbors fanned out across the community, some walking a few blocks away, others attending services at a more distant church. Some shifted from one church to another until they found one to their liking, leading frustrated pastors to complain of "church tramps."[35]

At the same time, the black community in general exhibited a strong pull, becoming the focus of identification for black Chicagoans. This was in part a function of white prejudice, which maintained the invisible walls of the ghetto, but there were more proximate reasons as well. One was the spatial compactness of the South Side Black Belt. Within this area, key public spaces attracted people from all over the community. Black Chicagoans told Drake and Cayton during the 1930s, "If you're trying to find a certain Negro in Chicago, stand on the corner of 47th and South Park long enough and you're bound to see him." In addition, communitywide events and institutions instilled a sense of collective identity. Beginning in the 1920s, the *Defender* sponsored an annual communitywide Bud Billiken Day Parade, named for the mascot of the newspaper's children's page. And, via newspaper ballots, black Chicagoans also elected a "Mayor of Bronzeville." The *Defender* itself was both a reflection of community solidarity and an agent in its creation. Around 1940, the paper's estimated readership was one hundred thousand, almost half the city's adult black population.[36]

Rather than being segmented into neighborhoods, the African-American community was multiple cities layered one upon another. Black Chicagoans were oriented to communities of interest or affiliation whose members might be drawn from all over the Black Belt. Its density and mobility made the Black Belt a cosmopolitan environment, one in which distinct ways of life coexisted in uneasy proximity. Within the rigid walls of the racial ghetto, boundaries were permeable: between sacred and secular, between respectable and underworld.[37] The result was a more diffuse community, one based on social connections that were more socially diverse and perhaps more transitory. Because the community was structured in this way, people more often encountered strangers; thus, status markers such as education became more valuable.

Status in the City

Working-class immigrants enjoyed collective status mobility as labor unions, the Democratic machine, and the Catholic Church gained legitimacy and prestige within the city. Nothing comparable occurred for African Americans. The institutions that gave immigrants status were far less hospitable to black Chicagoans. Their community had a complicated relationship with the labor unions. Black workers in the steel and meatpacking industries participated in the union struggles of World War I, and later in the CIO campaigns of the 1930s and early 1940s. Some in the union movement, however, regarded blacks with suspicion because of their early involvement in strikebreaking. This mistrust was reciprocated, for black Chicagoans were well aware of the racially exclusionary practices of many unions, especially those affiliated with the American Federation of Labor. The CIO's interracial organizing could not mend all these wounds.[38]

In politics, black voters were latecomers to the ascendant Democratic Party. In Chicago, the traditional tie of blacks to the Republican Party had been reinforced by allegiance to William Hale Thompson, a Republican who served as mayor in 1915–23 and again in 1927–31. Thompson opposed racial discrimination and appointed blacks to a number of city government posts, including the chair of the Civil Service Commission; indeed, his opponents called City Hall "Uncle Tom's Cabin." When Thompson ran against Anton Cermak in 1931, the majority-black sections of the city were the only ones he carried. Then the popularity of President Franklin Delano Roosevelt, a Democrat, spurred a gradual realignment among black voters. The Democratic mayor Edward

Kelly, who served from 1933 to 1947, cultivated black voters with favors and political appointments. As William Grimshaw describes, however, blacks remained second-class citizens in the Democratic machine, and the alliance with that organization required painful compromise: black politicians were subject to a "code of silence" on controversial racial questions.[39]

The growing strength of the Roman Catholic Church held little significance for black Chicagoans. Fewer than 10 percent of black churchgoers were members of predominantly white denominations, including Catholicism; the few black Catholics often faced racial hostility and exclusion in white parishes. Moreover, black Chicagoans' own church organizations did not give them status within the city. Most of the black Protestant churches were affiliated with separate conventions or denominations such as the National Negro Baptist Church, which had little visibility outside the black community. The "storefront churches" were socially marginal even within the black community and even more so outside it. Certainly, the church was clearly a prominent institution within the community: it is a measure of the gulf separating the black and white worlds that the black churches were of so little consequence outside the walls of the ghetto.[40]

A final contrast: as immigrant communities became more prosperous and established their own charitable societies, and as working-class wages rose, immigrants could more often avoid stigmatizing encounters with authorities and social workers. This, too, did not happen in the black community, where rates of poverty and dependence remained high. At times during the Great Depression, roughly half of the city's black population was on relief. In 1959, the poverty rate among black children was nearly 50 percent. Private black charities sought to ameliorate these conditions, but these organizations were small and vulnerable to economic downturn. Thus, there were few buffers between black Chicagoans and the city's courts, public welfare offices, and social service agencies. Many black Chicagoans encountered whites chiefly through stigmatizing interactions which cast blacks in dependent roles and reinforced racial stereotypes. A white social worker interviewed in 1957 reflected the perceptions that blacks were likely to face in these encounters: "All that these Negroes think about is making babies. After all, it doesn't cost them anything. They don't have to work because they are on ADC [Aid to Dependent Children] . . . Charity is only ruining these people." For the black community, education had value as a rebuke to such stereotypes.[41]

Conclusion

For black and immigrant Chicagoans, the meaning of education was tied to status both within the ethnic community and in relations to the dominant white American society. Ethnic elites believed education could confer status and counter the prejudices of the larger society.. For the working classes, the meaning of education was a more complicated question. Compared to blacks, immigrants were less exposed to elite influence, they were more oriented to the neighborhood and its close judgments of behavior, and they had other ways to gain status in the city. Working-class immigrants had status within the local neighborhood as persons of good character, and they entered the city under the banner of union, church, and party. Just as the labor market offered an economic position for less-educated immigrants, in unionized or skilled blue-collar jobs, so the ethnic community and the city offered a valued social position. In Chicago's black community, by contrast, elites were barred from assimilation, so they remained to advocate schooling. To a degree not found within the immigrant communities, educational credentials became coinage in the black community's social contests, as well as a weapon against racism. Education did not guarantee respect, any more than it guaranteed economic rewards—but for black Chicagoans there were few alternatives.

After World War II, the ways of life described in this chapter began to change. Racial transition in the city disrupted some previously stable immigrant neighborhoods and widened class segregation within the black community. Social and ecological change, in particular the growing concentration of poverty and the geographic and social isolation of the ghetto, must be taken into account when we consider the forces that sustain inner-city schooling. But these changes did not take place soon enough to explain the problems of inner-city schooling.

The first three chapters of this book lay a foundation for a history of education in the inner city. Some elements of these chapters, including the growing racial gap in schooling, the demographic change in the city, trends in school resources, labor market discrimination, and the distinctive economic strategies of the black and immigrant communities, become important components of this history. At the same time, these chapters rule out certain explanations of inner-city schooling. At least for Chicago, the origins of inner-city schooling were not simply a matter of money, because per-pupil expenditures rose in the 1940s and 1950s.

They were not simply a response to labor market discrimination, because the economic rewards for education were similar for black and immigrant workers. Nor does it appear that immigrant cultures embraced
education while African-American culture rejected it.

We cannot understand inner-city schooling without delving more
deeply into the history of the schools themselves. The next four chapters
come to terms with the school policies and practices that were most critical to the character of inner-city schooling in Chicago.

CHAPTER FOUR

Racial Segregation and Inequality

The next three chapters examine school policy and practice in areas critical to the formation of inner-city schools. In all three policy areas—race, vocational education, and remedial education—significant changes occurred between 1900 and 1960. Chicago public school officials recognized a problem, then began to cast about for a solution, sometimes going through a period of experimentation. New practices were adopted, sometimes modified, and over time became part of the taken-for-granted framework of the urban schools. As we will see, many elements of these policies were at least nominally race neutral, but because they were implemented in a racially divided and unequal city, they had racially disparate consequences.

In this chapter, we consider a set of decisions that explicitly concerned race. They include districting and resource allocation for black and white students, as well as the policies and practices shaping race relations in the schools. The Chicago schools, like most other northern schools, were officially color-blind, yet over time they became racially segregated and unequal. This chapter traces the rise of segregation, the emergence of racial inequality in the schools, and the political controversies over these problems, along with the intercultural programs adopted in response to racial tensions. These developments had implications both for the quality of education in black schools and for the legitimacy and trust that black parents and children were willing to give to the schools.

The Emergence of Segregation, 1900–1930

At the turn of the century, Chicago's public schools were not racially segregated; indeed, the schools had been integrated for decades. During the Civil War, Chicago had opened a "Colored School," but many of the city's black parents refused to send their children there; the school closed after two years. In 1874, the General Assembly of Illinois passed a law banning racial exclusion in public schools. In the early 1900s, although black families clustered together residentially, these clusters were small and scattered, and most school attendance areas were racially mixed. In 1915, only one school had a black enrollment of more than 90 percent.[1]

Chicago's racially mixed schools were not without tension, however. Demonstrations and fistfights might result when black children were assigned to attend a predominantly white school. Some white students refused to march next to black classmates at graduation. Racial conflict was more intense in the high schools, where black students were excluded from many extracurricular activities. Even so, the Chicago Commission on Race Relations heard in the early 1920s that young black and white children mingled comfortably in the classroom and on the schoolyard. "They don't understand the difference between colored and white children," said a principal of his kindergarten students. According to the CCRR, "The white children at a school 20 per cent Negro (Haven) were Italians, Jews, and Greeks, and all the races played so naturally together that passersby frequently stopped to watch them."[2]

Although racial exclusion was prohibited, there was no positive commitment to racial equality in the Chicago Public Schools. African Americans did not receive the same symbolic recognition via political representation given to other ethnic groups. The Czech, Polish, and Jewish communities all had representation on the Chicago Board of Education before 1900, and an Italian board member was appointed in the 1920s. By contrast, although black civic leaders began to lobby early in the century for a representative to the school board, that appointment did not happen until 1939. Also significant is the board's failure to curb racial discrimination in the employment of black teachers and administrators. Black men and women attended the Chicago Normal School in large numbers, but they faced racial barriers to professional employment in the public schools. In 1917, only forty-one black teachers were employed in a teaching force of more than eight thousand. Not until 1927 was the first black principal appointed.[3]

Nor did the Chicago Public Schools promote racial tolerance or integration. This reticence is striking given how readily local educators embraced other moral missions such as Americanization and character education. Indeed, some teachers believed the schools could not be truly democratic if they separated students of different social classes—a view repeatedly expressed in debates over vocational education and IQ-based tracking. But no one put race on the schools' moral agenda. When educators spoke of race at all, they disclaimed responsibility, blaming prejudice on factors outside the school. When the CCRR spoke with school administrators after the 1919 race riot, for instance, many said that racial problems in the schools "could not be solved until the prejudice and antagonism of adults had disappeared."[4]

Thus, Chicago educators had to reconcile legal and institutional pressures for race-blind policies with political pressure from a constituency ambivalent about racial integration. At first, school officials followed no consistent policy on racial matters, and at times accommodated white students' prejudices. When white students objected to black classmates joining their school's orchestra, for instance, the principal suggested that the teacher "fill the orchestra places by a general tryout, so understood, but really with the policy of excluding the colored." At other times, administrative convenience outweighed political pressure. During the early 1900s, for example, school officials allowed white students to transfer out of racially mixed schools, but when this practice led to overcrowding in white schools near the ghetto, it was suspended. Occasionally, school officials opposed segregation as a matter of principle. When Superintendent Ella Flagg Young learned that Wendell Phillips High School was holding segregated "social rooms"—classrooms where students socialized after school—she abolished these rooms rather than countenance the separation of the races.[5]

During the Great Migration of the 1910s and 1920s, residential segregation increased dramatically in Chicago. In the past, black Chicagoans had been scattered across the city, but this new influx, and the growing competition over jobs and housing, spurred white resistance. Racial tensions exploded in a riot during the summer of 1919, leaving thirty-eight dead and hundreds wounded after a week of street fighting. When black families moved into predominantly white neighborhoods, they often met violent resistance: windows were broken, homes were firebombed. New migrants had little choice but to settle in the predominantly black neighborhoods of the South and West Sides of the city. As Chicago's

African-American population grew from 44,000 to 234,000 between 1910 and 1930, the city's black neighborhoods became more segregated and densely settled, and the emerging ghetto expanded block by block as black migrants crowded in, black pioneers pushed at the boundaries of the ghetto, and whites fled. By the mid-1925s, white home owners began to implement restrictive covenants, or legal agreements forbidding property owners from selling or renting to blacks; these covenants halted the expansion of the ghetto.[6]

Because school attendance areas were based on the neighborhood in which the school was located, it was inevitable that the schools would also become more segregated. Indeed, the proportion of elementary school children attending predominantly (more than 90 percent) black schools rose from 8 percent in 1915 to 84 percent in 1930. Segregation would not have risen so quickly, however, without the connivance of school officials. During the late 1910s, several affluent white communities on the city's South Side, including Kenwood, Hyde Park, and Morgan Park, began to face racial transition. The white residents of these communities were organized and well connected, and saw school segregation as a way to keep their neighborhoods white. As the historian Michael Homel has documented, in these neighborhoods the school board began to adjust attendance-area boundaries and feeder patterns in ways that kept black and white students separate. When racial transition reached Oakland School, for instance, the board sent the school's white students to a nearby (white) school, keeping only the black students at Oakland. In another neighborhood, the board combined two racially mixed elementary schools into a single school; the principal then assigned most of the black students to one building and most of the white students to the other. As South Side elementary schools became predominantly black, they were reassigned to feed into Phillips, a racially mixed high school, instead of into white high schools.[7]

Immigrants were said to be more tolerant than other whites of black teachers and racially mixed schools. In many cases, however, working-class whites, southern and eastern European immigrants included, resisted integrated schooling, but they did not have the political leverage to prevail. In the impoverished and predominantly Italian "Little Hell" district, white residents protested in vain when black students began attending the local school. On the South Side, Wentworth Avenue divided the Black Belt from the white working-class neighborhoods to the west, but a number of elementary school districts straddled Wentworth,

TABLE 4.1:   **Location of Chicago public elementary schools with more than 1 percent black students, 1930**

	Percentage of black students in school		
	1–9	10–89	90–100
Middle-class neighborhoods	0	1	2
Working-class neighborhoods	6	13	6

Sources: Tabulations from Herrick, "Negro Employees," 92–105. Community area class status assigned based on proportion of professionals among employed males in 1920.

creating racially mixed schools. Unable to influence district policy, working-class whites resorted to informal means to maintain segregation. In Little Hell, sociologist Harvey Zorbaugh observed, "On the school and public playgrounds are re-enacted the scenes of a generation ago when the Sicilian was forcing out the Swede. The Negro child is often mistreated and ostracized. There are gang fights on playground and street." On the South Side around 1920, sixty black students transferred from Phillips High School to Tilden, a boys' technical high school just west of Wentworth Avenue. According to a local teacher, these students "were thrown out by the Tilden boys. They made it so hot for the colored boys that the sixty had to withdraw." Despite this informal resistance, however, school segregation remained far more extensive in middle-class than working-class neighborhoods, as table 4.1 shows.[8]

Ironically, school segregation in Chicago separated black and white children at the very ages when integrated schooling had the best chance to succeed. Race relations were less contentious among younger children, and racial attitudes were more malleable. Schooling remained racially mixed at the high school level long after the elementary schools were largely segregated. Phillips High School was located in the heart of the Black Belt, and by 1925 nearly all its students were black. Most black high school students, however, attended racially mixed schools. One-third attended Englewood, which was 70 percent white in 1930. One out of four black students attended high schools that were 90 percent or more white (see table 4.2). The racially mixed high schools were sites of significant tension over extracurricular activities and discipline policies. At Englewood, for instance, black students were prevented from joining the Honor Society and most other student activities. Black community leaders "charge[d] that Negro students are dismissed for of-

TABLE 4.2: **Segregation in Chicago public high schools, 1930**

	Percentage of black students	Estimated distribution of black students
More than 90% black		
Phillips	100.0	35.8
10–90% black	—	40.2
Englewood	30.0	33.1
Flower Technical High School for Girls	12.8	3.9
Medill	20.0	3.2
Less than 10% black	—	23.9
Fenger	2.4	2.2
Hyde Park	6.0	7.6
Lindblom Technical	1.1	1.8
McKinley	7.0	3.5
Morgan Park	5.6	3.0
Parker	1.5	0.3
Tilden Technical	3.0	3.7
Waller	2.0	1.1

Source: Herrick, "Negro Employees," 92–105.
Note: Schools in which black students are less than 1 percent of enrollment are included in the total for "less than 10% black" but not listed individually.

fenses so slight that white students would hardly receive a reprimand for them."[9]

School segregation met a mixed response in the black community. Some black parents believed that predominantly black schools provided a better educational environment, because their children were sheltered from the hostility of white classmates and the threats of white gangs. Segregated schools also provided employment opportunities for black teachers and other professionals such as librarians and school nurses. More generally, black Chicagoans may have felt a sense of ownership about their community's schools, just as they took pride in the growth of black-owned businesses and other local institutions. This sentiment is evident in the pages of the Intercollegiate Club *Wonderbook,* a precis of Chicago's black community printed in 1927 by an elite social club. The glossy volume included a section devoted to Phillips High School, featuring photographs of the marching band, prominent athletes, graduating seniors, and the school's majority-black office staff.[10]

A vocal faction opposed segregation in the schools, however. Some, particularly those active in the NAACP, held a deep commitment to racial integration as a matter of both principle and legal strategy. Their concern about segregation in the Chicago Public Schools was heightened as whites in northern and border states tried to draw the color line in new areas. During the 1910s, there were efforts to prohibit interracial marriage, mandate residential segregation, and even (in Chicago) to curtail the migration of black southerners. President Woodrow Wilson's moves to dismiss or segregate black employees in the federal civil service also provoked alarm. These developments, reported extensively in the NAACP magazine *The Crisis,* had particular resonance for the black men and women who had thought they left the South behind, only to find that Jim Crow had followed them to Chicago.[11]

The opposition to segregation was led by members of the black elite, who had the requisite financial and political resources and were well connected to the black civic organizations. Their motivation was heightened by the experiences many had as pioneers on the edge of the ghetto. Very often it was these black middle- and upper-class families who sought to move into white neighborhoods, whose children braved the hostile climate at Englewood High School, and who were most directly affected when school officials changed attendance areas or took other steps to separate black and white students. With no formal representation within the school leadership, these men and women filed lawsuits, organized protests, and petitioned city officials. Although their efforts could not prevent racial segregation in the schools, they did force school officials to abandon some overtly racially biased measures. In 1923, for instance, administrators at the predominantly white Parker High School on the South Side asked teachers to submit lists of all black students who did not live in the school's attendance area. The NAACP, anticipating a move to exclude the black students, protested this race-specific canvass, and the mayor cancelled it.[12]

Protests of segregation were less successful when school officials could provide a nonracial rationale for their actions. Consider a mid-1920s conflict in Morgan Park, a racially mixed area on the city's Far South Side. Until the mid-1920s, black children in that neighborhood attended Esmond School, a predominantly white elementary school. In 1926, the Board of Education built a new school and assigned to it all the neighborhood's black students, even those who lived nearer to Esmond. White students continued to attend Esmond School regardless of where they lived. It seemed clear that these districting rules violated the state law against racial exclusion in the schools. Joined by civic leaders from the Black Belt, African-American Morgan Park residents protested and the NAACP filed suit. The suit failed, however. The circuit court ruled that the NAACP had not proved discriminatory intent.[13]

The pattern of segregation that emerged in Chicago was driven primarily by residential patterns, aided and abetted by school officials' actions. This type of segregation might seem more benign than the overt racial exclusion of the southern Jim Crow schools. It preserved at least nominally the universalism expected of government institutions, and did not encode racial exclusion into law. The long-term consequences were considerable, however. As the Morgan Park case suggests, de facto segregation proved difficult to challenge legally. While the *Brown vs. Board of Education* decision in 1954 overturned segregation in the southern schools, it had no legal repercussions in Chicago. In addition, because of the legal and political sanctions against racial exclusion, school officials masked the actions they took; for them, segregation meant a stance of hypocrisy which became politically corrosive in school-community relations.

Racial Inequality and Political Protest, 1930–45

The black community's ambivalence about segregation persisted only as long as black schools were not conspicuously unequal to white ones in funding and other kinds of material resources. This state of affairs ended in the early 1930s. Inequality between black and white schools began to rise, with profound consequences both for the conditions of black education and for school politics in the black community. School officials dissembled, refusing to acknowledge the existence of segregation and inequality in the schools. These developments spurred a wider mobilization in the black community, eventually attracting white allies to the struggle to improve black schools.[14]

The rise in racial inequality began with a dramatic increase in overcrowding in black schools. During the 1930s, Chicago's African-American population grew by nearly 20 percent, but the ghetto could expand little: restrictive covenants covered some three-quarters of the residential property in the city. The population growth in black neighborhoods increased pressure on the local schools, but the Board of Education failed to respond. Pleading lack of funds, the board built few schools during this time. And although white schools near the ghetto had relatively stable enrollments (table 4.3), school officials refused to

TABLE 4.3: **Change in enrollment in selected Chicago public elementary schools, 1929–37**

	Enrollment		
	1929	1937	Change (%)
Black Belt schools	19,292	23,682	+22.8
Schools east of Black Belt	8,210	8,772	+10.0
Schools west of Black Belt	26,358	22,393	−15.0

Sources: Public schools selected based on listings in Wirth and Fuerz, eds., *Local Community Fact Book
1938.* Enrollment figures tabulated from untitled document providing enrollment figures for Chicago schools
between 1929 and 1937, Chicago Area Project, box 70, folder 3.
Note: Black Belt schools included all those in community areas 35, 38, and 40 as well as McCosh. Schools
east of the Black Belt included all those in community areas 36, 39, 41, and 42 with the exception of McCosh.
Schools west of the Black Belt included all those in community areas 34, 37, 60, 61, and 68.

let black students transfer there. The combined enrollment in twenty-four
Black Belt schools was reported to have risen by 65 percent between 1930
and 1940.[15]

Overcrowding created many problems. Classes grew larger. School
buildings deteriorated more quickly, and the cash-starved school board
provided little money for maintenance and repair. Some schools housed
the extra students in portable wooden classrooms, which were rat in-
fested and difficult to heat and cool; the children called them "dog-
houses." Most often, black schools were put on double-shift schedules.
This schedule, which cut the school day from five hours to four, created a
racial deficit in instructional time, a vital resource for education. It also
disrupted the school day—some students ate lunch very early, others
very late—creating problems especially for younger children. Students in
these schools could more easily play truant; if caught on the street during the day, they could simply claim to be attending on a different shift.
By 1940, *an estimated three-quarters of all black elementary-school students attended school on double shifts,* while only one white school had
this schedule. A few black schools were even on triple shifts.[16]

These disadvantages were compounded by a shift in the composition
of the teaching force. The black schools began to have trouble retaining teachers. Often, an observer noted, "beginning teachers stay only
a month or two in a Negro school before obtaining their transfers." In
1925, the proportion of novice teachers averaged 28 percent at both immigrant and black schools. By 1940, such novices comprised 39 percent
of the teaching staff at black schools, compared with 22 percent at immigrant schools. Because teacher salaries were pegged to seniority,
teachers at black schools were paid less, on average, than those at white

schools. More important than this salary gap was the gap in experience and maturity it represented.[17]

As school conditions worsened, black opposition to segregation widened. The Chicago Urban League began to protest school overcrowding in the early 1930s. Within a few years, it was joined by other organizations, including the NAACP, the Chicago Council of Negro Organizations, the National Negro Congress, the Interdenominational Council of Churches, and the Association of Colored Women. Local PTAs and neighborhood organizations mobilized as well, engaging in rallies and boycotts. The growing frustration in the black community is illustrated by an episode in the small middle-class enclave of Lilydale. Although Lilydale had no school of its own, the Board of Education had refused to let Lilydale students attend nearby white schools; instead they attended classes in several battered wooden portables. Petitions and protest were fruitless in getting a real school for the neighborhood. Finally, a group of teenage boys from the neighborhood torched the portables, and the conservative and law-abiding community of Lilydale, usually so vigilant against juvenile delinquency, stood firmly behind the youths. Less than two months later, the Board of Education broke ground on a school for the neighborhood.[18]

In general, however, black community protest won little. Powerful private and political interests were arrayed against desegregation. According to the Hyde Park–Kenwood Council of Churches and Synagogues, "whenever the School Board has considered redistricting of schools to [ease overcrowding], the restrictive covenant groups supported by the Chicago Real Estate Board and the University of Chicago have blocked the efforts." In addition, the black community had little leverage with the Democratic political machine that dominated City Hall after 1931. The school board, chaired by James McCahey, was appointed by Mayor Edward Kelly and was loyal to him. The grip of the machine tightened after 1936, when the board elevated its own candidate, William H. Johnson, into the superintendency. Mayor Kelly's few black protégés retained their positions only by backing the mayor and school board on controversial racial questions. Typical was Midian O. Bousfield, the first black Board of Education member, whom Kelly appointed in 1939. When black parents in West Woodlawn protested the double-shift schedule at their school, Dr. Bousfield refused to support them, stating that "Woodlawn mothers should not expect a full day for their children when most all of the other schools in Negro communities had double and triple shift."[19]

Black mobilization did, however, attract allies among the city's white liberal and left-wing activists. The late 1930s and early 1940s saw the formation of a number of organizations committed to racial equality, among them the Catholic Interracial Council, the Chicago Council Against Racial and Religious Discrimination, the Congress on Racial Equality, and the Mayor's Committee on Race Relations. These new organizations had a myriad of connections with one another and with the older civil rights groups. They were also allied with opponents of the Democratic machine, including the Chicago Schools Council, founded in 1933 to oppose school budget cuts, and the new Chicago Teachers Union. The campaign against overcrowded black schools joined issues of racial justice with a critique of the corrupt Johnson-McCahey administration, neatly bridging the agendas of groups within this loose coalition. Between 1940 and 1945, many organizations, including the Chicago Schools Council, CCARRD, CTU, and the MCRR, called for an end to overcrowding.[20]

The lines of conflict were evident at a 1944 MCRR conference on the subject of race relations. School board president James McCahey declared that "today [black students] have the same facilities, they have the same type of education, the same everything, that any other student in any other part of Chicago has." Although he acknowledged that black schools were overcrowded, he denied that school boundaries had been gerrymandered, and claimed that nearby white schools could not absorb additional students. Contending that Chicago's black students were much better off than they would have been in the South, McCahey distributed a pamphlet juxtaposing pictures of southern black schools—mere shacks—with the impressive school buildings that Chicago's black students attended. Twenty years earlier, this visual argument might have been persuasive. It wasn't now. Irene McCoy Gaines, a black civic leader, retorted that visitors to Chicago's ghetto schools "could easily imagine, from the lack of facilities, that they were in one of the backward sections of the South." Edwin Embree, chair of the MCRR, rebuked McCahey: "It is not a proper answer to point out that children receive a better education in Chicago than they do in rural Mississippi—any more than it would be to point out our advantages over County Cork or the more dilapidated sections of Poland. Education in Chicago must be judged by Chicago standards."[21]

In less than a decade, racial segregation became linked with widespread inequality between black and white schools. The Board of Education could have alleviated this inequality by changing school boundaries to allow black students to attend nearby white schools. Its decision to preserve segregation at the cost of black children's education severely damaged the legitimacy of Chicago public school leadership. This political damage was compounded when school officials refused to acknowledge this inequality. The growing anger and cynicism in the black community—what Irene McCoy Gaines called a mood of "smoldering resentments and hatreds"—extended even to schoolchildren, who participated in protests and boycotts and who experienced at first hand the material deprivation of black schools.[22]

Segregation and Inequality after 1945

For a brief period after 1945, some change in this pattern of segregation and inequality appeared possible. The McCahey-Johnson regime began to collapse when a National Education Association investigation was sharply critical of the Chicago Public Schools; indeed, Johnson became the first NEA member to be expelled from the organization for unprofessional conduct. When the North Central Association of Secondary Schools threatened to withhold accreditation for the city's high schools, Johnson and the Board of Education were finally asked to resign. A new superintendent, Herold Hunt, arrived in 1947 with broad support and a reputation as a liberal on racial issues. A 1945 Illinois law reaffirmed the state's prohibition of racial exclusion in the schools. By 1950, civil rights activists across the state would form the Committee to End Segregation in the Public Schools of Illinois.[23]

   Emblematic of the altered political environment was the response to a series of student strikes in 1945. White students at Englewood and Calumet High Schools staged a strike to protest rising black enrollment at their schools. The city's Commission on Human Relations (as the MCRR had been renamed) immediately met with the mayor, school board members, and the police commissioner and got their assurances that "the departments of the city would stand solidly against the action of the students, and that all procedures of the Board of Education, e.g., the handling of absentees as truants, etc., would be carried through promptly." Within two days the school board, at the urging of the CHR, released a public statement explaining that segregation was illegal and urging the students back to school. The police dispersed the striking students; those arrested were brought to the precinct station with their parents for a lecture from CHR members "to show these students and their parents that they were wrong in taking the action they did; that the state law forbade segregation; that the Negro students at a given high school were residents of the district and belonged in the high school and would remain there; that continued absence from school would result in action being taken against them as truants."[24]

Facing intensifying crowding in the schools, and what seemed to be a favorable political climate, Hunt decided to revise the school attendance areas. To advise the redistricting, he asked for help from the Committee on Education, Training and Research in Race Relations at the University of Chicago. Faculty from this committee, including the sociologists Louis Wirth and Philip Hauser and the anthropologist Sol Tax, formed a Technical Advisory Committee on Intergroup Relations. Wirth and a team of graduate students studied the city's neighborhoods and school zones and developed a redistricting plan that proposed boundary changes for 102 elementary schools. Although its aim was relief of overcrowding, not school desegregation, the plan did bring about significant racial change at four schools and more modest change at a number of others. Hunt implemented the plan in 1950. At the Technical Committee's recommendation, he also eliminated most of the "neutral areas"—neighborhoods in which residents could choose which of several schools to attend.[25]

This redistricting proved highly controversial, and Hunt earned the respect of the black community "for his courage in carrying out the plan." White parents, however, were not so pleased, especially when redistricting led to racial change. These parents had become accustomed to informal accommodation of their racial preferences. Although school policy forbade interschool transfers motivated by race, in practice school officials often bent the rules, and several thousand students were said to attend school out of district. Many parents opposed redistricting even when it did not alter their school's racial composition. As the Technical Committee warned in 1948, "The school districts are regarded in many local communities as being fixed, sacred entities." Because of parent resistance, redistricting was partly rescinded at one school and never implemented at another. A plan to redistrict the high schools was completely scrapped.[26]

The Technical Committee's activities also met opposition from school administrators. Helen Amerman, a graduate-student observer, noted that "although [Hunt] is nominally chairman of the Human Relations Committee, certain members of the Subcommittee are very often (one gathers, *usually*) consulted by the secretary before she 'bothers' the chairman with any item, and in that way a matter may not even come to the attention of the chairman." She added, "It seems especially necessary to give special attention to the orientation of strategically located administrators in the system who are in a position to block the human relations program by resistance or to penalize those who cooperate by using negative sanctions against them." Hunt's deputies resented the interference of these university outsiders. At a stormy 1951 meeting, assistant superintendent Don Rogers "stated that the Technical Committee had done more harm than good, related how they had sent (instead of Mr. Wirth or Mr. Hauser) 'a snip of a girl who came down and blew smoke through her nose' at a meeting of District Superintendents to consider school boundary changes. . . . He especially criticized the elimination of neutral areas, which he considered the best plan they ever had. He accused 'five or six men' of being convinced that the school administrators were 'a bunch of segregationists,' and denied that they were."[27]

For their part, the graduate students on the Technical Committee were frustrated and bewildered at what seemed very much like obstruction on the part of Hunt's administrators. In February of 1952, the students were startled to discover that the planned boundary changes at one school had not been implemented at all. One of them, Leonard Breen, wrote to Wirth, "[School officials] have obviously been talking through the sides of their mouths to us, and haven't gotten into the spirit of the thing in the way which we would all like to see them do. . . . Are we to exist to assuage their conscience and to be a buffer between them and the public, or are we to be constructive-technical-advise [*sic*] givers?"[28]

In the end, Hunt's intentions for more lasting change were thwarted. In 1950, the Technical Committee recommended that Hunt's staff take over the task of redistricting; two years later this still had not occurred, and Hunt told the Technical Committee that "the schools would need the assistance of the Committee for sometime to come." Wirth died unexpectedly a few months later. Hunt resigned his position the following year, driven out by controversy over his liberal views.[29]

Hunt's replacement, Benjamin Willis, took office at a time of rising enrollment and rapid change in Chicago's racial ecology and built environment. The economic boom of World War II set off a massive migration from the South which continued after the war's end, spurred by the mechanization of southern agriculture. The restrictive covenants that had walled in the black ghetto were finally overturned in 1947 by the Supreme Court. The suburbs grew, attracting whites from the city and opening vacancies in city neighborhoods outside the ghetto. In 1950, three years before Willis took office, 51 percent of black Chicagoans lived in the old Black Belt; in 1960, only 21 percent did. This depopulation, along with Willis's ambitious campaign of school construction, reduced crowding in the most densely packed ghetto schools. By 1940, ten Black Belt schools had been grossly overcrowded, with up to twice as many students as there were seats available. By 1964, the combined enrollment in these schools had dropped by 42 percent.[30]

Racial segregation remained, however. As the historian Arnold Hirsch has described, Chicago's civic elites guided urban renewal to create a "second ghetto" bounded by expressways and anchored by highrise public housing projects. The same expressways and other ecological barriers that separated black and white neighborhoods also made convenient and readily justifiable school boundaries. In this new built environment, school segregation could be maintained without school officials taking a visible (and politically vulnerable) role. In 1964, for the first time, the Chicago Board of Education published racial statistics for the schools. At the elementary school level, segregation had increased slightly since 1930; the proportion of black students in segregated (at least 90 percent) black schools rose from 84 percent to 89 percent (see table 4.4). There was more change at the high school level. During the

TABLE 4.4: **Racial segregation in Chicago public elementary schools and non-vocational high schools, 1930–64**

	School segregation (Percentage of black students)		
	0–9.9	10–89.9	90–100
Elementary schools			
Percentage of schools			
1930	87.1	5.3	7.6
1964	52.6	11.0	36.3
Percentage of black students			
1930	0.3	15.6	84.2
1964	0.5	10.3	89.2
High schools			
Percentage of schools			
1930	85.0	10.0	5.0
1964	69.7	14.5	15.8
Percentage of black students			
1930	23.9	40.2	35.8
1964	2.2	30.4	67.3

Sources: The 1930 figures are calculated from Herrick, "Negro Employees," 92–105. The 1964 figures are calculated from "Here's School-by-School Breakdown on Racial Head Count," *Chicago American*, October 14, 1964. *Note:* In the 1964 figures, branches are counted as separate schools.

first half of the century, fewer than half the city's black high school students had attended segregated high schools. By 1964, the proportion had risen to 67 percent.[31]

Black and white schools also remained unequal in a number of other aspects. Although their overcrowding had declined, black schools were still more likely to be on double-shift schedules. In 1957, 40 percent of these schools operated on double shifts, compared with 19 percent of racially mixed schools and 2 percent of white schools.[32] In addition, black schools continued to have a more transient and less qualified teaching staff. During the 1950s, the district was scrambling to find teachers. Enrollments had risen sharply and class sizes were cut, requiring the district to expand its teaching force by more than 50 percent between 1950 and 1960. At the same time, suburban districts offered attractive new employment opportunities. To retain teachers in the city, Willis adopted a new procedure for assigning them to schools:

> In 1953 [and before], teachers received an assignment through the mail; in 1955, the procedure now in use was introduced. Under this system each teacher is invited in the order of his rank on the eligible list to the Bureau of Teacher Personnel; here he is shown a large map of the city on which all vacancies are indicated. From this, the new teacher may select the school he wishes.

This procedure made it easy for teachers to avoid placement in black schools, and many did. In 1961, some 3,500 of the 18,000 teaching positions went unfilled, most of these in the inner city. In a number of schools, more than 20 percent of teaching positions were staffed by substitutes. In a few schools, more than half were.[33]

The black community became increasingly frustrated by Willis's failure to respond to their concerns. Although the *Brown* decision had no legal implications for Chicago, it sparked a renewal of local civil rights efforts to address racial segregation and inequality in the schools. The Illinois NAACP focused on a few downstate districts where de jure segregation offered a promising legal target, while the Chicago branch of the association focused on the city. When the Chicago Board of Education claimed that no data were available on the racial composition of the city's schools, the branch's Education Committee ferreted out figures from its network of PTA councils. (White researchers for the NAACP also queried the school engineers, who were only too eager to complain about racial change in "their" schools.) The resulting report, issued in

1957, estimated that 87 percent of Chicago's black elementary school-children attended segregated schools, and documented widespread racial inequality in school resources. The *Defender* missed no opportunity to remind Chicagoans that more black children attended segregated schools in Illinois than in Arkansas.

Despite this evidence, Willis remained unresponsive. School officials maintained that no more than half of Chicago's black children attended segregated schools. What segregation did exist, Willis claimed, was "a circumstantial thing." As he said in response to the NAACP report, "We are not concerned with race when we build new schools. We build schools where there are students. We try to keep up with a school population increase of 15,000 a year and cannot consider racial motives in doing so." As the NAACP found, however, in a number of instances school siting and districting decisions appeared to be driven by race.[34]

Willis could withstand political pressure because he was protected by Chicago's political machine. Richard J. Daley was elected mayor in 1955; his black "sub-machine" kept dissent in line. After the NAACP report was released, William Dawson, a Black Belt ward committeeman, engineered a takeover of the Chicago branch by a more moderate leader, while Mrs. Wendell Green, an African American whom Daley appointed to the school board, repeatedly defended Willis. The growing anger in the black community could not be contained indefinitely, however. In 1963, when Mrs. Green spoke at a high school graduation ceremony, she was booed and hissed by black students inside the hall and picketed by protesters outside. Sponsors of the demonstration included the NAACP, CORE, the Negro American Labor Council, and the Student Nonviolent Coordinating Committee, and "children as young as 6 or 7 joined with adults in the pickets' parade." Only a few months later, some two hundred thousand students walked out—in the largest school boycott in Chicago's history—to protest conditions in the city's schools.[35]

Nonetheless, in the years after World War II, despite the efforts of Herold Hunt and the Technical Committee and the protests of the black community, racial segregation and inequality became more entrenched. With change in the city's built environment, school segregation could more readily be blamed on residential segregation, allowing school officials to claim race neutrality in student assignment and resource allocation. The cost, beyond the continuing deficits in black schools, was a growing anger and cynicism in the black community.

Race Relations in the Schools

Even in a largely segregated district, black students encountered white teachers and even white students, and the character of these encounters conveyed much to them about the public schools' commitment to fairness and to the education of black children. During the early twentieth century, the Chicago Public Schools took no responsibility for promoting interracial understanding and inclusion. Indeed, many school actions, such as tolerating the exclusion of black students from proms and other extracurricular activities, implicitly condoned white students' racial prejudice. Beginning in the late 1930s, however, the public schools faced rising pressure to improve race relations in the schools. The political climate had changed with the mobilization of civil rights and progressive groups during that period. No longer was it acceptable for educators to sidestep the question of racial tolerance. Then the question of race relations gained visibility as a wave of racial transition rippled through Chicago neighborhoods during the 1940s and 1950s, bringing black and white students in contact at least temporarily. In response, the Chicago Public Schools embarked on a program of intercultural education which aimed to promote racial and ethnic tolerance among teachers and students. Like Herold Hunt's redistricting effort, however, the program was limited both by political obstacles and by its own modest vision, and proved largely ineffective at improving race relations within the schools.[36]

Intercultural education first appeared at the Chicago Teachers College, in a new curriculum to prepare teachers for work with "underprivileged" black and immigrant children. John Bartky, then college president, observed that teachers' cultural ignorance and intolerance often led to classroom conflict. The old curriculum, he wrote, "never mentioned underprivileged communities and the educational problems unique to them. . . . It was only thought worth while to discuss the geography of Chicago." The new curriculum at the college, introduced in the late 1930s, attracted national recognition. Student teachers worked at settlement houses and toured black and immigrant neighborhoods. Jules Karlin distilled twenty years of urban sociology into a companion text, *Chicago: Backgrounds of Education*. But not all students were receptive. One commented, following a neighborhood tour: "We ate at a Mexican restaurant where we were served a typical Mexican meal consisting of tortillas, hot peppers, and other highly spiced foods. Because

most of us had never tasted food like that before, we left rather hungry."
Yet for most students, Bartky reported, the curriculum had the desired
effect, a cultural relativism epitomized by this response: "What interested most is the fact that people in slums have a way of living all their
own. I used to think that they did not act as we do just to be contrary.
I learned that their way of acting is no different in their eyes than ours
is in our eyes. I will no longer laugh at their customs or blame them for
some of their so called 'delinquencies.'" [37]

In the schools themselves, intercultural education grew out of the
"Americanism" campaign of the early 1940s, which aligned school programs and activities with the war effort. In service of the "Good Neigh-
bor" policy, Superintendent William Johnson penned articles about
Latin American countries, and children wearing sombreros danced at
school assemblies. After the war, with support and prodding by organizations such as the National Conference of Christians and Jews, the
Chicago Board of Education shifted its focus to domestic affairs and intergroup relations. The schools' monthly Americanism bulletin encouraged celebration of Brotherhood Week, Negro History Week, American
Indian Day, and I-Am-An-American Day with ceremonies of cultural
inclusion. Gospel choirs performed and rabbis made speeches. The
Chicago Public Schools added units on Negro history (these developed
by teachers at several Black Belt schools) and on the cultural heritage of
the city's immigrant groups. By the early 1950s, about half of Chicago's
schools claimed to have human relations committees, and one-quarter
had staff with human relations training. [38]

This approach to intercultural education was grounded in psychological theories of race relations, which viewed racial prejudice as an
irrational belief that could be modified with proper information. Intercultural education sought to correct stereotypes with two kinds of mes-
sages. First, the schools highlighted the literary, artistic, scientific, and
political achievements of each ethnic or racial group, along with a roman-
ticized folk culture drawn from the safely distant past. Here the schools
took their cue from ethnic and black elites, who had long promoted such
idealized accounts of their cultural heritage. [39] Second, intercultural education portrayed contemporary racial and ethnic differences as shallow
or illusory. For instance, Sema Williams Herman, a first-grade teacher,
asked her students if "they ever saw a dog or kitten decline to play with
another member of its family simply because the stranger had a spot-
ted coat of hair instead of a plain one. This always brought smiles or

a sally of laughs, but the children got the point." High school students were taught that their prejudices were irrational and without foundation in modern science. Students at Senn High School, for instance, read selections about race from biology, anthropology, and sociology: "After reflecting on these studies, followed by carefully guided discussion, students were convinced that scientists had exploded the 'myth of racial superiority.'" In a late-1940s survey of Chicago high school students, 93 percent dutifully expressed disagreement with the statement that "your mental ability depends on your race."[40]

Now and then, Chicago educators took cautious forays into the more sensitive terrain of their own city. Two tenth-grade classes at the racially and ethnically mixed Wells High School conducted a study of their neighborhood, sending small teams of students to visit local organizations (including the "glamorous editorial quarters" of *Ebony Magazine* and the *Negro Digest*). According to a teacher's account, "Everywhere our committees went they asked about discrimination; and everywhere the answer was, 'We welcome all races and creeds.' They realized they were talking to socially conscious, thinking persons; and they also realized there are not enough thinking people in the world."[41]

Intercultural education had some good effect. It began to shift the boundaries of polite speech and create a context in which overt and public expression of racism was unacceptable. The value of this should not be underestimated. Also, like the redistricting effort, intercultural education created some goodwill in the black community. In 1944, for instance, the Urban League's A. L. Foster noted that "the present system of conducting tours for students in the Normal College is an excellent beginning. And the Superintendent of Schools and the School Board should be commended for the introduction into the elementary grades of supplementary reading about the accomplishments of Negroes—again a good start."[42]

In general, however, by presenting such a simplistic view of racial and ethnic issues, the intercultural education program failed to address the lived realities of Chicago students. There was little mention of fraught questions such as racial and ethnic discrimination in the workplace or battles in neighborhoods over residential segregation and racial transition. Instead of providing a venue and an acceptable language for engaging these experiences, intercultural education silenced talk about race and ethnicity that went beyond the simple pieties of the curriculum. The content of the curriculum was further circumscribed when Superintendent Hunt began to press for a more diffuse conception of intercultural education, instructing that "intercultural relations should rarely be stressed *directly* in work with pupils, nor should attention be drawn to either the shortcomings or advantages of any particular groups." With the public silence over matters of race, class, and poverty, these issues were expressed only through a covert culture of resentment and misunderstanding. For teachers as well, intercultural education was of limited use. It did not, for instance, tell naïve young teachers how to cope when troubling manifestations of inner-city life made their way into the classroom. In interviews conducted around 1950, teachers in inner-city schools reported that even young students might bring weapons and drug paraphernalia to school. As one teacher said, "Sometimes I'm afraid to ask them what they've got with them this time—I'm afraid to find out what it is." [43]

The limitations of the intercultural education program were no surprise to local race relations experts, nor to the Technical Committee, which had promoted a more serious engagement with racial issues. In addition to developing Hunt's redistricting plan, the committee had held workshops for administrators and teachers in schools undergoing racial transition, and conducted surveys of students and teachers. Minutes of the meetings suggest a relatively candid discussion. Among parents, also, there was an appetite for more serious discussion. Around 1950, Mary Herrick, a seasoned educator and long-time civil rights advocate, led a series of talks with PTA members. These events attracted a growing number of parents from a total of thirty-six schools, most of them from the South or West Side and undergoing racial transition: "Because the group wanted it so, the class was continued for four extra sessions and the enrollment has increased considerably after the first sessions." [44]

There were limits, however, to how frankly educators could engage questions of racial inequality and racial tension. When Hunt tried to modify the high school curriculum to include more "relevant" material about contemporary race relations and urban issues, his efforts led to heated controversy. Herrick, who had led the PTA discussion groups, was replaced with an inexperienced staff member, and the results were dismal: "The Board of Education staff member, Miss Rowland, is far inferior to Miss Herrick as a discussion leader. The class drifted and a session on the way in which the PTA can initiate community action became an aimless series of confessionals." [45]

Intercultural education had another weakness: its reliance on instruction instead of direct contact with people of various backgrounds. Only a few elements of the program actually brought students of different races together. There was a "Companion Plan" in which students from paired white and black schools visited each others' campuses, but these visits were few and brief. Here, too, the Chicago Public Schools' program was at odds with the advice of race relations experts. In 1954, the psychologist Gordon Allport published his book *The Nature of Prejudice,* which contended that, under specific conditions, equal-status contact between the races would reduce prejudice. Even before that, experience had suggested that instruction and exhortation had limited impact—instead, experts emphasized the "fait accompli" as the way to change racial attitudes. When Louis Wirth was asked to endorse a bill requiring Illinois public schools to teach "racial amity and understanding," he refused. "I should not fail, as a student of race relations, to express to you my doubt as to whether 'racial amity' can be taught any more than any other virtue can be taught by a course of study," he wrote to the politician who had asked for his support.[46]

More generally, intercultural education had little impact on the schools' racial practices. Even as educators taught students about racial tolerance, their actions undermined it. A prime example is districting policy. There were a few cases in which schools were integrated carefully and with success. For instance, Edwards School was located in a closely knit Polish neighborhood on the Southwest Side. In the late 1940s, a racially integrated public housing project, LeClaire Courts, was built nearby over community opposition. About fifty black students from LeClaire Courts were sent to Edwards, making its enrollment about 14 percent black. Robert Reinsch, the school's principal, spoke frankly with the teachers and PTA members: "The opposition to the project in general was acknowledged but the existance [*sic*] of the project was a fact as well as the coming of the pupils and if the parents would refrain from voicing their oppositions in front of the children and not cause them to carry a chip on their shoulder much would be gained. The members of the [PTA executive] board graciously offered to come to school on opening day and welcome the parents of the new pupils." As Reinsch described later,

> Our first Negro children arrived on October 4th, a brother and sister who were in seventh and fifth grades respectively. When they were taken to the rooms and introduced to their teacher children quickly took over and showed them their locker and made them feel at home. The first day they held them-

selves off to one side at recess and noon but the next morning Larry was seen playing football with the rest of the boys and to date we have had no difficulties that might be inferred to be racial, among the pupils.

Under favorable conditions, racial integration could have a lasting benefit. In its 1957 report, the Chicago NAACP noted that Waller High School, 20 percent black, was characterized by relatively good race relations. The reason? Waller was fed mostly by racially mixed elementary schools, in which black and white children had the opportunity to develop friendships and intercultural understanding.[47]

In most cases, however, school officials sacrificed race relations to political and logistical expedience. Although both research and long experience had shown that school integration was more likely to work when it began with younger students, segregation remained far more extensive at the elementary than the high school level. In addition, when schools were integrated, the process was rarely managed as carefully as it had been at Edwards School. More typical was the experience of the racially mixed Wells High School, located in an immigrant working-class neighborhood. The school was abruptly sent large numbers of students from two segregated black elementary schools. Riots ensued, and many of the most experienced teachers quickly left.[48]

The everyday practices of Chicago schools were also inconsistent with the credos of intercultural education. Staff in racially mixed schools were reluctant to challenge traditional racial mores. In one high school, the white girls refused to swim at the same time as black girls. Instead of insisting, the school segregated the swimming classes: "In order to make it look right, they assign a couple of white girls to the Negro class, but then they don't go in. They always have an excuse, so it looks all right, they just come in and sit on the side." The views underlying these actions are suggested in the debate at a 1950 meeting of the schools' Committee on Human Relations. According to the Technical Committee member at the meeting, a "piperoo" of a discussion broke out over interracial dancing at school-sponsored events. Paul R. Pierce, a senior administrator, "summarized the gist (his interpretation of the gist) of the meeting by saying that we can't force people into anything, even democracy. Children must not be made to feel they have to 'carry the torch all the time, they must be allowed to have times when they can be with their friends, without feeling that there is pressure on them to be or to do something else.'"[49]

The atmosphere was especially tense in schools that were racially mixed or undergoing transition. Most teachers in racially mixed schools were white (91 percent, compared with 43 percent in black schools), and many were insensitive on matters of race. Englewood High School is a case in point. The school had been racially mixed since the 1920s, and had long been known for its poor race relations, including harsh discipline aimed at black students. Twenty years later, the situation had changed little. The proportion of black students rose during the mid-1940s, and white students had gone on strike to protest. In 1946, an observer in the school noted "the amount of aggression and the repressive attitude directed toward Negro youth by white teachers and 'counselors.'"[50]

Without a positive effort to promote interracial contact, black and white students in racially mixed high schools remained largely separate from one another. At Morgan Park High School, the NAACP commented in 1957, "the atmosphere is that of two schools, one Negro and one white, housed in the same building and taught by the same white teachers." At another racially mixed high school, a longtime resident observed, "very little integration has taken place, *except on the athletic fields*. Otherwise, a kind of peaceful coexistence would be the best way to describe relationships. White and Negro teenagers, except in a few isolated instances, have little communication." Yet underlying this "peaceful coexistence" was tension and distrust. Small conflicts escalated quickly. At Fenger High School in 1957, a black student knifed a white student during a dispute over a locker; the next day antiblack epithets were painted on the sidewalks, and white students shoved black students in the hallway and called them names. At Lindblom in 1958, after a fight between a white girl and a black girl, more than a hundred white students rioted and three black students were seriously injured.[51]

Despite its limitations, intercultural education had some impact. It acknowledged a responsibility on the part of the Chicago Public Schools for teaching racial tolerance—a significant change. It muted some of the more overt expressions of racism, and introduced white teachers and students to an African-American perspective on history. The initiative also provided a small opening for more candid discussion of the problems of race relations and inner-city education. In the end, though, its platitudes were inadequate to the moral and social complexity of racial encounters in the schools and city. The program was limited both by educators' naïveté about the difficulty of changing race relations and by constraints on what was considered politically acceptable. As an exercise in public relations, intercultural education was a partial success, but the reality fell far short of the new liberal ideals.

Immigrants and Ethnic Politics in the Schools

The experiences of African Americans in the public schools contrast sharply with those of the southern and eastern European immigrants. Unlike the black community, the immigrant communities had a voice in school policy, with representation on the school board from the early years of the twentieth century or even before. Moreover, immigrants' primary points of contention with the public schools—compulsory education and nativist and anti-Catholic bias—diminished over time. Compulsory education became less salient as employment opportunities for young adolescents disappeared and the incomes of working-class parents became more stable; there was less economic incentive to evade the truant officer. Over time also, the public schools began to accommodate immigrants' efforts to preserve their cultural heritage. Beginning in the 1910s, the Chicago school system allowed its high schools to offer language classes in Polish, Italian, and Czech, and to organize nationality clubs and host ethnic celebrations. Later on, intercultural education acknowledged the folk cultures and the artistic and literary heritage of the city's nationalities, even as immigrants themselves became more Americanized and less concerned about preserving ethnic culture. Although few children were taught by teachers of southern or eastern European origin, growing numbers of public school teachers were Catholic, bringing cultural styles familiar to the largely Catholic immigrant populations.[52]

On matters of racial segregation and desegregation, it is true, the Board of Education did less to "protect" the largely working-class immigrant communities than it did to protect middle-class and predominantly native white ones. The impact on immigrants was small, however. Relatively few southern and eastern European immigrants lived directly adjacent to Chicago's black neighborhoods, thereby facing their children's assignment to racially mixed schools. Those who were had the option of attending the local parochial school or of seeking a transfer to another public school. In 1958, in fact, only about 8 percent of nonblack students attended elementary schools that were more than 10 percent black.[53]

The racial politics of schooling may have had a more diffuse impact beyond those students and families directly affected by racial transition.

During and after World War II, working-class immigrants were beset by pressure for racial tolerance and integration from CIO organizers, the Catholic Interracial Council, and the interracial and interfaith task forces trying to manage neighborhood racial transition. With the intercultural education program, teachers and school officials symbolically aligned themselves with this pressure, and may have attracted some resentment as a result. Yet despite immigrants' possible objections to the rhetoric, in reality there was little change in school practice.[54]

Conclusion

The schools' response to race had consequences on several levels. The inequality in school resources—especially the deficits in instructional time and in qualified teachers—was surely detrimental to academic achievement. Many black children entered the schools with disadvantages stemming from poverty and migration; yet instead of getting more resources to compensate for these disadvantages, they got less. There were also symbolic and political consequences. School officials had countenanced segregation in defiance of law and precedent, even though it led to significant racial inequality, and then denied responsibility for it. As a result, the public schools lost legitimacy in the eyes of the black community. Schoolchildren, who had firsthand experience of the deficiencies in black schools, and who sometimes joined their parents in demonstrations and boycotts, learned that the schools were not to be trusted. Finally, the effect of these political battles was reinforced by the schools' uneven and largely ineffective efforts to improve race relations. The racial insensitivity and hostility that black students faced in school undermined their trust of the schools and gave emotional force to the larger patterns of segregation and inequality.

The racial segregation and inequality described above were compounded by changes in the curriculum and structure of schooling. As the next chapter describes, the emerging system of vocational education was, to a large extent, formally race neutral. However, because it was implemented in the context of racially segregated and unequal schools and a discriminatory labor market, this race-neutral system had very different implications for black and immigrant youth.

CHAPTER FIVE

Vocational Education

In the early years of the twentieth century, Chicago's public schools took on a new function: they began explicitly to prepare students for the labor market. The school system's new vocational curricula blended academic education with commercial and technical training, and were particularly attractive for students from modest backgrounds, as so many black and immigrant students were. For educators, these curricula offered a way to retain and motivate students. In this chapter, we follow the Chicago Public Schools as it constructed—and reconstructed—its system of vocational education, and show how the consequences differed for black and immigrant youth.

The Rise of Vocational Education

At the turn of the century, the city's public schools did very little to train students for jobs. The local high schools offered a handful of vocational classes such as surveying and bookkeeping, but their curriculum was largely classical, with an emphasis on Latin, Greek, and the humanities. For their part, employers paid little attention to school credentials. For skilled or professional positions, training took place largely through formal or informal apprenticeship. During the late nineteenth century, the Chicago Board of Education took a few steps to develop a more practical kind of education. Beginning in 1886, it opened a repair shop to boys from the surrounding schools who elected manual training in lieu of academic work for half the day. In 1890, the board opened the English High and Manual Training School, a three-year program with a curriculum that was about half shop courses with no foreign languages. On a very limited basis, the elementary schools also began to introduce "manual training." Such training did not prepare students for specific jobs, but did introduce them to the use of tools and construction materials.[1]

It was only after the turn of the century that the Chicago Board of Education began to offer vocational training on a larger scale. There are several reasons this happened. One was an increase in the demand for school-based training. The need for clerical labor had grown rapidly around the turn of the century. This demand had been met largely through recruitment of women to staff the more routine clerical positions. But turnover among female employees was high; most left their jobs after marriage, and employers themselves often imposed age restrictions and marriage prohibitions on clerical workers. As a result, training costs became a more serious concern. At the same time, typewriter keyboards and shorthand methods became standardized, enabling clerical skills to be taught in school rather than by the employer.[2]

The labor market changed in other ways as well. Professional associations and state governments had begun to set minimum licensing standards for many occupations. By the early twentieth century, for example, the State of Illinois established licensing requirements for a wide range of occupations, including real estate agents, accountants, plumbers, embalmers, and barbers. These laws created a demand for vocational courses that would prepare students for licensing exams or fulfill certification requirements. Even when such training was not required by law, it might be adopted to raise an occupation's prestige and standardize skill requirements.[3] The growth of corporations also opened new opportunities for credentialed labor. Where family connections or long service had once sufficed, now training in finance or marketing became de rigueur for aspirants to management. By 1908, schools of commerce had opened at the University of Chicago, Northwestern University, and the University of Illinois.[4]

During the late nineteenth century, businessmen began to lobby the public schools to provide students with vocational education. Organizations such as the National Association of Manufacturers pressed for this program at the national level. The National Society for the Promotion of Industrial Education was established in 1907, gaining support from both business and labor. At the local level, the Chicago Board of Education formed an advisory committee on vocational education, joined by representatives from business organizations and the Chicago Federation of Labor.[5]

The public schools were also motivated by competition from the private sector. In the nineteenth century, when the Chicago Board of Education declined to expand vocational education, businesses turned to private schools for well-trained future employees. In 1884, Marshall Field and other prominent businessmen established the secondary-level Chicago Manual Training School. Phillip Armour of the meatpacking family donated funds to establish the Armour Institute of Technology in 1893. The Lewis Institute, another technical school, was founded in 1896 with a bequest from Allan C. Lewis, a wealthy businessman. The Pullman Free School of Manual Training, associated with Pullman Co., opened in 1915. Proprietary "business colleges" sprang up to provide commercial training. Vocational training was also provided by denominational schools, including the YMCA's Association Institute, St. Stanislaus Kostka (a Polish Catholic academy), and the Christian Brothers' De La Salle Institute and St. Patrick's Academy. A number of Catholic elementary schools offered two-year commercial programs. All of these private-sector programs tailored their curricula to the requirements of businesses, trade organizations, or certification exams. The Armour Institute, for instance, worked with the National Board of Fire Underwriters to develop a course of study in fire protection engineering. The Association Institute developed courses preparing students for the CPA, civil service, and real estate examinations. The business colleges put businessmen on their boards of examiners and consulted them on curricula.[6]

This competition became more threatening when some private schools began to add college-preparatory curricula. At the time, most midwestern colleges, including the University of Chicago, Northwestern University, and the University of Illinois, granted admission "by certificate," accepting any graduate of a high school accredited by the North Central Association of Schools and Colleges. The Association Institute's day school graduates were accepted by the city's law and medical colleges; by 1908 these graduates were also admitted to liberal arts colleges. Later on, the institute's evening high school was the first in the city to be accredited, beating out the public evening schools by several years. The Pullman Free School added a college-preparatory course soon after its founding, and the Armour Institute established a secondary-level Scientific Academy preparing students for technical colleges.[7]

Enrollment figures suggest that private schools were significant players in the educational marketplace. Between 1900 and 1910, enrollment growth in the Catholic high schools exceeded that in the public ones (by 95 percent, compared with 74 percent). Although we do not have systematic data about trends in other private schools, the scattered evidence indicates both high enrollments and rapid growth. Between 1880 and 1910, the number of private business colleges rose from five to forty. In 1910, when the public high schools enrolled about 17,800 students, the YMCA's Association Institute enrolled 1,700 students and private business colleges were estimated to have 19,000 students.[8]

After the turn of the century, vocational education began to seem more acceptable to public school educators. Although some defended a broad academic education for all students, others promoted a more utilitarian approach. Students who were not bound for college, they argued, did not need the academic curriculum of humanities, math, and foreign language; they needed a more specific and practical kind of training. Research by the educational psychologist Edward L. Thorndike, which seemed to show that learning in one domain did not transfer well to other domains, strengthened the case for teaching students only what they would need in adulthood. Vocational education gained legitimacy from the Douglas Commission of Massachusetts, which in 1906 issued a report promoting it. In Chicago, these ideas were championed by Edwin Cooley, who was superintendent of schools from 1900 to 1909.[9]

School officials and child welfare advocates also saw vocational education as a way of keeping adolescents in school. Youth aged fourteen to fifteen years were of particular concern, because they were old enough to leave school but too young for apprenticeships and stable factory or office work; their job prospects had diminished with the passage of stricter child labor laws in 1903. These young workers typically held unskilled jobs and were often out of work; roaming the streets, it was feared, they might be drawn into delinquency. Child welfare advocates such as Jane Addams thought a more practical course of study might keep these youth in school and out of trouble.[10]

Shortly after the turn of the century, the Chicago Board of Education began to expand vocational education in the high schools. In 1901, the board introduced commercial classes into the regular high schools on an elective basis. In 1903, the English High and Manual Training School got a new name (Crane Technical High School), a larger building, and a four-year curriculum. Over the next ten years, the board opened two more technical high schools for boys, Lane and Tilden, and one, Lucy Flower Technical High School, for girls. The general high schools added more commercial classes, and in 1913 established a four-year commercial course of study.

The four-year technical and commercial curricula were broad and relatively academic; indeed, Crane adopted a four-year program partly to allow time for more academic courses. The technical curriculum qualified students for the new engineering colleges such as Armour and Lewis, and also for postsecondary education in fields such as teaching and home economics. The commercial course of study was aimed at future businessmen and included courses in commercial geography and law. Some technical and commercial courses let students take two years of a foreign language, thus qualifying for admission to a liberal arts college.[11]

Vocational education expanded more rapidly after 1910, when Superintendent Ella Flagg Young introduced two-year vocational programs into the general and technical high schools. Students taking these programs graduated after completing the tenth grade. The two-year courses of study were less academic than the four-year courses; they offered business English and shop math, and allowed no time for foreign languages. The vocational training in the two-year courses also was narrower, because students could not complete the full circuit of shops and related courses in their field. Two-year graduates from technical programs, for instance, might choose among programs in electricity, mechanical drawing, machine shop, or cabinetmaking, while four-year technical graduates received training in most or all of these areas. By 1925, the public high schools were graduating students in a number of technical and commercial fields (see table 5.1), as well as a five-month certificate in stenography. The Board of Education also expanded vocational programs for part-time students already in the workforce, including continuation schools (a one-day-per-week program required of fourteen- to seventeen-year-olds not in school), evening schools, and the apprentice education housed primarily at Washburne Continuation School.[12]

Although the elementary schools did not offer commercial or technical training, they expanded manual training in the upper grades. By 1909, seventh and eighth graders in most schools received manual training once a week, as long as they remained in good academic standing;

TABLE 5.1:   **Types of high school diplomas awarded in June 1925, Chicago Public Schools**

Four-year degrees	Two-year degrees
General	Accounting
Architecture	Automobile mechanics
Art	Cabinetmaking
Commercial	Carpentry
Household arts	Electricity
Normal preparatory	Mechanical drawing
Technical	Stenography
	Woodworking

the boys worked with simple hand tools and the girls cooked and sewed. Shortages of space, equipment, and trained teachers slowed the expansion of manual training, although by the early 1930s all boys in grades six through eight took a shop course, usually woodworking. Children in the younger grades were given "construction work" or arts and crafts, but the curriculum allowed little time for these activities, and teachers seldom integrated them into the rest of the curriculum as manual training enthusiasts desired. Among elementary schoolchildren, the most intensive manual training was given to over-age sixth through eighth graders in the twenty-three "industrial schools." These students spent one-quarter to one-half of their time in shop work.[13]

High school students responded enthusiastically to the vocational courses of study. Adolescent boys crowded into the technical schools, drawn by "lots of machinery and no girls." Lane Technical High School, the largest and best equipped, opened in 1908 with an enrollment of 1,200 and reached 7,000 by 1930, with the overflow housed in portable classrooms and nearby elementary schools. The response to the initial commercial courses was also positive: one early report described their success as "phenomenal" as students thronged to the classes despite limited space and equipment. By 1915, if we include both two-year and four-year degrees, half of the high school diplomas granted were vocational; in 1925, almost 60 percent were (fig. 5.1).[14] As educators had expected, the technical schools attracted students with weaker academic skills; among incoming ninth graders at Tilden, for instance, the median student tested at the sixth-grade level in reading and at the seventh-grade level in mathematics. Nonetheless, many vocational graduates found work in their field of training.[15]

Chicago educators disagreed about whether the schools should guide students' choice of curriculum. During the 1910s, social efficiency experts advocated sorting students into curricula based on their academic prowess. When standardized intelligence and achievement tests began to be used in the schools in the early 1920s, educators saw the potential of using test scores to guide students' curricular choices. However, many teachers remained ambivalent about choosing curricula for students. Tracking students in this manner remained controversial among the public, and the labor unions strongly opposed it.[16]

Yet even if Chicago educators had agreed on tracking students based on academic achievement, they would have been hard-pressed to do it. The schools simply did not have the capability. The Bureau of Vocational Guidance, established during the 1910s, had a small staff which worked primarily to discourage students from dropping out. The bureau also processed employment certificates for students leaving school and helped physically disabled youth find work. With these and many other responsibilities, the office could not advise students individually on their courses of study. By the mid-1920s, the Bureau of Vocational Guidance had grown to forty-seven employees, and each high school had at least a part-time vocational counselor. One counselor, however, could accomplish little in a school of several thousand students. Nor could standardized tests be used to select a student's course of study; regular testing was rare and systematic record keeping even rarer.[17] The following advice, given in 1923 by an elementary school principal to his eighth-

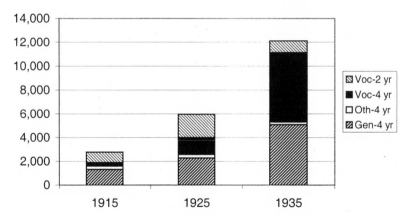

FIGURE 5.1 Number of degrees by type, Chicago public high schools, June 1915–35. Source: Tabulations from Chicago Board of Education, annual *Proceedings* volumes.

grade graduates, suggests that students were more or less on their own in choosing a curriculum. On the first day of high school, the principal wrote, students should

> go direct to the assembly hall, where all newcomers, called Freshmen, will meet. Remain there until the principal or his assistant tells you where to go. The principal or someone in charge will then ask all those who wish to take a Four-Year Technical Course, etc., to stand. Then you will be counted off in squads of thirty and sent with a teacher to some room . . . Make up your mind as to just what course you intend to follow: i.e., Two-Year Commercial, Two-Year Accounting, Four-Year Commercial, Four-Year General, Four-Year Science, Four-Year Normal Preparatory, Four-Year Technical, etc. You will have no time to ask questions the first day. Don't ask any. Listen, keep quiet and cool, and go where you are told at the time you are told, and wait.

Undoubtedly, there were instances in which teachers or guidance counselors steered students to one course of study or another, but the high schools did not have the capability to do this en masse.[18]

Vocational education helped Chicago's public schools attract students and quell private-sector competition. Between 1910 and 1930, enrollment grew by 484 percent in the city's public schools, compared with 121 percent in its Catholic high schools. The public schools' new curricula also spurred private schools to drop their secondary school programs and focus on postsecondary training, where they remained competitive. Indeed, while a diminished business college sector continued to attract students, the Board of Education's own Medill College of Commerce and Administration closed in 1925 because of low enrollment. Thus, for vocational training at the high school level, the public schools became dominant, and the vocational programs changed the character of the high school curriculum in a very short time.[19]

Stratification of the High Schools

Although the vocational curricula helped the public schools gain ground against the private schools, this very success jeopardized the economic value of the program. As the rate of high school enrollment rose, the population of high school graduates increased and the schools risked flooding the labor market, thereby diluting the value of their high school

credentials. In the early 1900s, when public schools began to implement vocational education, high school graduates were a select group
and their credentials were scarce, giving them a competitive advantage
in job seeking. However, as figure 5.1 shows, the number of vocational
graduates rose dramatically between the 1910s and the 1930s. George
Strayer, who led an extensive survey of the Chicago Public Schools in
1932, warned against "training too many boys for certain occupations.
It is not good public policy to duplicate needlessly industrial courses and
train a surplus of young workers." At the time of his survey, almost four
thousand boys were studying printing, and more than six hundred were
studying Linotype and presswork. Industry, he wrote, could not possibly
absorb so many.[20]

The market for clerical workers gives a striking example of the problem of declining selectivity. Around 1910, most firms hired eighth-grade
graduates for "general office work," but preferred stenographers to
have some high school training: "Good stenographers are always in demand, but the girl who has not had the proper educational background
can never become a good stenographer . . . The market is flooded with
inefficient girls, who are too incompetent to be recommended for good
positions and who are lowering standards of work and wages." The public schools began to train two-year (tenth-grade) stenography graduates
to meet this demand, but as high school enrollment rose, these two-year
graduates became a less select group. In a 1927 canvass of employers,
"the mention of stenography brought about, invariably, a discussion
of the deterioration in quality of the present day high school product."
By then employers might hire a tenth-grade graduate for general office
work, but for stenography they preferred the twelfth-grade graduate:

> She represents a more carefully selected group. She has, at least, held to her
> choice in vocation and worked toward one end for four years; she has benefit-
> ted by the background of the school training and the contact with teachers
> and classmates. As a rule, she comes from a home which recognizes the ad-
> vantages derived from a broader education.

Then came the Depression, and competition for jobs intensified. The
tenth-grade commercial graduates could not find work at all, and the
Board of Education discontinued the two-year degree. The number of
four-year commercial graduates grew dramatically, however, to more
than 3,400 in June 1935 (see fig. 5.2). Now surveys of businesses revealed

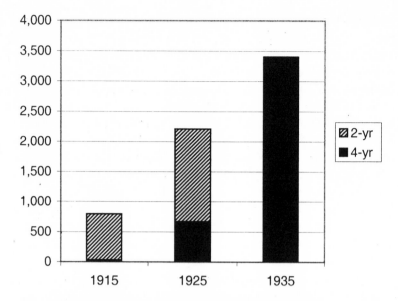

FIGURE 5.2 Commercial graduates from Chicago public high schools, June 1915–35. Source: Tabulations from Chicago Board of Education, annual *Proceedings* volumes.

dissatisfaction with the four-year graduates: employers complained they had "inadequate skill and occupational intelligence." A 1940 study of a Chicago high school found that 81 percent of commercial graduates believed clerical job-seekers needed postsecondary training. One student reported, "It seems that most large firms will not even take your application unless you have graduated from high school and business college."[21]

Colleges also faced a problem of declining selectivity. As more students graduated from high school, the pool of potential enrollees became larger. By the 1930s, college officials began to worry about certificate-based admissions, which guaranteed a seat to any graduate of an accredited high school. In 1933, the Carnegie Foundation, which had spearheaded the earlier standardization of college admissions, recommended that the old system give way to "more flexible, individual, more exact and more revealing standards of performance as rapidly as these may be achieved." Chicago colleges began to experiment with standardized tests and other new admissions criteria. By 1935, the University of Chicago added a "quality criterion"—enrollees had to have finished in the upper half of their high school class—and began to use standardized tests. In 1936, the Armour Institute of Technology began to require that incoming freshmen take standardized tests in silent reading, vocabulary, mathematics, and science achievement, as well as an American Council on Education test of "mental ability." Armour officials were chagrined to find their freshmen scoring only at the median on the ACE test. As a college historian wrote, "One year later, due perhaps to an unconscious raising of standards by the admissions office, the score was raised to the seventy-fifth percentile, a most gratifying improvement."[22]

A major revision in the high school curriculum, begun in 1937, addressed the glut of high-school-educated workers by stratifying both the vocational and the academic programs. School officials began by eliminating the four-year vocational courses of study at the general high schools. Students there could still take vocational classes as electives, but the more specialized vocational courses were discontinued.[23] These changes had only a modest impact on students in the technical and household arts courses; two-thirds of them had already taken their training in the technical high schools. But the changes had a dramatic impact on the number of commercial graduates. In 1935, 36 percent of all four-year graduates from the general high schools had taken the commercial course of study. After this option disappeared, the number of graduates with vocational diplomas fell sharply between 1935 and 1945, alleviating the oversupply of vocational graduates (see fig. 5.3).

The specialized technical high schools, on the other hand, continued to offer the intensive vocational courses of study. Here a two-tiered

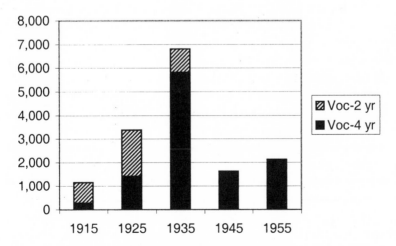

FIGURE 5.3 Total vocational degrees from Chicago public high schools, June 1915–55. Source: Tabulations from Chicago Board of Education, annual *Proceedings* volumes.

system began to emerge. The upper tier included vocational schools and programs that were selective, admitting students on the basis of academic achievement. This practice began in two new vocational schools. The first, Jones Commercial High School, opened in 1937 and became the only public high school in the city to offer a four-year commercial curriculum. Representing an effort to restore business confidence in the public schools' commercial training, Jones admitted students on the basis of academic aptitude, vocational interest, and "employability," or motivation and personality. The effort was a success: Jones graduates were much in demand at Chicago firms, which petitioned the Board of Education to expand enrollment at the school. The second selective high school, Chicago Vocational School, opened in 1941 on the city's South Side. It was better equipped than the older technical schools, and provided a more intensive training program, awarding four-year degrees in specialized subjects such as electricity, foundry, tailoring, and aircraft mechanics. CVS admitted students based on their school records (grades, test scores, attendance) and interviews. In later years, the district opened other selective vocational schools, and some existing ones—notably Lane Tech—also began to require entrance exams. When the high schools introduced a new Distributive Education co-op program to train students for sales jobs, it, too, limited enrollment based on academic record, personality, and attendance.[24]

At the same time, Chicago school officials expanded a second tier of nonselective vocational high schools. These schools were created from the "prevocational" classes established years ago for over-age high school students. Their trade training included janitorial engineering, tailoring, and commercial cooking, and 75 percent of the school day was spent in shop work. Students with low achievement test scores were channeled into these schools, where the meager and outmoded shop equipment gave students little opportunity for obtaining marketable job skills. While the selective technical high schools offered a wide range of specialized courses, the nonselective schools offered far fewer options. Under this two-tiered system, the public schools could protect the economic value of credentials from its flagship technical schools while providing at least nominal access to vocational training for large numbers of students.[25]

When the Board of Education dropped the technical and commercial courses from the general high schools, the number of students in the general course of study increased rapidly, making more students

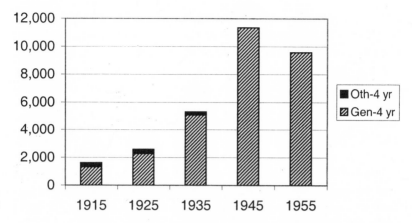

FIGURE 5.4 General and "other" four-year graduates from Chicago public high schools, June 1915–55. Source: Tabulations from Chicago Board of Education, annual *Proceedings* volumes.

eligible for certificate-based admissions to college (see fig. 5.4). At the same time, however, the public schools began to stratify the curriculum of the general high school. Although many colleges continued to require foreign language and mathematics for admission, the new high school curriculum made foreign language optional. As a Board of Education report explained in 1937,

> The parents and the student must understand that a high school diploma will not necessarily admit its holder to college. It will admit him to college only if the entrance requirements of the college he expects to attend are met in his high school work. Since these entrance requirements vary among the colleges and according to the different courses within a single college, the student should learn early in his high school work what are the requirements of the college he expects to attend, and should elect his work to meet them.

The high schools also made enrollment in foreign language and advanced mathematics courses contingent on achievement test scores. Consequently, the pool of graduates eligible for college entry became smaller and more selective.[26]

Ultimately, however, the high schools lost the right to be arbiter of a student's fitness for college. More and more colleges abandoned certificate-based admissions in favor of test scores or other indicators of academic achievement. By 1949, the University of Chicago evaluated applicants on the basis of reading and writing tests and a "mental test," having found that "simple tests of these three abilities have a higher correlation with marks in all courses than any other measure they have used." In 1950, a committee of state educators urged public universities to abolish subject requirements and to substitute a combination of standardized test scores and high school transcript. The University of Illinois, which for decades had admitted any graduate of an accredited high school, began to require entrance exams for applicants graduating in the lowest quarter of their class. Despite an acute teacher shortage, beginning in 1957 the Chicago Teachers College required entrance exams for *all* applicants, with the lowest scoring candidates denied admission and some others required to take remedial work.[27] Students who aspired to college but could not meet these requirements could fall back on the city's junior colleges, operated by the Board of Education. These colleges had originally offered an academic curriculum. In the late 1930s, as it became clearer that most of their students would not transfer to four-year colleges, the junior colleges introduced "terminal" courses of study: junior technology, junior chemistry, nursing, merchandising, and banking. Between 1940 and 1960, enrollment in Chicago junior colleges rose from 6,200 to 23,000.[28]

The stratification of the high schools shifted control over curricular choice from the student to the school. School staff used students' school records, including standardized test scores, grades, and teachers' comments, to make up the course schedules. To defuse resentment about this restriction of choice, the schools emphasized the objective bases of curriculum and career placement through guidance and "self-appraisal" activities. In the junior year, after a round of achievement testing,

> results in percentile scores are returned to the students for self-appraisal. The students make their own profiles on profile sheets provided for the purpose. Interpretation of the test data is made to them and they are invited to locate their strong and weak areas. They then write notes on their reactions to the results, their interpretation of the factors that may have caused the weakness, and their requests for assistance, in order that their successful pursuit of education may be promoted and their deficiencies removed before graduation.

Most seniors took a career guidance course which involved another round of testing; students again made profiles of their scores and compared their own scores with the requirements of various occupations. This self-appraisal invited them to attribute responsibility for their own academic and career trajectory to their standardized test scores.[29] At the same time, the schools highlighted the elements of choice that remained. At "Parent Interview Day," for instance, teachers used the cumulative record data to make recommendations about the high school course of study. As Superintendent William Johnson wrote, "If the child and his parents decide on a specialized course inconsistent with the data on the child's aptitudes and abilities, a notation is made and retained in the elementary school for future reference . . . It is not the purpose of the conference to guide the pupil and parents in their choice but rather to present all the available facts to them."[30]

Race, Ethnicity, and the High School Curriculum

African-American and immigrant students, most of them from working-class backgrounds, were exactly the kinds of students that Chicago educators had in mind when they expanded vocational education. The schools offered training for technical or commercial jobs that were better than the jobs most students' parents held. Yet black and immigrant students did not benefit equally from vocational education, and this differences grew over time as the system became more stratified.

For the few who were bound for college, the turn-of-the-century academic curriculum served black and immigrant students equally well, even after the high schools began to add vocational curricula. If students had the financial and academic wherewithal, the path from high school to college was smooth. Note this account by the daughter of the civil rights activist Ida B. Wells-Barnett:

> My mother didn't want me to be in a coed school, so for two and a half years I stayed at Lucy Flower [Technical School] and had a good time . . . And when my brother, my older brother, then told Mother that he thought that I could weather the storm of a coed high school, I transferred to Wendell Phillips High School, named for the outstanding abolitionist. Because I had so many technical courses at Lucy Flower, I didn't need many years of work, and so I graduated from high school in three and a half years. Then I went over to the University of Chicago. At that time a high school diploma was automatic admission to a college. There were no entrance exams. I had no problem, I simply registered and started going to school at the University of Chicago.[31]

College was irrelevant, however, for most immigrant and black high school students. Only a small minority had even graduated from high school, and even fewer could afford higher education. Little scholarship support was available. Some of the ethnic societies provided grants or loans for immigrant students, but these were very limited, so most worked their way through college. A number of eastern European immigrants went to Indiana's Valparaiso University, known informally as "potatohead university" or "dishwashers university" because so many students earned their fees by working in the kitchens. For black students as well, financial aid was limited to a handful of scholarships from high schools, sororities and fraternities, and other private sources. For both immigrant and black students, the public colleges were more affordable. In a survey of Chicago-area colleges conducted in 1909, almost half of the black and immigrant students attended the University of Illinois, which had schools of medicine and pharmacy in the city. A number of black students attended the city's junior colleges and the Chicago Normal School, neither of which charged tuition.[32]

Vocational education was especially important for students with no prospect of attending college. Here the contrast between black and immigrant students was striking. From the beginning, when the high schools introduced the vocational curricula, immigrants were heavily represented in these courses of study. High schools that were predominantly attended by children of southern and eastern European origin had the highest proportions of graduates in vocational studies. If we compare the general high schools, in 1925 51 percent of the graduates of Phillips—the only predominantly black high school—earned vocational diplomas, compared with 68 percent of students in heavily immigrant working-class high schools. By 1935, the difference had widened: 29 percent at Phillips and 66 percent at immigrant, working-class high schools graduated with vocational degrees.[33] Black students were also poorly represented at the four specialized vocational schools, which offered the best technical and household arts training. Of these schools, Lane, Crane, and Flower were located at a distance from the South Side neighborhood where most black families lived. Tilden was located very close to the Black Belt, but in a notoriously hostile neighborhood. As chapter 4 recounts, when sixty black students transferred to Tilden in order to take the technical coursework, the white students forced most of them to leave. In 1930, only 3 percent of Tilden students were black.[34]

Black students were also deterred from taking the vocational course of study by racial discrimination in the labor market. Those with vocational degrees found few opportunities, as anecdotal evidence attests.

In 1913, a young black man who had graduated from a technical high school "was sent with other graduates of his class to a big electric company where in the presence of all his classmates he was told that 'niggers are not wanted here.'" It was the same for African-American girls with commercial degrees: "High school girls of refined appearance, after looking for weeks, will find nothing open to them in department stores, office buildings, or manufacturing establishments, save a few positions as maids placed in women's waiting rooms." During World War I, when black women were hired into clerical positions, there was a surge of interest in the high school commercial course, but enrollments dropped again after the war. Black men gained entry into some manufacturing jobs during the war, but not into the skilled blue-collar jobs that required outside training. A 1920s survey of the alumni of a technical school included a black man who had spent four years learning drafting and sheet metal work. His recommendation: "More music for colored boys. That is the only thing they can use to make money."[35]

After 1937, black and immigrant students faced an increasingly stratified curriculum in the high schools. The onus was now on students and their parents to learn about college entrance requirements, but given their parents' modest backgrounds, immigrant and black youth had little access at home to information about college. On the other hand, immigrant students appear to have negotiated the stratified vocational system with relative ease. Graduation lists show that many students of southern and eastern European origin attended the selective vocational schools such as CVS and Lane.

Black students did not fare as well. Both geographic inaccessibility and racial barriers prevented them from taking full advantage of the selective trade and technical schools. The Lane campus was relocated during the 1930s and was now quite distant from the South Side Black Belt. Crane and Tilden were closer, but they dropped their vocational programs in the 1950s. CVS initially did not admit black students. Very few black students attended Washburne Trade School, a training school for apprentices; it remained virtually impossible to secure a place there without informal connections in the skilled trades.[36] The Chicago Board of Education was chastised by the North Central Association of Secondary Schools and by the Illinois State Office of Public Instruction for the limited vocational training provided to black students.[37]

The only bright spot was Dunbar Trade School on the South Side. During the 1930s, Dunbar had been a school for over-age students,

offering only limited facilities and a curriculum that did not meet licensing requirements for state-certified occupations. After community protest and pressure from the state, the Chicago Board of Education reconsti-
tuted Dunbar as a trade school. Like its predecessor, the new Dunbar was
poorly equipped, but it was fortunate in its leadership. Clifford Campbell,
an African American, had a background in architectural drawing and
years of experience in school administration. He recruited an impressive
staff, sought donations of equipment, and turned Dunbar into a serious
trade school with a curriculum whose range rivaled that of CVS. Dunbar
trained students both for lines of work traditionally open to blacks, such
as cosmetology and masonry, and for nontraditional occupations such as
plumbing, electronics, and aircraft mechanics. With an excellent reputation and a job placement rate of 90 percent, the school attracted black students from all over the city; enrollment rose from several hundred in the
early 1940s to more than two thousand in the 1950s. With more applicants
than it could accommodate, Dunbar began to select students based on academic record, although it sometimes waived its admissions standards.[38]

Even with Dunbar, black students remained disproportionately represented in the lower-tier vocational schools. In 1963, among students
in vocational, trade, or technical schools, 87 percent of white students
attended CVS, Dunbar, Jones, Lane Tech, or Prosser—the most selective vocational schools—while only half of all black students did so. At
a time when public school enrollment was nearly half black, as figure 5.5

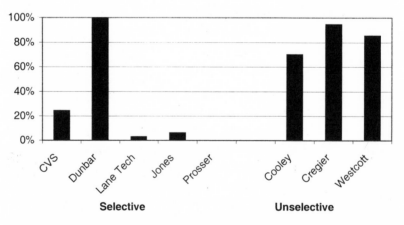

FIGURE 5.5 Black representation in Chicago public trade, vocational, and technical high
schools, ca. 1963. Source: Havighurst, *Public Schools of Chicago,* 247–49. Racial composition for Lane is from "Here's School-by-School Breakdown." Note: Tilden is excluded,
because it was in the process of shifting from a technical to a general curriculum.

shows, black enrollment in most selective vocational schools was quite low, while the three lower-tier schools were all predominantly black.

When the public schools developed their vocational curricula, they also set forth a model in which students would use the schools' assessment, guidance, and course offerings as a way to select and prepare for their "life work." This structure gave meaning to the high school experience for many students. The following selections are survey responses of students at Hyde Park High School (predominantly white) and brief autobiographies from Morton High School (a predominantly eastern European school just outside Chicago):

> Before entering high school I had not decided what I would do after I graduate from high school. Last summer I thought I was near a decision. Then when I entered high school I chose to take a commercial course. Now I wish I had chosen an art course because I think now I want to become an artist.

> My vocational choice was teaching. Then my father made me take a commercial course. Now he wants me to change back to a teaching course and continue on in college. I think it would put me too far behind. What shall I do?

> I chose aviation because I have always been interested in aircraft; because of the high pay; and because my parents advised me to take this. Recently some friends have argued against it and I am a little disturbed by this.

> My ambition increased and I took subjects that were necessary for an engineer such as machine drawing, three years of mathematics, and a foreign language . . . When I finish high school I expect to go to college for an electrical engineering course.

Although their decisions could be a source of anxiety or family conflict, these students took seriously their deliberations about curriculum and occupation. These were meaningful choices.[39]

For black students, however, this model was empty. Students with high achievement scores, who could qualify for college-preparatory academics or top-tier vocational training, were discouraged by labor market discrimination. In response to the Hyde Park High School survey, a black sophomore wrote, "Because my skin is not the same color as that of the majority of these students there are certain vocations practically closed to me. Some of the things I want most to do are impossible because of this."[40] Students with low test scores faced a disheartening choice between the degraded curricula of the unselective vocational schools, which prepared students for lower-tier jobs, many of them racially stereotypical, and a nonvocational curriculum that prepared students for nothing at all. Adding insult to injury, the schools' apparatus of self-appraisal placed the blame for blocked opportunity on students themselves, by framing test scores as a determinant of occupational opportunity.

Conclusion

The Chicago Public Schools expanded its vocational curricula rapidly after the turn of the century, and within two decades, more than half the graduates from the city's high schools earned vocational diplomas. When the success of these programs jeopardized the economic value of their credentials, the schools created a two-tiered structure in which access to college-preparatory or top-tier technical and commercial programs was contingent on academic achievement. Low-achieving students, disproportionately black, were relegated to a degraded second tier. For immigrants, vocationalization made school more attractive; they fared relatively well in the two-tiered vocational system. Black students did not. As high school enrollment became the norm, this difference became even more consequential, with the most significant impact on low-achieving students. High-quality vocational education could have given these students a sense of purpose in school and a modest economic boost after school. Yet those who might have gained the most from this program were denied it.

Vocational education offers one example of how black students could be disadvantaged by policies that were ostensibly race neutral. Because of racial inequality in school and the labor market, vocational education had very different implications for black and immigrant students. As the next chapter shows, we see a similar pattern for remedial education. Inner-city students were more likely to need this program, in part because of the widespread poverty and disadvantage in their neighborhoods, and in part because of the educational damage done by the schools themselves. What the Chicago schools provided, however, fell far short of what those students needed.

CHAPTER SIX

Remedial Education

Differences in student achievement were not a new condition in Chicago's public schools. There had always been students who struggled academically. In the nineteenth century, however, most of these children dropped out of school before long. Then, when compulsory education laws became stricter, low-achieving students became more visible, and more troublesome. Beginning in the early twentieth century, Chicago's school administrators went through an elaborate period of trial and error as they developed new strategies for dealing with low-achieving students. This chapter follows the city's educators and district officials as they explored new approaches, such as ability grouping and social promotion, then settled on a set of policies that would last with little alteration from the late 1930s through the 1960s. As the chapter describes, the schools' approach to remedial education may have been adequate in some schools, but it was an abject failure in the schools of the inner city.

The Problem of School Failure

At the turn of the century, the schools managed achievement differences among students with grade retention and acceleration. At the end of each semester, when teachers made their promotion decisions, a student might be held back, promoted to the next half grade, or given a double promotion. Unlike the practice in some cities, such as New York, Chicago's teachers did not base promotion decisions on standardized exams. Instead, promotion was determined by semester grades, with all students who earned 75 or above proceeding to the next grade. Relying on grades allowed some discretion, however. Noting "the pleadings that seek to soften the teacher's heart," one teacher commented, "how often does she indeed pass one who really does not deserve it, but knowing the circumstances she closes one eye and marks him seventy-five!" Teachers also complained of pressure from administrators to promote students to make room for the incoming ones.[1]

Turn-of-the-century school officials did not view school failure as a problem. Indeed, schools enacted their high academic standards by holding some students back. Moreover, as a response to achievement variation, retention and acceleration had a practical advantage. Instead of tailoring the curriculum and teaching methods to variations in students' aptitudes and learning styles, the schools simply sorted children into classes at different grade levels. Whatever its implications for learning, this "batch processing" was more economical—and in a school district scrambling for money, that was a compelling argument for its use.

This view began to change in the early 1900s. School failure gained national attention when a spate of studies, including Leonard Ayres's 1907 *Laggards in Our Schools,* startled educators with evidence of how common grade retention was. Under the new rubric of efficiency, that policy began to seem wasteful, because students were being taught the same material twice or even more often. Given the financial strains they faced, school officials were sensitive to the implications for the cost of education. Grade retention also seemed inefficient in the deeper sense that teaching the same curriculum at the same pace to students of divergent abilities was bound to be wasteful—unnecessarily slow for some, dauntingly fast for others. Teachers began to see problems with grade retention when the district cracked down on truancy and dropping out. Student absence and attrition had long been essential, if unacknowledged, elements of the schools' response to low achievement: failing students often truanted or dropped out altogether. Keeping them in the classroom created problems of morale and discipline.[2]

Explanations for school failure ran the gamut. Teachers had some notion of differences in intelligence among their students, reflected in their casual use of terms such as *fast* and *slow, bright* and *dull,* but acknowledged many other causes of low achievement. From their own observation, they recognized the impact of poverty, hunger, illness, child labor, poor housing, foreign birth, and the distractions of street life in the slums. Whereas some teachers faulted students for lack of effort, others faulted the school system for flaws in the curriculum, failure to give them the time to assist struggling students, and pressure to promote students who weren't ready. From their own classroom experience, teachers acknowledged the stigma and embarrassment felt by students, repeatedly been held back, who attended school with much younger children.[3]

The schools began to look for alternative ways to handle failing students. At the time, perhaps the most effective measures to address school failure aimed at alleviating poverty, hunger, and illness. In 1908, a local charity provided a penny lunch of oatmeal mush, bread, and milk to students in a poor immigrant neighborhood; their teachers reported significant improvements in students' attention span and academic work. Over the next several years, the School Children's Aid Society and local women's clubs began to support penny lunches, donations of shoes and clothing, and "visiting teachers" who referred families to relief agencies and free clinics.[4]

The schools also organized special classes for students who had been held back repeatedly. A handful of elementary schools began to provide an "industrial" curriculum in grades six to eight. The over-age students in these classes spent up to half of their school day in household arts or manual training. The Board of Education also expanded the numbers of "ungraded" or "subnormal" classes for low-achieving students. Half the size of regular classes, these provided a combination of academic instruction and manual training, and allowed students to return to the regular classes if their academic work improved. Ungraded classes for younger children were housed in the elementary schools. Over-age students of high school age attended ungraded "prevocational" classes at the high schools.[5]

Educators believed that students in these classes could make at least modest academic progress: "The majority of subnormal children if sufficiently aroused and interested, and properly taught, learn to read concrete reading material and to perform the mechanical operations of number work with ease and skill." The prevocational classes were thought to raise morale by moving over-age students into high school with their age peers: "Transplanting the retarded children into the soil of an active vigorous high school, and encouraging them, soon has a marked effect." Educators expected at least some of the students in ungraded classes to return to the regular classroom.[6] The impact of these classes was modest, however. The industrial curriculum was available only to students in the upper grades in about 10 percent of the elementary schools. The ungraded classes were expensive because they were small, and many schools didn't have room for them. Although the number of ungraded rooms grew significantly during the 1910s—rising from 25 in 1911 to 92 in 1920— they housed fewer than 1 percent of all elementary school students.[7]

Concern about school failure grew during the 1910s. By 1920, Chicago schools began to gather statistics about nonpromotion, and to question teachers about their reasons for retaining students. In responding to low achievement, however, educators were limited by the rigid organization of the city's school system. The schools were like a conveyor belt moving at uniform speed through the curriculum. If a child didn't learn quickly enough, he was plucked off the belt and set back at an earlier point. If the pace was too slow, the schools might skip him ahead. There was no other way—apart from the small numbers of industrial schools and ungraded classrooms—to deal with students for whom the pace was wrong. The solutions proposed at this time all took the "conveyor belt" as a given, making only minor changes within the existing structure of schools. Not until a few years later would educators begin to think about modifying this structure.[8]

Preventing Failure

During the 1920s, Chicago educators began to explore new techniques for "failure prevention." Their experiences were widely reported in the pages of the *Chicago Schools Journal,* the monthly magazine of the Chicago Normal School, which highlighted new or exemplary practices and provided a forum for principals and teachers to share ideas and experiences.[9] As the *Journal* shows, standardized intelligence and achievement tests had a powerful influence, and a complex one, on how educators viewed students' academic achievement.

The testing movement in education began when the "group" IQ tests, developed for use in the U.S. Army, were adapted after World War I for use in the schools. In 1921, the Chicago district office established a Bureau of Standards and Statistics to administer standardized intelligence and achievement tests to the city's students. During the 1920s, regular testing took place only in Chicago's junior high schools, although the district conducted occasional rounds of achievement testing in all the elementary and high schools, and some schools undertook their own programs of testing. Intelligence testing was less common and perhaps more controversial; in the early 1920s, when the district conducted these tests in the high schools, participation was voluntary, and only 15 of the 24 schools took part. To help teachers understand the new standardized tests, the *Chicago Schools Journal* published short articles about statistics and test reliability and validity, and the Chicago Normal School added courses in educational measurement.[10]

Intelligence tests were important, however, because they gave scientific legitimacy to educators' folk categories of bright and slow, lending them a new precision and causal weight. In her typology of students, for instance, Lillian Tobin drew a qualitative distinction between normal students and those she called retardates, "those slow reaction individuals with I.Q.'s usually lower than [other low-achieving students], who must not only jog along at a lesser pace but must live their experiences in a little different manner." Many educators assumed that IQ tests provided a true and exact measure of a student's academic potential. For instance, after a round of intelligence testing, the principal at Ray School noted that a student with low reading scores was discovered to have the second-highest IQ in the class. "As she was strong and healthy," he wrote, "we concluded that she was just plain lazy and told her so, with the result that she has much improved."[11]

Nonetheless, Chicago teachers were far from reaching a consensus on the importance of IQ to school performance. Indeed, W. J. Bartholf, a high school principal, complained in 1925 that "there is too much talk about mental tests and subnormal children. The greatest number of subnormal pupils is always found where there is the most subnormal teaching and supervision . . . If by skillful work we make practically all the pupils succeed we shall be relieved of the embarrassment of explaining by mental tests why so many fail."[12] Most educators continued to see IQ as only one of many determinants of school performance. Some also recognized that IQ test scores reflected English language fluency, a factor that disadvantaged many immigrant students in the city's public schools. Carl Brigham's book *A Study of American Intelligence,* which purported to demonstrate racial and ethnic differences in intelligence, got only a brief and dismissive review in the *Chicago Schools Journal.*[13]

The impact of intelligence tests was also tempered by the widespread use of standardized achievement tests. During the decade, educators began to conduct test-retest studies of student achievement, many of which seemed to show that this achievement was malleable and could be influenced by curriculum or teaching methods. Two central office administrators, Ambrose B. Wight and Edward E. Keener, promoted this idea, contending that achievement tests could help teachers improve instruction by encouraging the trial of new teaching methods. As Wight wrote, "The thought and the discussion which have been aroused by tests seem to be one of the greatest values derived from their use. Whether the results have been received without question, taken with a grain of salt, or entirely rejected does not alter the fact that teachers have been led to reflect upon the status of pupils and effectiveness of instruction in the subjects for which tests have been used." Early studies seemed (to them) to vindicate their enthusiasm. Wight and Keener reported instances in which average test scores rose more than one grade level from one year to the next. They attributed this extra gain to rising efficiency among teachers who used the test results to improve their teaching.[14]

During the early 1920s, achievement tests became the basis of a small flurry of instructional research in the Chicago Public Schools. Wight and Keener created a demonstration site at the city's Corkery Elementary School for what they called "measured teaching." Using standardized achievement tests, teachers at Corkery evaluated the effectiveness of various curricula and teaching methods. Their demonstration work attracted much attention. Local principals, administrators, and Chicago Normal School classes visited the school to learn about measured teaching. It soon became the norm to justify new teaching methods with evidence about rising test scores. In an eighth-grade remedial class at Corkery School, for instance, teachers reported that after eight weeks of intensive work the students' median reading score jumped from 4A to 9A—a startling five grade levels.[15]

No doubt, some of this remarkable progress was spurious. Among other threats to validity, students became "test-wise" when teachers let them practice on old versions of the tests. And with empirical social science in its infancy, there was little check on educators' naïve enthusiasm.[16] Nonetheless, this applied research was significant. It offered a counterweight to the pessimism suggested by IQ tests, and seemed to show that—under the right circumstances—low-achieving students could be helped and disparities in school achievement could be narrowed. It was a tentative beginning for a science of education grounded in the classroom.

Techniques of Failure Prevention

During the 1920s, Chicago educators tried out new approaches to cope with achievement variation and aid low-achieving students. The resulting "failure prevention" movement was not centrally coordinated; most experiments were small in scale and initiated by teachers or principals. They represented a variety of approaches. Some built on the casework approach of professional social work. For instance, Emma Levitt, who taught in an ungraded room, had the school nurse and a cooperating physician screen new students for "eyesight, hearing, tonsils, adenoids, condition of teeth, nutrition, and any other defects." Given the widespread poverty and rudimentary medical services of the time, it was not unusual to find students who were given only coffee for breakfast, or who had undiagnosed problems with vision or hearing. *Chicago Schools Journal* articles described the dramatic improvements in scholastic achievement that could result when a student in need received a pair of eyeglasses or a hot breakfast.[17]

Schools also provided new kinds of academic assistance. Some organized tutoring clubs in which low-achieving students were coached by their peers. The junior high schools, and a few high schools, brought failing students in for counseling, and readjusted course schedules to provide a "double dose" of subjects that presented difficulty. Hoping its students would find a more applied math curriculum more engaging, Tilden Technical High School let them take "shop math" instead of algebra, and found their achievement improved.[18]

In the English Center project, a small group of schools tried a more ambitious redesign of classroom practice. This demonstration of progressivist techniques, led by James Fleming Hosic of the Chicago Normal School, emphasized classroom participation and reading materials drawn from everyday life. Teachers replaced conventional recitation and textbook exercises with "socialized recitation" (class participation in discussion and critique), free reading in library books, and projects such as class newspapers and letter writing. Teachers found the new methods particularly helpful for low-achieving children. One teacher tried the new methods with immigrant children who had already failed a semester, and enthused that "in my years of experience teaching the primary grades, I have never had a class which could read as readily or grasp the thought of the lesson as clearly as these little children now can."[19]

Much work in failure prevention reflected the view that schools should adapt the curriculum to differences in students' mental ability rather than asking all students to learn the same material at the same pace. This was not a new idea, but standardized tests gave it new force with dramatic evidence of the achievement differences among children in the same grade. Very quickly it became an article of faith that students learned better with curricula calibrated to their aptitude or achievement level.[20]

Chicago educators tried several ways to adjust academic demand based on individual differences. One approach was the multitiered curriculum, with "minimum essentials" specifying the skills and knowledge required to pass from grade to grade. Minimum essentials appeared in the late 1910s as an effort by the National Education Association and by local and regional associations to standardize the curriculum and pare away antiquated material. In Chicago, committees of teachers defined minimum essentials for subjects including English, foreign languages, and math. During the 1920s, some Chicago schools began to use the these essentials as a simplified curriculum for slow learners. At Harrison High School, for instance, "teachers adjust[ed] their courses by enriching the work for the brighter, and scaling down to minimum essentials for the duller groups." A major curriculum revision begun in 1926 aimed at a three-tiered set of courses, with "minimum essentials" for the lowest third of students and enrichment for the top third. This three-tiered curriculum could be used in mixed-ability classes, with the enrichment material providing "busy work" for bright students.[21]

A second approach, individualized learning, was inspired by the well-known Dalton Plan developed by Helen Parkhurst, a Massachusetts educator. Under this plan, students developed monthly contracts for their academic work, which they completed independently, rotating through a series of laboratories and consulting with teachers as necessary. Several Chicago schools tried a modest version of the Dalton Plan, allowing students to move at their own pace through a sequence of written lessons and exercises. At Wentworth Elementary, where James McDade was principal, children worked individually through a series of "learning units." They took turns distributing and grading the lessons, freeing the teacher to coach students who needed help. McDade contended that individualized education was more efficient and promoted student independence and motivation. At Wentworth, he found that the individualized approach helped low-achieving students catch up with their peers.[22]

A third way to fit the curriculum to the child was "homogeneous grouping," in which children of the same grade were sorted into classes that were differentiated by ability or achievement. The pace of instruction or the difficulty of the courses could then be adjusted to the students' aptitude or achievement level. The editors of the *Chicago Schools Journal* endorsed homogeneous grouping and often reported on other cities' experiences with this practice.[23] In Chicago during this time, however, only the junior high schools used homogeneous grouping consistently. (Before they were closed in 1933, the junior high schools enrolled about one-third of all students in grades seven through nine.) Students entering junior high school were ranked by IQ and sorted on that basis into their classes. Students in the more able classes received an enriched curriculum, and some were also accelerated to complete the three-year program in five semesters. At the elementary and high school levels, there was no districtwide policy of homogeneous grouping, although a number of schools experimented with it.[24]

In Chicago, homogeneous grouping became highly controversial. Many teachers were wary of it. Some worried that teaching low-achieving students would hurt their efficiency ratings, or that principals would reward their favorites with "bright" classes and punish their critics with "dull" ones. Some felt it gave too much emphasis to innate intelligence in determining students' potential for learning. Still others saw grouping as undemocratic, because it might limit the educational opportunities of working-class students, or separate students of different social classes. Homogeneous grouping was one issue in the heated controversy over the junior high schools, with the Chicago Federation of Labor mobilizing labor and teachers in opposition. A 1924 rally to protest junior high school testing and tracking attracted over four thousand teachers, more than one-third of the city's teaching force.[25]

These doubts notwithstanding, some local educators came to believe that homogeneous classes made teaching more effective and eased problems of classroom management. Various research seemed to support this view. An early study of eight schools reported that using intelligence tests to classify students "increases the output of the school sufficiently to justify the additional expense involved." There were hints that grouping was especially beneficial for low-achieving students. The principal of Ray Elementary School, which tried IQ-based grouping in the early 1920s, described its tonic effect: "The slow children are getting more for their time, for they cannot now depend upon the bright children to do all the work and reciting. They do not feel out of place and they work with more zest. These slow children when placed with the brighter ones usually slump, will not take part in the class activities, get dissatisfied, and frequently become chronic troublemakers." Remedial efforts often began by grouping low-achieving students together for intensive review or an alternative curriculum. To secure the benefits of homogeneous grouping, Chicago educators urged that grouping schemes should allow students to change classes when their achievement rose, and that "slow" classes should be smaller to facilitate remedial work.[26]

The district continued to place some low-achieving students in ungraded rooms. These classes may have had a remedial effect for some children. During the 1920s, a large minority of students in the ungraded and prevocational classes improved enough to return to the regular classroom. These classes became particularly important as the district coped with black students who had recently migrated from the South. Disadvantaged by the very poor quality of southern schools, many of these children achieved well below grade level. Yet the Chicago Commission on Race Relations reported that some caught up very quickly if they were sent to the ungraded rooms "where they are advanced through several grades as rapidly as possible." At Doolittle, where the CCRR found six ungraded classes, "the teacher said that many of these children who were unable to read or write when they came up from the South showed remarkable progress in a few months, and in less than a year were able to do fourth-, fifth-, and sixth-grade work."[27]

Stalled Reform

The 1920s were a time of new ideas and informal experimentation in education, accompanied by some excitement at the progress that low-achieving students could make under the right conditions. George Prinsen, a high school teacher, wrote in 1926:

> As teachers, it behooves us to abandon the notion that fate has predestined some of us to eternal mathematical hopelessness, others to everlasting grammatical uselessness, and a chosen few to general brilliance! Strengthening the weak spot in time to prevent a series of weak spots, fortifying the loose foundation in time to prevent a landslide, all this is possible in education. It is right and proper for the teacher and school to regard failure prevention as one of the highest forms of professionalism.

By the close of the decade, however, none of the failure prevention measures had been adopted districtwide. One reason was the resistance of

William McAndrew, who served as superintendent from 1924 to 1927. He contended that efficient teachers who adhered strictly to the prescribed curriculum could get good results even in large classes. In his view, close supervision of teachers, combined with testing to ensure accountability, was the best way to raise student achievement. When Harrison High School tried to reduce the size of its classes for slow learners, McAndrew's budgetary rules prevented it.[28]

More generally, resource limitations made it difficult to adopt new failure prevention strategies. During the 1920s, the district faced growing enrollment, overcrowded buildings, and deepening debt. Many failure prevention strategies were costly, because they relied on small classes, new curricula, standardized testing, or extra administrative support. The small innovations of the failure prevention program became increasingly vulnerable as the district's financial difficulties mounted. The junior high schools, one site of experimentation in failure prevention, were closed during the budget crisis of 1933 and never reopened.

Homogeneous grouping illustrates the financial and logistical costs that made the schools slow to adopt new means of failure prevention. Grouping was generally based on standardized tests, but not all schools conducted such tests regularly, and even fewer entered test scores in students' permanent records. In addition, while homogeneous grouping was administratively feasible in elementary school, it was a much more daunting task in high school. Given the multiple courses of study and large numbers of students, constructing schedules for students was already a challenge; sorting students by test score added an intractable layer of complexity. As Helen Richards wrote in 1924, reporting on the experience of Austin High School, "There seems little doubt but that the theory of differentiated classes is sound and sane, but the innumerable obstacles we are actually encountering in trying to administer such a program subtract materially from the practicality of the theory."[29]

Homogeneous grouping might also require differentiated curricula, and this, too, was costly. In 1926, the Chicago Public Schools began to revise its curriculum with the intent of developing one that had three tiers. Although a small curriculum bureau to facilitate this work was established in 1928, the district continued to rely heavily on time donated by teachers and administrators. The new curricula were designed, printed, tested in the schools, revised based on teachers' comments, and then printed and distributed systemwide. By 1930, new courses of study had been produced for some subjects but not all. New curriculum development was slowed by budget cuts and then suspended in 1933, when the curriculum bureau was temporarily dismantled.[30]

The spread of standardized testing during the 1920s had left educators keenly aware of individual differences in the classroom. As a principal wrote in 1931, "We are all familiar with the fact that the average intermediate grade room has a spread in reading ability of six years and a spread in arithmetic ability of four years." But absent any systematic change in the structure of schooling, teachers were left to struggle alone with these differences. Charlotte Rowe, who taught General Science at Sabin Junior High School, gave reading tests at the beginning of each term to identify students likely to require special attention. She asked rhetorically, "Must Eugene, a 9A pupil, with the reading ability of a 4A pupil, sit idle always and become a menace to the peace and progress of his class?" Writing for the *Chicago Schools Journal,* she described many ad hoc adaptations she had made to individual differences in her classes, noting that "all of this is an acid test of the instructor's adaptability, resourcefulness, and knowledge of science facts and sources of information."[31]

Accommodating Failure

Beginning in the late 1930s, the schools finally began to make systemwide changes to respond to student differences. Much of this policy change occurred under William H. Johnson, who served as superintendent of schools between 1936 and 1946. An infusion of resources helped Johnson move as quickly as he did. By the time he took office, enrollment had begun to drop and the worst of the schools' financial troubles were over. The district also benefited from federal programs such as the Works Progress Administration, which provided professional staff and an army of clerks and typists to Chicago's Bureau of Child Study. Moreover, a new technology—Hollerith cards—made it easier to tabulate the results of standardized tests. Johnson's impact also reflected his ruthless use of political power, based on strong ties to the school board and the Democratic machine. In the Depression-era labor market, teachers and administrators were loathe to jeopardize their jobs by opposing him.[32]

Most components of the new approach were familiar from the experimentation of the 1920s. It would be a mistake, however, to view Johnson's reforms as simply the fulfillment of the failure prevention movement. There were important differences. During the 1920s, a concern with remediation animated the failure prevention movement. Johnson's reforms were more fatalistic. Their thrust was not to reduce disparities in achievement, but instead to create channels through which low-achieving children could move through the grades with other students of the same age. This orientation appears in the changes made to curriculum, grading, promotion policies, and ability grouping in the regular classroom; in the provisions for remedial education; and in the failure to invest in instructional research.

The Regular Classroom

Under Johnson's administration, the elementary schools took several steps to accommodate low-achieving students. The first change concerned "social promotion," or the practice of passing students grade to grade with their age group. Social promotion had certainly occurred in the past, but only as an administrative convenience. Now the school district legitimated it. Milton Cohler, an influential elementary school principal, made the case for social promotion as early as 1931. Studies of grade retention, he wrote, showed that when students were held back, "about equal numbers of pupils do worse or the same caliber of work; and the smallest percentage does better work." In 1937, a committee of elementary school principals affirmed Cohler's position. Incoming first graders, they wrote, should be given a reading readiness test. Children who scored low should take a semester of "pre-reading activities," called 1C, before beginning the first grade. After that, the committee recommended, students "regardless of their placement or accomplishments [should be] advanced with their chronological age groups up to and through the third grade." [33]

Changes in student evaluation were also significant. In a new report card adopted in 1937, the schools broadened grading criteria to include more indicators of social behavior, diluting the emphasis on academic performance. The old report card had only recorded absences, tardiness, dismissal, and deportment; the new one assigned marks for eleven "personal qualities," including cooperation, courtesy, industry, and dependability. More important, instead of assigning a percentage grade for mastery of the material, the new report card assigned marks of Satisfactory, Improving, or Unsatisfactory, reflecting a student's achievement relative to his or her intellectual capacity. As a school principal explained the new cards, "Pupils that have done the best work they are capable of should not be compared with pupils of a much higher mental level." In 1947, the schools modified this scheme to reflect both absolute and relative criteria: "Grades of *excellent* and *good* indicate those levels of achievement in relation to grade level standards, *fair* represents acceptable progress 'all things considered,' and a grade of *unsatisfactory* is given when poor work is produced as a result of lack of application on the part of the pupil." Teachers found this hybrid scheme confusing, and many continued to weigh students' effort heavily in their evaluation.[34]

Taken together, these changes meant that students who worked hard and complied with school rules could be passed grade to grade even if their academic performance was weak. Classes remained academically heterogeneous. Johnson established a small two-track program in which high-achieving elementary school students were grouped into accelerated classes, but the program didn't last. Instead, the district supported ways of teaching classes with a wide range of achievement levels. Many schools began to use individualized instruction like that developed by James McDade a decade earlier, which let students work at their own pace. By 1939, with the help of its WPA clerks, the Bureau of Child Study had developed individualized lessons in reading and spelling, and two-thirds of the elementary schools used these lessons in all grades. Elementary school teachers also grouped children by ability within classes, forming instructional groups which moved at different paces. Teachers were encouraged to use the "project" or "experience" curriculum, in which students worked in mixed-ability groups and "each pupil may do the thing best suited to his needs and ability." Finally, the district simplified its K–8 math curriculum, deferring more complex topics to later grades.[35]

The high schools followed a different strategy to accommodate low-achieving students. First, school officials made high school easier. Under the new core curriculum introduced in 1937, students taking a general course of study no longer needed a foreign language to graduate. They could meet the science requirement with "General Science" rather than a laboratory course, and could even substitute industrial or household arts for one semester of science. The new curriculum gave credit for required courses in physical education, health, music, and art that previously had been noncredit. Johnson also encouraged teachers not to assign homework, and instead to have students do their practice exercises in class. Under this new curriculum, students took more general and introductory courses and fewer specialized and advanced courses. Enrollment rose in General Science, for instance, but dropped in courses such as physics, physiology, and geology. Concern grew during the 1940s and early 1950s about lax academic standards, but these graduation requirements remained in place through 1958.[36]

While the curriculum change made high school easier for all students, Johnson's administration also brought homogeneous grouping and a differentiated curriculum to all Chicago high schools. This differentiation began on a trial basis in 1938, when Johnson inaugurated "English R," a ninth-grade remedial English class for students with low reading scores. Next came a sophomore-year "minimum essentials" English course and "essential mathematics" courses for freshmen and sophomores. By 1940, four high schools were piloting a "minimum essentials" course in ninth-grade science. Describing the situation as urgent, Johnson pressed the high schools to improvise homogeneous classes whenever they could.[37] His efforts were extended by later superintendents. By the early 1960s, most Chicago high schools offered five levels of English and mathematics:

Advanced placement—college-level courses

Honors—for students with achievement a year or more above grade level and an IQ of 110+

Regular—for students with achievement at or slightly below grade level

Essential—for students with achievement at sixth- to early eighth-grade level at high school entry

Basic—for students with achievement below sixth grade level.

The history curriculum had three levels; freshman biology had four. Foreign language courses became limited to those in the regular track or above. Unlike most districts, however, Chicago did not assign students to the same level in all subjects; for instance, a student could be placed in both Honors English and Essential Mathematics.[38]

To develop curricula for these differentiated classes, Johnson expanded the curriculum bureau, tripling its staff in 1937. These changes were also supported by an elaborate program of intelligence and achievement testing. In 1939, for the first time, the public elementary schools sent the high schools reading scores for all the incoming freshmen. By 1945, reading achievement tests were given every year; intelligence tests were given in the fourth and eighth grades and usually in high school as well. Test results followed students in a "cumulative record folder," which also included grades, attendance figures, information about family background and health, and student interest questionnaires. To support this program of testing, Johnson expanded the Bureau of Child Study dramatically: from five psychologists in 1935 to forty-two in 1939, along with thirty-eight WPA-supported psychologists and statisticians. In 1939–40, the WPA Adjustment Service Project scored and recorded more than 628,000 standardized intelligence and achievement tests and produced 1,650,000 individualized lessons.[39]

Remedial Education

During the late 1930s, Johnson's administration introduced new provisions for low-achieving students. Building on the casework model of the 1920s, Johnson assigned each school an "adjustment teacher," recruited from the teaching staff and trained by the Bureau of Child Study. That teacher was to evaluate students who displayed academic or behavioral problems, find the cause of these problems, and refer students to school psychologists, medical clinics, or charitable agencies. For a student needing remedial education, the adjustment teacher would prepare individualized lessons for the classroom teacher to administer; the child might also be tutored by the adjustment teacher.[40]

The Chicago Public Schools did not, however, set up specialized classes for low-achieving students. The reason given was that remedial classes would segregate the low-achieving students and "encourage the regular teacher to teach classes instead of children." For children of normal intelligence, the 1C classes and the adjustment service were to be sufficient. For these students, the adjustment service was expected to bring academic achievement up to grade level by the time they entered high school, so that eventually the high schools could phase out the English R classes.[41]

The ungraded classes were now reserved for students with an IQ score between 50 and 75. Although the classes included reading and other academic subjects, they were no longer intended as remedial. As Johnson wrote, their students were of such low mentality that it was futile to expect them to rejoin a regular class. Because the ungraded classes had become a long-term home rather than a remedial way station, the schools differentiated these classes by age group, organizing primary and intermediate ungraded classes for students aged six to twelve years, Lower Vocational Centers for students aged twelve to fourteen years, and Upper Vocational Centers for students aged fourteen years and over. The classes remained small, and incorporated more and more "shop work" as students moved through the sequence. Students in the Upper Vocational Centers could earn an eighth grade diploma or a Smith-Hughes vocational certificate.[42]

Research and Innovation

During the 1920s, Chicago educators had used a nascent social science to evaluate new instructional techniques. By the late 1930s, quantitative social science had advanced, and the schools' testing program provided a wealth of new opportunities for the "measured teaching" Wight and Keener had promoted more than ten years earlier. But the Chicago schools did not build on this model. Johnson, in fact, was dismissive of such research:

> No attempt has been made to evaluate the progress of children under the stimulus of the Chicago Developmental Reading Program by means of *standardized* tests. Of course, individual schools and districts have undertaken isolated appraisal studies which in every case have shown a marked improvement in reading ability. It is inadequate, however, to judge growth in reading power solely in terms of an individual's test performance. Achievement in school subjects, success in personal and social relationships, and a more intelligent use of the reading tool for citizenship in a democracy are objectives of an evaluation program appropriate to the concept of developmental reading.

While Johnson promoted school-based research, most such projects were simply descriptions of student attitudes or compilations of practice, lacking even the simple test-retest or comparison-group designs of a decade ago.[43]

Nor did the Chicago schools collaborate with college- or university-based researchers on studies of curriculum and instruction. The Chicago Teachers College remained an inhospitable climate for educational research; most instructors at the college did not have doctoral-level training, and in any event their teaching load left little time for research. Although Johnson hired psychologists from the University of Chicago to develop new standardized tests, he did not invite its researchers into the schools, nor were they eager to go. Like most elite schools of education, the University of Chicago's prestigious Department of Education pursued laboratory studies rather than applied research in the classroom.[44]

An episode from the late 1950s illustrates the schools' arms-length relationship with academic researchers. When the City of Chicago was awarded a research grant of $600,000 from a new U.S. Office of

Education program that was intended to promote partnerships with universities, colleges, and state educational agencies, the Chicago Board of Education bypassed local universities such as Northwestern and the University of Chicago to negotiate a pass-through arrangement with the Illinois Superintendent of Public Instruction. Faculty from the Chicago Teachers College had an advisory role, but the funding went primarily to teachers and central office administrators. Noting that other Office of Education projects were university based, an assistant superintendent in Chicago expressed confidence that the backgrounds of personnel for the city's project "can be compared with pride with the qualifications of any research team any university is likely to assemble." The resulting study, however, had a flawed research design, and critics questioned its results.[45]

During the 1920s, teachers' classroom innovations received moral and technical support from administrators such as Wight and Keener, and the context of the times encouraged teachers to think of students' academic achievement as malleable. By the late 1930s, that sense of possibility had diminished. The decline of instructional research gave teachers nothing to offset the fatalism implicit in Johnson's reforms. The school system provided little support for new practices to prevent failure or minimize disparities in achievement. Standardized tests were used primarily to diagnose the subnormal and to track high school students. The schools had already chosen a response to achievement inequality, one that offered little encouragement and few classroom contexts for new remedial measures. Teachers didn't stop experimenting in the classroom, but their efforts rested only on individual initiative, without institutional support for testing these school-based innovations or communicating them to other teachers.

Johnson's Reforms and the Inner-City Schools

During the 1940s and 1950s, Johnson's reforms were put to the test and found wanting in the inner city. Although they may have been adequate in some schools, these remedies were ill suited to the conditions of education in Chicago's predominantly black neighborhoods. Although some inner-city students performed academically on par with white students, a large share of their classmates faced deep educational disadvantages. Half lived in poverty. Many were ill housed and lived in crowded and rapidly shifting ghetto neighborhoods. Some had begun their education in the substandard Jim Crow schools of the South. Many, especially those from the South, used language styles that were misunderstood and stigmatized by their teachers.[46] Compounding these disadvantages, racial inequality in Chicago's schools denied an equal education to black students.

As a result, inner-city schools served many students whose academic achievement fell far below their own grade level, producing a wide achievement range in any given classroom. In high schools in poor black neighborhoods, some 40 percent of ninth graders read at or below the sixth-grade level. At the Burke Elementary School in the early 1950s, half of the sixth, seventh, and eighth graders read at or below mid-fourth-grade level. At the Howland School, the principal reported, "The range of reading achievement was so wide that ordinary groupings were not adequate."[47]

Under the conditions that existed in inner-city schools—including high enrollments, large classes, double-shift schedules, and frequent turnover among teachers and students alike—Johnson's model for remedial education simply broke down. The problem was one of scale. The adjustment service had been designed for situations in which only a handful of students needed remedial help. As late as 1959, the *Chicago Schools Journal* published a sentimental cameo of an adjustment teacher who tutored a single "defeated boy." While the story exemplifies Johnson's original model, it was unrealistic even in an average school, where the adjustment teacher "seldom [got] beyond the first stage of the program—that of administering, scoring, and interpreting standardized tests." In the predominantly black schools, where the enrollment might exceed one thousand students and where perhaps half the student body performed significantly below grade level, this model of one-on-one tutoring was absurd. The adjustment teacher faced a daunting number of academically needy students under very unfavorable conditions. Moreover, because of high rates of teacher absenteeism, the adjustment teacher often substituted in the classroom. With transient students, the cumulative records were often missing or incomplete. And with large classes and high levels of academic need, it was difficult for the classroom teacher to supervise remedial lessons, even if the adjustment teacher had had time to develop them. It is no wonder that Gloria Williams, principal at a predominantly black school, concluded that "'coaching' as an approach to the reading problems in a school as large as ours (865 students) is ineffective."[48]

A generation earlier, Chicago's public schools had used ungraded classes for remedial work with children of normal intelligence, some of whom improved enough to return to the regular classroom. Now the ungraded classes were intended only for "subnormal" students, those with low IQs. School administrators, however, took advantage of the fact that the IQ scores of many inner-city children were depressed by "the complete lack of the experiential background on which intelligence tests are based." At Smyth School around 1940, almost half of the students had tested IQ's under 80; nearly one in four Smyth students was in an ungraded class, while many more awaited evaluation by a school psychologist. Of the students referred to the ungraded classrooms in the mid- to late 1950s, 44 percent had been born outside Chicago, and 25 percent had attended schools outside the city.[49]

However, the ungraded rooms—now called rooms for the educable mentally handicapped—did not suffice. The EMH curriculum was not designed to bring students back up to grade level; instead, the intent was to give "mentally handicapped" students the skills required to live productive and independent lives. And even if the curriculum had been more suitable, there were not enough classes to meet the need in inner-city schools. Overcrowded schools had little room for these small classes, and qualified teachers were in short supply; in 1964, nearly half of all EMH teachers were uncertified. In addition, staff shortages at the Bureau of Child Study meant delays in getting students into EMH classes: in 1964, about fourteen thousand students were waiting to be evaluated. In the late 1950s, the schools tightened eligibility criteria for the EMH program, leading to a drop in the number of students in these classes.[50]

Although the inner-city schools made extensive use of the ungraded and 1C classes, the regular classes still had a wide range in scholastic achievement. At the elementary level, teachers had to choose between keeping pace with the regular curriculum or slowing down to accommodate low-achieving students. Most slowed the pace. A teacher interviewed around 1950 reported,

> In a school like the D [Negro school] you're just not expected to complete all that work. It's almost impossible. For instance, in the second grade we're supposed to cover nine spelling words a week . . . the best class I ever had at the D—— was only able to achieve six words a week and they had to work pretty hard to get that. So I never finished the year's work in spelling, I couldn't. And I wasn't really expected to.

As students in these schools reached the upper elementary grades, their teachers sacrificed the grade-level curriculum to work on basic skills:

> It's not like at a school like S—— [middle school] where they have science and history and so on. At a school like that they figure that from first to fourth grades you learn to read and from fifth to eighth you read to learn. You use your reading to learn other material. Well, these children don't reach that second stage while they're with us. We have to plug along getting them to learn to read. Our teachers are pretty well satisfied if the children can read and do simple number work when they leave here. You'll find that they don't think very much of subjects like science, and so on. They haven't got any time for that.

Conscientious teachers spent evenings and weekends adapting the curriculum or developing their own materials. Others, according to a teacher interviewed in the early 1950s, "starting with the conviction that Negro children can't come up to the scholastic level of white children, don't try to teach them much of anything."[51]

Although many elementary school students had not mastered the material expected for their grade, grading and promotion policies in the Chicago Public Schools allowed them to be passed along. As a principal from an inner-city school acknowledged, "At the Carter we cannot reach the standard therefore our children transfer out with Gs and Es in relation to himself but is actually much lower in relation to the norm." A teacher at a predominantly black school, interviewed in the early 1950s, "does not believe any of her pupils do superior work, but she does give some of them superior grades, because then they work harder—'Negro children react to praise.'" Even so, failure rates in elementary school doubled between 1950 and 1958, from 3.1 to 6.4 percent. In four schools, all of them "high transiency" (a common euphemism for *inner-city*), failure rates exceeded 20 percent.[52]

The inner-city high schools could group students by achievement, reducing the heterogeneity in levels of learning that created such problems at the elementary level. The problem in the high schools was that, as Robert Havighurst reported in 1964, "courses, textbooks, and materials are appropriate primarily for students working at grade level or above." Teachers complained that the prescribed curriculum was too difficult for many students. One of Havighurst's research staff noted,

> It is disturbing to observe classes of tenth graders who read at the fifth- or sixth-grade level stumbling line by line through a history textbook appro-

priate for the average tenth grader . . . [Many teachers] working with poorer
students seem to have little knowledge of how to proceed. Many merely read
the textbook through line by line with the students and give only short-answer
quizzes. Some do nothing at all; their students can be seen dozing or staring
into space.

Not surprisingly, 44 percent of teachers in Basic or Essential English and
35 percent of teachers in Basic or Essential mathematics said they never
used the curriculum guides. Although students could transfer to the regular track if their achievement rose, the only records Havighurst found
showed a transfer rate of less than 3 percent.[53]

Because the high schools passed failing students along, new problems
arose at the college level. In 1959, Wilson Junior College, a South Side
community college that enrolled many black students, began to offer
remedial instruction to those with low scores on an English placement
test—about one-third of its incoming freshmen. Eighty percent of these
remedial students were graduates of Chicago public high schools, and
40 percent had been in the top half of their graduating class. Reportedly,
students were "shocked" by their low scores, and some became demoralized by "the fact their apparent success in high school was a delusion."[54]
A 1959 article in the student newspaper of DuSable High School hints
that some students sensed how much their education had been watered
down. In "Seniors Offer Ideas for Improving DuSable," the students
proposed "Be more strict," "Give more homework," "Have classes on
college level for seniors," "Have periods longer than 50 minutes," and
"More courses in math and science." The article went on to explain, "A
majority of the seniors felt that they had waited too long before deciding
to study and they wanted the incoming students to be aware of what is
expected and have them begin to work in the first semester instead of
waiting until their last year."[55]

Because the schools' remedial program was so inadequate, a few
inner-city teachers improvised their own solutions. These teachers abandoned the district's model of one-on-one or individualized instruction
in favor of group-based or whole-class activities. In 1943, for example,
two teachers at Colman Elementary School organized a remedial class
for students who were very far behind in reading. The teachers used a
phonics approach with enunciation drills; group work allowed for student participation and for tailoring instruction to individual needs. The
teachers started with a class of thirty students; by the end of the year,

twelve children had improved so much they returned to the regular grades, and twelve others were selected to take their places. The program became so popular that it grew to 150 students by 1949, and some Colman teachers applied the same techniques in the regular classes.[56]

To take another example: in 1938, Wilhelmina Williams at Douglas Elementary School—in one of the poorest neighborhoods in Chicago—faced a class in which reading vocabularies ranged from 3B to 7A. For a twelve-week exercise in remedial reading, she divided the class into instructional groups at roughly the fourth-, fifth-, and sixth-grade levels, and assigned different kinds of work to each. Williams developed her own materials for the project, collecting sample books sent out by publishers and reviewing curriculum guides for all three grades. She used group work as well as student presentations:

> The individual child's understandings were checked at a round table discussion to which all the children participated. The teacher glanced at the record of individual reading and asked a child to tell what he has learned about bears from his reading. He rose, consulted his notes, and began to talk or read . . . As he talked, if the class did not know one of the new [vocabulary] words, which he must always use, he was halted and the meaning asked. If no one stopped him, he then tested the class to see if they really knew the words or were simply "sleeping" as he talked.

Williams reported that most children raised their reading score by more than twelve weeks, with some gaining a year or more in grade level.[57]

A few inner-city schools tried schoolwide interventions. Burke Elementary School set up homogeneously grouped reading classes for students in grades six through eight, half of whom read at or below the mid-fourth-grade level. The students in these grades were grouped into nine reading classes on the basis of reading achievement scores. Those who made progress during the year moved up to a higher group. The lowest two reading classes were much smaller than the others—25 to 30 students, compared with 40 to 45. The reading teachers met regularly to talk about curriculum and teaching methods. At the same time, Burke's teaching staff agreed on new standards for promotion and graduation. For over-age students, the reading standard was set first at 6.0 (beginning sixth grade) and then raised over time to 7.5. Students knew their own score as well as the new standards. Those who made significant progress received praise and prizes: "We explain that we are just

as happy with the 2.0 readers who have 'jumped' to 3.2 as we are with
the 9.0 readers who have progressed to 10.2." In three years, the median
reading achievement of Burke's graduates rose from 6.3 to 8.3, and the
school added homogeneous grouping in math.[58]

Although the district didn't forbid these kinds of innovations in remedial education, it did little to support or encourage them. As the teachers at Colman wrote, "We had no precedent to guide us and we had to
formulate a flexible program which would meet our particular needs."
Resources for these programs came from the teachers themselves, who
either gave up their planning periods to work with small groups (as at
Burke), accepted larger regular classes so that remedial classes could be
small (as at Colman), or developed their own materials (as at Douglas).[59]

During the 1950s, central office administrators introduced some new
elements to respond to the difficulties faced by Chicago's inner-city
schools. The district opened Upper Grade Centers, schools for grades
7 and 8 only that used homogeneous grouping; about three-quarters
of these centers were highly segregated (more than 99 percent) black
schools. For younger elementary students, the district piloted a "continuous development plan" that replaced the first three grades with nine
achievement levels through which children moved at their own pace.
Young students were grouped based on achievement, not on age, an arrangement which permitted more homogeneous grouping. Responding
to the problem of teacher turnover, Superintendent Willis began a "master teacher" program in thirty-four schools; experienced teachers were
relieved of classroom duty in order to supervise and train the substitutes and novices who taught most classes. Special service teachers were
added at some schools to attend to children substantially above or below
the level of their class. More than earlier reforms, these new elements acknowledged the systemic problems faced by inner-city schools, but they
were too little and too late to make much difference.[60]

Conclusion

The Chicago Public Schools began to adopt new measures aimed at low-
achieving students in response to the growing heterogeneity of scholastic
achievement in the classroom, and to growing sensitivity about school
failure. During the 1920s, local educators embarked on a period of trial
and error, experimenting with a wide array of measures that might help

low-achieving students catch up with their peers. Yet the measures that were finally chosen, during the 1930s, allowed little genuine remediation. Selected by school managers, not educators, these measures accommodated low-achieving students through social promotion, relative grading, and a differentiated high school curriculum while doing little to address learning problems. These measures failed most spectacularly in the inner-city schools, where high rates of school failure were compounded by conditions such as overcrowding, high enrollments, large classes, a deficit of instructional time, and high turnover among both teachers and students. These conditions, which helped cause low achievement in the first place, also hamstrung the schools' efforts to remediate it. Ultimately, the schools' race-neutral remedial policies had racially disparate consequences, because they were implemented in an environment that—both inside and outside the school—was profoundly unequal.

The failure of remedial education had obvious consequences for achievement in inner-city schools. As the next chapter describes, the Chicago Public Schools' treatment of low-achieving students also shaped classroom dynamics. Instruction that was so unresponsive to students' learning problems, that gave children so few opportunities to succeed, eroded the trust and cooperation essential to learning in school. Chapter 7 explores how the district's policies concerning remedial education, as well as race and vocational education, shaped the environment in which teachers and students worked together.

CHAPTER SEVEN

Classroom Dynamics

Chapter 7 returns to the problems of authority and engagement with which we began the book. By the early 1960s, Kenneth Clark wrote, inner-city schools were characterized by what teachers framed as problems of discipline, including tension and distrust between teacher and students, resistance to schoolwork, and disruption in the classroom. Not all teachers faced these problems, but by the early 1960s, they were a recurrent theme in observations of inner-city schools, and continue to be so today. This book has argued that problems of discipline and disengagement emerged in inner-city schools because teachers' strategies for authority and engagement were undercut by school policy. This chapter enters the classroom, linking reports of discipline problems to the features of urban context and school policy discussed in the earlier chapters.

We begin with a few simple observations about classroom life. First, learning is voluntary; it will not happen unless students choose to cooperate with the teacher. In school, learning is a group activity, which brings added challenges. Students differ in their interests, learning styles, and levels of achievement; a single curriculum or teaching method may not work equally well for all. Students also distract one another, and one or two students can disrupt learning for everyone else.[1] In this context, teachers use two main strategies to get students' cooperation. One rests on authority: students give attention and effort because the teacher directs them to. The other rests on qualities of the lesson: students are motivated by interest in the curriculum, by engaging teaching methods, by gratification from growing mastery, or other aspects of the lesson. The teacher's authority and the qualities of the lesson—the push and pull of the classroom—complement and support each other. Authority aids engagement by creating a calm and orderly environment so students can concentrate, and by directing students to work so the lesson itself can take hold. The influence is reciprocal: engagement aids authority by providing another support for student cooperation. If students become interested in the lesson itself, they will pay attention and work hard. An engaging lesson also creates a small stock of trust and goodwill. If the students have been assigned a task and find it rewarding, they will cooperate more readily the next time. The two sections that follow examine in more detail the bases of authority and engagement, and consider how Chicago educators approached these matters.

Authority

Although we associate authority with unequal rank and power, it rests on the consent of subordinates, in this case students. In school, genuine authority relations imply that students are drawn to share at least some commitment to the goals of education. Authority is important, because it means students will comply even with instructions that the teacher cannot directly monitor, such as paying attention in class or studying at home.[2] Authority requires trust, as the anthropologist Frederick Erickson writes:

> Assent to the exercise of authority involves trust that its exercise will be benign. This involves a leap of faith—trust in the legitimacy of the authority and in the good intentions of those exercising it, trust that one's own identity will be maintained positively in relation to the authority, and trust that one's own interests will be advanced by compliance with the exercise of authority.

If children do not trust the teacher, they may be reluctant to follow her instructions. This may lead to overt conflict; more often, the class will appear to fritter away time getting organized rather than learning. As teachers and students work together over time, they negotiate a relationship with stable expectations and patterns of behavior, a relationship that reflects their interaction together as well as their separate past experiences in school. The result is what Arthur Powell, Eleanor Farrar, and David K. Cohen call a "treaty," a shared and largely tacit understanding of what teacher and students expect of one another.[3]

Even when authority relations are strong, the need for discipline still arises. To prevent or punish misbehavior, and to enact their commitment to school goals, teachers may use social sanctions, creating a normative climate in which students are deterred from misbehavior by concern about the opinion of others. Alternatively, they may use coercive penalties such as detention or suspension. As Mary Haywood Metz has pointed out, regardless of which approach a school takes, its disciplinary strategies become more vulnerable when disobedience is more widespread. In Metz's evocative phrase, schools may seek to "institutionalize innocence," creating a context in which students don't even think of disobeying. If students observe others misbehaving, these social sanctions become weaker. The same applies to a coercive approach. If enough students challenge the school's authority, the limits to schools' coercive resources become more evident. In schools that rely on coercion, teachers often punish small infractions severely to create the impression of abundant coercive resources and thereby deter an escalation of disorder. Schools may also exclude students via suspension or expulsion, or isolate them from other students, to prevent the contagion of misbehavior and to conceal the vulnerability in the school's armamentarium.[4]

A teacher can seek students' cooperation using her own personal resources, such as intellect or personality. For instance, she may try to inspire students with her erudition or love of learning, making the goals of education more compelling. She may deploy her expertise to gain students' confidence. Or she may present a stern façade to make punitive sanctions more credible. Individual qualities are not all that matter, however. Teacher-student interaction sits within a larger institutional and social context. Teachers commonly claim the right to govern by virtue of their formal position as teachers, as official representatives of the school. In this way, authority relations depend on the legitimacy of the school in the eyes of students and parents. If the school loses this legitimacy, teachers' connection to the school may hurt rather than help. In addition, authority relations in school may be strengthened by "social capital," particularly by relations between parents and teachers. Trust and normative consensus between parents and teachers buttress the school's authority by giving school norms greater force. These social connections improve the monitoring of behavior.[5]

In the Chicago Public Schools, educators gradually shifted from coercive control and exclusion toward an effort to promote genuine authority and mobilize social sanctions. In the early years of the twentieth century, as one teacher noted, "teachers seemed to expect before they entered the Chicago schools that [discipline] was going to be hard and it was a challenge to them to be able to master that situation." Most relied on intimidation and on punitive measures such as detention or suspension. They might resort furtively to corporal punishment, which by then was against school rules. Schools also relied heavily on exclusion: troublesome students were suspended or expelled, or more often simply dropped out.[6] When school officials began to enforce compulsory schooling laws more strictly and to discourage suspension and expulsion, discipline problems increased. In 1913, the director of compulsory education observed that "the question of discipline in the schools has become as great as the question of truancy." In response, the district began to send disruptive students to ungraded "industrial" or "truant" rooms, usually at a different school. According to the Board of Education reports, the truant rooms were "not to keep boys interested by teaching them different things, but rather to give boys a changed point of view and to make conduct habitual to this end." The stigma of being sent away was expected to deter misbehavior while the regimented routine was to inculcate a respect for authority. "For the first time, the boys became conscious of the power of the state to control their actions," noted a school official at the time. "They lived at home and all were anxious to return to their own schools." Repeat offenders might be sent to Parental School, a residential facility on the outskirts of the city.[7]

Space in the truant rooms was limited, however, and Chicago educators began to look for new approaches to classroom discipline. What they found was "character education," a national movement with both academic and popular dimensions. University researchers analyzed the dimensions of moral behavior and developed character education curricula while organizations such as the Character Development League and the National Honesty Bureau promoted moral instruction in the schools. Character education was often taught without much subtlety. Many teachers used "direct instruction," in which students memorized slogans and pledges or extracted moral lessons from bits of history or literature. Indeed, a Chicago student complained during the 1930s that "all [teachers] think and talk is discipline and good citizenship. Go in the algebra class and get a lecture on being a good citizen—no thought about algebra. The same with the other classes."[8]

For other educators, however, character education was a rubric for deeper reflection about student motivation and moral learning. Dissatisfied with the old-style punitive methods, they began to articulate a more positive approach that rested on students' respect and esteem for the teacher. Writing about the modern high school, a committee of high school principals in Chicago criticized discipline based on coercion and punishment. "How much history will a boy learn," they asked, "who is kept after school to make up a lesson on the day that he has planned to play ball? Or what does it do to a pupil to force him to apologize for behavior that he feels was justified?" Instead, teachers were to use more subtle diplomacy. If plagiarism were suspected, for instance, the teacher might say, "'You wrote so brilliantly last week, I have a special topic I believe you can handle.' If he falls down miserably on the assignment, he knows that you know, and he will be grateful for your tact in not exposing him to class ridicule."[9]

Character education also harnessed students' relations with their peers, adding social sanctions to the schools' array of coercive tactics. Student government, extracurricular activities, and student monitors were to teach students that "the self interest of each is best served by cooperation with the social group to which he belongs." By 1933, almost two-thirds of Chicago's elementary schools had some form of student government, as did 95 percent of the junior high schools and 83 percent of the high schools. Use of student monitors was also widespread. Susan Gorman, principal at Smyth School, declared that because of the school's student monitors, "there is no class at the Smyth which is not proud to be able to conduct itself even if no teacher is present."[10]

By the 1930s, character education had become the approved approach to discipline. In a 1933 piece for the *Chicago Schools Journal,* a local administrator contrasted old and new styles: "Discipline, a century ago, was a hard-fought battle between children and teacher, in which physical force was the deciding factor, and silent uniform rigidity the highest desideratum . . . Discipline, in those days, was largely negative, discouraging disorder, preventing movement; now it is largely positive, establishing individual self-control in a social situation." Students at the Chicago Teachers College learned "not to use the old-fashioned things such as making them write sentences a hundred times or doing the multiplication tables a hundred times." Punitive methods lost their luster even for students in the truant classes, who before had faced a harsher regimen. "The formerly feared 'hooky cop' has become a social worker," wrote the director of compulsory education in 1939. At Montefiore, a new school for truant and incorrigible students, "there was no military discipline, informality was the rule, teachers were friendly and sympathetic . . . Many of the boys had deep misgivings in adjusting to the new situation because it looked more like a settlement house than a place of detention for 'bad boys.'"[11]

Although ideals had clearly changed, practice lagged behind. Coexisting with character education was a covert culture of old-style disciplinary tactics that relied on coercion and exclusion. The Chicago Area Project noted in 1940 that "children who present problems which threaten classroom discipline frequently are transferred from one school to another by teachers who wish to place responsibility for dealing with the problem elsewhere. Or, as is often the case, they are demoted, as a form of punishment. The practice of using promotion to coerce children is common in both public and parochial schools. In one instance, a boy was demoted six months because he damaged the teacher's car." Teachers also threatened to send misbehaving children to "the dummy room." When the new-style approach proved ineffective, teachers resorted to old-fashioned ways: as a young teacher reported, "I just threw the progressive out and went back to my own school days for methods."[12]

Engagement

Authority is not the only way teachers might gain students' cooperation in learning. Another approach is through engagement, in which students are motivated by an interesting or rewarding lesson. Here the focus is on a student's relation to the material, not to the teacher (although the teacher still has a crucial role to play in selecting, presenting, and pacing the lessons). Education research shows that a lesson is more engaging when the content is relevant to students' lives, or when it incorporates novelty, cognitive complexity, or stimulating connections with other domains of knowledge. Students may also be motivated by the promise of extrinsic rewards, such as getting a job or going to college. Teaching methods such as discussion, laboratory work, or group projects are said to be more engaging because they respond to student questions and perspectives and allow students to take an active role.[13]

Lessons may also engage students by giving them a sense of accomplishment and growing mastery. To motivate students in this way, a lesson

should be challenging enough to provoke interest, but not intractably difficult. Thus, the match between the difficulty of the lesson and the student's
aptitude is important. Also, students may vary in their willingness to take
on a given level of challenge. Those who believe that academic success
reflects innate ability rather than effort, or who have often experienced
failure, may be particularly wary. Students can be inventive at evading
academic demands, sometimes with help from teachers who want to avoid
embarrassing them. Fear of failure can set off a self-fulfilling prophecy in
which students withhold engagement and therefore fail to learn, deepening their reluctance to engage.[14]

Like authority relations, student engagement reflects the teacher's
own knowledge, skill, and personality. School policies also matter, however, by setting the parameters within which teachers work. It is usually
district officials who choose curricula, determine class size, decide how
children are grouped by age and aptitude, and provide resources for remedial education. Through its teacher training, the district may support
some teaching methods and not others. Finally, schools offer a context
of meaning that shapes whether children and parents interpret academic
performance as innate or effort driven, fixed or malleable.

Unlike authority, engagement was not a focus of concern for Chicago
school administrators. Indeed, the doctrine of mental discipline, which
had many adherents during the nineteenth century, held that students
were better served by learning material they disliked. This view began
to shift around the turn of the century with the influence of progressive educators such as John Dewey, but curricula and teaching practices
changed more slowly. Classes were large—up to forty-eight students in
elementary school—making innovative methods difficult to use. By reputation, the Chicago schools remained old fashioned in their pedagogi-
cal approach.

Concern with engagement was most evident in two specific areas.
One was vocational education. Educators believed that vocational education could motivate students because of its instrumental value and its
more active style of instruction. In the continuation classes sponsored
by the Swift meatpacking plant, for instance, "[the] discipline problem is
mainly to absorb the new boys who have failed in public school and are
filled with a dislike for all schools in general . . . The problem of motivation is solved by making the subject matter apply to the packing business as much as possible." This complaint by a working-class student in
Chicago exemplifies what educators believed about student motivation:

What's the good of geography or arithmetic or any of those other things? They don't do you no good. When you grow up you're supposed to forget 'em anyway. I just go to school when they're having manual training. I'm building a windmill. I like that. We have that on Mondays so I always go then. I wish we had that all of the time, then I'd always go.[15]

As chapter 5 describes, the Chicago schools expanded manual training and vocational education significantly over the first few decades of the twentieth century.

The other area in which administrators actively addressed engagement was in "failure prevention." Many such measures aimed at matching the curriculum to the child. A child's misbehavior, educators wrote, often reflected frustration or boredom over lessons that were too difficult or too easy. When this mismatch was corrected, as the *Chicago Schools Journal* often recounted, both achievement and behavior improved. For instance, when a "problem boy" was given individualized lessons,

> The pose of indifference and boredom disappeared, and the boy truly became interested in his work. He was no longer expected to keep up with those who were two, three, or four years ahead of him in achievement . . . Gone was the feeling of discouragement resulting from so many constant failures, and in its place, a feeling of mastery. He is probably realizing success for the first time in his school life. Consequently, he is no longer a discipline problem in his reading class; he is kept so busy doing something he can do, that he is no longer interested in disturbing his neighbors.

Also under the rubric of failure prevention was an array of measures that addressed nutritional or medical causes of school failure. Here, too, school performance and behavior often improved in tandem.[16] Chapter 6 recounts the 1920s experiments with failure prevention, and then the adoption in the 1930s of the "adjustment service," high school tracking, individualized lessons, and other means of fitting the curriculum to the child.

Classroom Dynamics in Inner-City Schools

The Chicago Public Schools' strategies for authority and engagement rested on conditions that were not always met in Chicago's inner-city schools. Racial segregation and inequality undermined school legitimacy and thereby weakened authority. Black children's trust of the schools was further eroded by the insensitivity they sometimes experienced in encounters with white teachers, principals, and students. Character education depended on the moral credibility of teachers and principals, but was thrown into question by school policy. Character education also sought to harness relations among students, but in racially changing schools those relations were shot through with distrust and division. For all these reasons, authority was more fragile in inner-city schools. When teachers and principals did maintain authority, it was largely through their own character, demeanor, or skill; they got little help from the institution around them. The schools' strategies for engaging students were also weakened by conditions in inner-city schools. Chicago educators hoped to improve engagement through vocational education or techniques of failure prevention, but neither of these measures was fully available to inner-city students. Students' academic difficulties were all the more demoralizing when teachers assumed their achievement was limited by low innate intelligence or cultural deprivation. "I don't mean to say that Negroes don't have the same ability as whites because they do, naturally," one teacher said. "Race has nothing to do with intelligence. But the Negro hasn't had the opportunities that the white has, and you can't expect him to do as well." [17]

Corresponding to the unfavorable turn in school policy during the 1930s, anecdotal evidence suggests a gradual shift in the classroom dynamics of inner-city schools. In the early years of the twentieth century, there was no sign that black students were perceived as particularly difficult to discipline. When the Chicago Commission on Race Relations surveyed teachers and principals after the 1919 race riot, its investigators found a telling lack of consensus about black children and discipline. Some teachers believed that only "military discipline" would work with black students; others said these students could not be scolded but must be "jollied along"; still others saw little difference in how black and white children should be disciplined. When they did occur, discipline problems were sometimes sparked by a perceived slight or insult. According to the CCRR, "In one case the teacher threw a paper at a boy instead of handing it to him, and the boy had refused to recite to her ever since. He went to school but recited to his mother at home." Teachers' stereotypes of African-American children, however, did not include defiance or intractability. [18]

This perception had changed by the early 1950s, as is clear from interviews with teachers conducted around that time by University of Chicago researchers Howard Becker, Virginia Johnson, and Miriam Wagenschein. Problems of discipline and disengagement appeared frequently in teachers' accounts of black schools. As one recalled, "I thought I'd go crazy those first few months I was there. The room was never really quiet at all. There was always a low undertone, a humming, of conversation, whispering, and shoving." Teachers commonly complained that black children were not motivated to learn, or even that "some of them are actively opposed to learning." A teacher interviewed in the early 1950s reported that "a great many of them don't seem to be really interested in getting an education. I don't think they are. It's hard to get anything done with children like that. They simply don't respond." Mary Herrick, a veteran teacher at DuSable High School, reported about her three-period remedial class:

> It was all right for the teacher to want the class to do something; that is what she was there for. But that was no sign they were going to do it, even it [*sic*] was something they had said they wanted to do. Slouching physical posture and heads on desks indicated both real and physical weariness and lack of any personal motivation. The group resented being in the core [remedial] group. They wanted to learn how they could get out. Their nervous inability to concentrate made definite class control necessary or there would have been no results but [*illegible*] confusion.

As early as 1940, John Bartky, head of the Chicago Teachers College, wrote that disorder and resistance were characteristic of "Negro underprivileged schools." In this context, he observed, teachers who were particularly inexperienced and fearful might face "what is unprofessionally termed 'a runaway room' in which the children completely disregard instructions from the teacher. If this occurs in a first grade division, the children become habituated to this disregard of teacher and it becomes most difficult even for an experienced teacher to exert any control over them." [19]

Problems of discipline could even lead to physical threat. Bartky warned of the risk that ineffective disciplinarians might face: "On several occasions the writer has seen teachers emerge from rooms as low as third grade level with their clothing torn, their hair disheveled, and their faces scratched." By 1955, teachers had become so concerned about such threats that the Chicago Teachers Union began to collect information on school attacks and altercations, most of them described as "assault on teacher," that were taken to court. Of the forty-two incidents taking place between 1955 and 1961, two-thirds occurred in predominantly black schools, at a time when only 40 percent of public school students were black. Of course, only a small minority of teachers faced physical assault by their students, and assaults occurred in white schools as well as black schools. Yet stories of such incidents, circulated among teachers, undoubtedly created anxiety and reluctance to work in inner-city schools.[20]

Accounts of discipline problems in black schools suggest a collective and context-specific phenomenon. Note Herrick's observations about the students in her remedial class: "Their attitude toward the teacher is contradictory. None were rude or uncooperative in individual contacts, in the hall, or before or after class. In class, the group was a unit against the teacher, and rudeness was common." She tried to break up this group dynamic by rearranging tables and chairs so students did not face each other, but the daily process of moving furniture consumed excessive time and became yet another occasion for noncooperation.[21] Herrick was a seasoned and well-liked teacher; that she had trouble inside the classroom and not outside it suggests that students' peer sanctions discouraged public acquiescence to school authority.

There were hints, also, of a racial dimension to discipline problems in inner-city schools. Black students were reported to accept discipline more readily from black teachers. As Wagenschein noted, "Some [white teachers] reported that in Negro schools the Negro teachers 'can get away with hitting them, but we wouldn't dare.'" In some cases, student defiance may have been triggered by a teacher's insensitivity. Despite the intercultural movement, some teachers were said to use racial epithets or insults in class. More common was unintentional offense by white teachers who understood little of the lives and sensibilities of their black students. Yet these interpersonal tensions were not only about the actions and attitudes of individuals; suspicion of white teachers was heightened by their status as representatives of a racially inequitable school system. Tensions between black students and white teachers were accentuated at racially changing schools, where students could readily observe racially disparate treatment.[22]

When an inner-city school could make up for what the district failed to supply, authority and engagement might improve. Sound remedial programs, for instance, could promote engagement by responding to the challenges students faced in learning. As Chapter 6 describes, teachers at Colman School developed an intensive remedial class to address the needs of children with severe reading difficulties. As the teachers observed, students initially entered the remedial class feeling demoralized by their difficulties in school: "The children needed to be made to *feel capable of doing.* Too many of them were so far behind the children in the regular grades that they felt it was useless to try. They had to be taught how to study. Many had failed to do any real thinking for so long a time that they did not know how to get their minds working." By their report, the remedial work improved morale: "I have seen children change gradually from irritable, restless, careless little beings to earnest, careful, industrious workers. These children had considered themselves failures. Now they have confidence in themselves. They not only know how to read and work, but they welcome new and harder assignments." Children were so enthusiastic about the remedial program that those who returned to the regular classroom tried to secure places in the remedial class for siblings or friends.[23]

Dunbar Trade School provides a different kind of example. As chapter 5 describes, the school offered black students vocational training that paid off in the labor market. Dunbar had another asset in its principal, "a tall, deep voiced, 48 year old Negro educator, Clifford Campbell, who himself has come up the hard way." Campbell, described as "an artist in human relations," would undoubtedly have been effective under any circumstances. In a segregated school district with few African Americans in positions of leadership, he was a particularly compelling role model. Dunbar students' respect for school leadership was illustrated in an incident that occurred in 1952. After a basketball game at Dunbar against predominantly white Lindblom High, there was a fight in which several Lindblom players were assaulted. As an investigation later revealed, Lindblom students had assaulted Dunbar players the year before and no action had been taken against them. Campbell and his staff immediately questioned Dunbar students about the incident, and asked faculty for help "in arousing in the hearts and minds of our students a feeling of acceptance of responsibility for advancing such information as they might have concerning the identity of the person or persons responsible for this act." Despite the apparent double standard in discipline, Campbell got full cooperation from the student body. The Student Council agreed to offer a $100 reward for information about the incident, and within a day the reward had been raised from student donations. Even before then, Campbell had learned the identity of students involved and had spoken to their parents, who "cooperated with us to the fullest."[24]

Home-School Relations

Social capital—the relations of communication and trust between parents and teachers—can be an important support for school discipline. Inner-city schools were at a disadvantage when it came to this resource. Although parents didn't experience the day-to-day reality of the school as their children did, they did have an eye on the politics of race and resources. Many northern-born black parents had attended school in Chicago during the era of racial integration; they knew what they had lost as those schools became segregated and unequal. At a practical level, parents struggled with the disruption of double-shift schedules; at a symbolic level, they resented it. Some were involved directly in demonstrations and boycotts to protest segregation and inequality. The stonewalling and hypocrisy of school officials further eroded parents' trust in the public schools.

Relations between teachers and inner-city parents were burdened with other tensions as well. One was miscommunication over children's academic progress. Because of social promotion and relative grading, a student's academic difficulty might be masked until he or she was assigned to an ungraded or lower-track class. For instance, a principal at the predominantly black Kozminski Elementary described her quandary when a fifteen-year-old student transferred to her school reading at a third-grade level and his father "all along assumed the child was doing well and could prepare to be a druggist." In dealing with southern migrant parents, principals complained of problems such as "parents wrongly interpret recommended transfer to voc. prep. schools as punishment" and "resentment at use of lower grade reading units." This kind of misunderstanding may have become more common over time as school signals about student performance became more ambiguous.[25]

Home-school relations were also complicated by the role the schools took in dispensing assistance and advice to poor families. School administrators and teachers often worked with relief and charitable associations to supply food and clothing to poor students. At Smyth School, for example, when a truant officer brought in a cash donation, the principal went to the nearby Maxwell Street market and bargained with street vendors for thirty-five pairs of new shoes. Teachers also instructed students in proper hygiene; lacking facilities at home, some students even took baths at school. Many families desperately needed this help. Yet the schools did not always offer it with much tact or sensitivity. When black children from a public housing project enrolled at a nearby white school, for instance, parents took offense when the teachers tried to "clean up" the new children. The principal noted, "There is still one mother who thinks we 'should teach and not smell her child.'"[26]

Black parents' wariness was compounded by the high turnover among young teachers. While long-time school staff might gain parents' trust, the brief tenure of many teachers made it difficult to build constructive relations with parents. Margaret Bradburn, a white woman, was a truant officer in the Black Belt during the 1930s; she had worked in the neighborhood for more than thirty years and knew everyone: "As she walks down the street nearly everyone whom she encounters greets her." In contrast, many new teachers were fearful of inner-city communities and poorly equipped to reach out to parents across race and class lines. As one teacher noted around 1950, her colleagues were "worried about being in that neighborhood, so they all jump in a car together, making sure no teacher has to leave the neighborhood by herself."[27]

Scattered evidence suggests that parents' support for the schools did indeed decline. In the early years, black parents were described as supportive of school discipline. For instance, from the Chicago Commission on Race Relations, in 1922:

> In most cases the high schools were receiving splendid support from Negro parents in matters of discipline. "I have never had a case where the parent did not back up the teacher in the treatment given to a colored child," said one principal, speaking of cases where children had got into difficulty when they complained that the teacher had "picked on them" because they were Negroes. The parents always made the child withdraw the statement and admit that the trouble was not due to color at all.[28]

In the 1940s and 1950s, many teachers saw the situation differently. According to Virginia Johnson, teachers at a predominantly black school believed that

> the parents do not back up the teacher on discipline. The Negro parents are likely to take a reprimand or act of punishment against their child as

discrimination against the child because he is Negro. Thus, it is the parents who are 'race conscious,' and who develop this in their children. The children themselves, say teachers, have no consciousness of race, but the parents promote race consciousness.

Likewise, Bartky commented in 1940 that the black child "is warned to beware of the white man and many of his attitudes toward public institutions are colored by this caution. Teachers 'pick on him' not because he misbehaves, but because he is black . . . The Negro boy is drilled in what his rights are. Every teacher of a Negro class knows that the first reaction of a Negro when she threatens to punish him is to say, 'The law won't let you hit me.'" A black teacher told Johnson that "our children are taught to be on the defensive when the teachers holler insulting things to them. They sometimes holler right back at the teacher. I don't blame them one bit. It's more out of place for a teacher, who has a college education to holler insulting things than it is for young children to do that." Black parents did not oppose strict discipline, or even corporal punishment. The problem was that trust was low: parents were not confident that school discipline would be fair, and conveyed that caution and skepticism to their children.[29]

Teachers' Response

The district offered little support to teachers facing discipline problems in inner-city schools. When the reality of inner-city classrooms fell short of the ideals of character education, teachers and principals were left to their own devices to solve the resulting problems. Unfortunately, the solutions that many adopted may have made matters worse. Teachers commonly responded to classroom disorder and defiance with old-style discipline. Although trained in the progressive approach, they came to view this approach as ineffective in the inner city. Drawing on their own school experiences, or practices of older colleagues, teachers tried to maintain order with an intimidating style, vigilant rule enforcement, and teaching methods that left little room for student initiative. As one teacher advised, "You can't let them get started; you have to have complete silence, or the whole class goes haywire." New teachers were warned by those more experienced: "I have friends who are teachers and they told me about it. Some of them went to C.T.C. three years ahead of me and so they were out teaching and they told me about conditions . . . they told me to go right in and get control right away, or I would never have control over my class." This approach may have contained disorder, but at a cost. With rigid control as their imperative, teachers were reluctant to use methods such as discussion or small group projects. As an inner-city teacher remarked, "With forty-five [students] you can't be forever motivating small groups. No thanks, it just doesn't work. You may get half of the class motivated and then the other isn't so what are you doing [*sic*] to do with the ones you do if you have to stop and work with the others?"[30] Thus, their approach to discipline tied their hands pedagogically, preventing them from experimenting with teaching methods that might have been more engaging.

Some teachers also employed harsh punishment, learning from colleagues how to avoid running afoul of school regulations:

> Technically you're not supposed to lay a hand on a kid. Well, they don't, technically. But there are a lot of ways of handling a kid so that it doesn't show—and then it's the teacher's word against the kid's, so the kid hasn't got a chance. Like dear Mrs. ——. She gets mad at a kid, she takes him out in the hall. She gets him stood up against the wall. Then she's got a way of chucking the kid under the chin, only hard, so that it knocks his head back against the wall. It doesn't leave a mark on him. But when he comes back in that room he can hardly see straight, he's so knocked out. It's really rough. There's a lot of little tricks like that that you learn about.

Most principals turned a blind eye to their teachers' use of corporal punishment. One teacher, a black woman, told Becker what happened when she handled a defiant fifth grader a little roughly. The girl rushed out to the principal's office. At the end of the day, the principal brought the girl back to the classroom:

> Mrs. W—— looked at her and said, "Shirley, I want you to apologize for the lie you told on Mrs. X—— when you were down in my office." I don't know what Shirley had said about me, but it might have been true because I had handled her. But Mrs. W—— told her to beg my pardon. Shirley looked at us, practically in tears, you know, and said, "But it's the truth, Mrs. W——. She did hurt my arms bad." Mrs. W—— looked at her hard and said, "*Shut up!* Do you hear me, Shirley, *Shut up!* Keep your mouth shut! Now beg Mrs. X——'s pardon and don't give me any more backtalk."[31]

Although teachers wanted support from their principals, some hesitated to report discipline problems for fear it would lower their efficiency ratings. School principals, in turn, were said to avoid reporting violent incidents to the police because it might damage their own reputations. Thus, teachers punished students within a context of denial and concealment, which heightened the illegitimacy of punitive actions for both teachers and students.[32] Teachers may have felt their harsh tactics were justified, but they also felt professionally isolated by the pressure for secrecy and by the sense that district officials did not understand the challenges they faced. For students, this denial and concealment signaled that the school would not protect them.

While some teachers pursued a strategy of intimidation and rigid control, others offered tacit "treaties," exchanging slack academic demands for classroom order. This approach may have been more common with older students, whom teachers could less easily intimidate or punish physically. One of Becker's interviewees noted, "I subbed at [the black high school] DuSable once. I was really cracking the whip, letting them have it. Well, I got called an S.B. I learned that you don't act like that around there. One of them hollered it in through the door. I didn't know who did it, but if one had the nerve to do that, I figured the rest of them were thinking it, so I eased up." Another teacher observed that at DuSable, teachers "just try to keep the kids busy and out of trouble. They give everyone in the room some kind of little job—one takes care of this, another takes care of that. Everybody's busy, they like having the honor of the little job." Such treaties may account for the perception among black teachers that white teachers were reluctant to exert academic pressure on their students. Leroy Lovelace, a veteran teacher at DuSable, observed that "white teachers tend to give up too easily on the kids. They take the kids' resistance as not wanting to learn. But as soon as the teachers stop pushing, the students say that teachers didn't care because if they had they would have kept on pushing them."[33]

Inner-city schools with exceptional leadership or creative teaching could establish authority and engage students. Yet the conditions in these schools made it difficult to attract and retain such staff. Teachers burned out at or avoided inner-city schools because they were stressful environments in which to work. As Becker wrote in his study of Chicago teachers, most teachers in inner-city schools could derive little sense of accomplishment from students' academic progress. Some adapted by emphasizing character building instead, but discipline problems jeopardized this source of motivation as well. The consequent "policeman" role was at odds with the ideals some had learned to value for classroom relations. At one predominantly black school, Johnson heard, some teachers "find their jobs unsatisfying. They feel they're not accomplishing anything. They have to be so concerned with discipline, that they can't do any real teaching; they can't 'reach' the children; they can't 'mold character.'"[34] These conditions became self-perpetuating. Because new teachers expected problems, they were on guard when they entered the classroom. They responded to disorder with repressive discipline or, alternatively, excessive laxity. These classroom dynamics left a residue of distrust that made it increasingly difficult for teacher and students to renew good intentions and work together.

Classroom Dynamics in Immigrant Schools

Conditions in immigrant schools were different because these students were not disadvantaged by school policy as black students were. In the early twentieth century, however, there were particular tensions between immigrant families and the public schools that might have led to problems in the classroom. Immigrants resented the public schools for their nativism and anti-Catholicism. Jacob Horak, who studied Chicago's Czech community during the 1920s, wrote that "I heard very often such teachers who are prejudiced against the foreign born child being very mercilessly criticized by the little ones." Although the public schools made concessions to the preservation of ethnic cultural heritage, for instance by allowing the high schools to teach language classes in Polish and Italian, many teachers and staff remained dismissive of the culture and customs of working-class immigrants.[35] Yet as the immigrant community became more assimilated, and as the schools employed more Catholic teachers, these cultural tensions diminished. Indeed, the schools' intercultural education became an occasion for celebrating the ethnic heritage of Chicago's immigrant students.

Also in the early twentieth century, compulsory education was an irritant for immigrants, who were accustomed to children contributing economically to the family. These tensions are illustrated in an incident that occurred shortly after the turn of the century, when a young truant officer tangled with an Italian family. When a boy in the family was sentenced to Parental School, his mother "had hysterics on the spot, climaxing the attack with the statement that the disgrace was too much and that she was going over and throw herself under a train . . . Much moved by his mother's demonstration, [the truant officer] said that she went to the judge and pleaded for probation. This the judge finally granted." A few days later, the truant officer "was pleased to hear about the neighborhood that the judge and the truant officers were just a couple of fools, that all that was necessary to prevent a child from being sent to Parental School was to make a sufficiently impressive scene in the courtroom." This incident could be multiplied many times: immigrant parents engaged in tactics of evasion and resistance as they tried to prevent interference in what they viewed as a private family matter. Yet this source of conflict, too, diminished over time. Rising wages among adult men took pressure off the immigrant family economy, while the collapse of the youth labor market removed the impetus for flouting the compulsory schooling law.[36]

When we consider direct evidence about discipline and disorder in immigrant schools, we find no indication that teachers regarded their students as particularly difficult to discipline, or that they avoided immigrant schools for this reason. True, classic studies by Frederick Thrasher and Clifford Shaw portray adolescents in working-class immigrant neighborhoods as joining gangs and engaging in petty theft, gambling, drinking, and sexual delinquency. Long after children stopped evading school in order to work, truancy remained an expressive behavior. For some, the most engaging thing about school may have been plotting to escape it. Yet inside the classroom, immigrant students were said to be compliant. John Bartky, who worked in the Chicago schools for more than twenty years, noted that while Polish students might cut classes or vandalize the school, they were seldom disruptive inside the classroom. There were similar reports about Italian students. When Howard Becker interviewed Chicago teachers in the early 1950s, most agreed that working-class or "in-between" children—most of them from immigrant backgrounds— were well-behaved.[37] There were also few complaints about immigrant parents' support for the schools. A teacher interviewed by Miriam Wagenschein singled out the "foreign parents" as cooperative: "They demand that their children look up to authority. They are very easy to deal with." An Italian man referred to what he called the "European hand": "You went to school, you came home and talked about a teacher picking on you, you would have gotten a few more whacks from your parents."[38]

Likewise, academic difficulties were not attributed to students' resistance. If there were a stereotype about immigrant children, especially those of Eastern European descent, it was of dullness and passivity. A teacher interviewed by Becker complained about "these Polish or Bohemian children who just sit and look at you and don't say anything at all." This perception of passivity appears again in descriptions of teaching in a working-class school: "Here you present, and maybe you catch a gleam in four or five children's eyes. Then you present again. A few more catch on. Then you present a third time. Then you present again. By that time most of them have got it. Then you have to start working extra hard with the ones that still don't get it." Although this view of the students is not flattering, there is no hint in these accounts of the opposition that teachers perceived in the inner city.[39]

Conclusion

Antagonism and disorder are common threads running through descriptions of inner-city schooling. The drama of the struggle between teacher and student draws attention to the moment of defiance and sanction within the classroom. To explain this struggle, however, we must look beyond the classroom to school and district policies, and to policy domains far beyond discipline. Chicago's public schools built their strategies for authority and engagement on foundations that were undercut by the realities of inner-city education. The motivations that induced other students to comply were weak in inner-city schools. In the end, there was simply too little these schools could offer.

No doubt, the evidence in this chapter must be read cautiously.[40] Most reports on classroom dynamics came from teachers, who may have attributed discipline problems to students. (The fact that the students were often blamed for classroom disorder reflects who was telling the story.) To make this evidence useful, we must reframe it: what it provides is evidence of trouble in the relationship between students and teachers. And while some teachers succeeded in a difficult situation while others did not, or could not, it is ultimately the district that bore responsibility for making that situation difficult. School policymakers were the unseen actors in the classroom. Their decisions made it much more difficult for inner-city teachers and students to work constructively together.

Conclusion

This book seeks to explain the origins of the troubles of inner-city schooling that emerged in the 1940s and 1950s, coinciding with the changing urban conditions of the post–World War II era. These problems cannot be attributed to urban change alone. School policies are a critical part of the explanation. We might suppose, for instance, that cities after 1945 were hampered by a shrinking tax base and by rising numbers of disadvantaged students. There is no question that inner-city schools were handicapped by resource scarcity. The problems of poor facilities, overcrowding, inexperienced teachers, and double-shift schedules were only too plain. These resource deficits did not result from economic and demographic change, however: after 1945, Chicago's public schools had more money, not less, to spend on education. Instead, these deficits reflect decisions made by school officials about how to allocate funds and students. Students were segregated by race, and fewer resources were allocated to black schools.

Another possible explanation highlights labor market discrimination. In this account, black students became indifferent or hostile toward school because they did not expect their education to pay off when seeking employment. As this book shows, racial discrimination had a profound effect on Chicago's black community, but its effect differed by class. For relatively advantaged students, discrimination didn't negate the economic value of education. In fact, educated black workers sought paths into the white-collar labor market for which their schooling could be a shield against discrimination, hence their strong representation in civil service and the professions. For disadvantaged black Chicagoans, however, the aspiration for education was largely empty, because higher education was so far out of reach. If they did continue to subscribe to education as a strategy for mobility, it was because there were so few alternatives in the blue-collar world.

A third account concerns the cultures of urban minority communities. It holds that prejudice and racial segregation promoted an oppositional culture in which students saw academic achievement as antithetical to their racial identity—as "acting white." In contrast, immigrants could readily assimilate into the American mainstream, and thus held more positive orientations to American institutions such as education. Both the immigrant and the black communities were internally diverse, however, and the differences between them were more subtle and contingent than the contrast between assimilation and opposition suggests. In both kinds of communities, the elite members were strong advocates of education, but the character of class relations in the black community gave the advocacy of its elites greater force. In addition, differences in the internal organization of these communities and in their relation to the white American majority affected the salience of education. Black Chicagoans used education to bid for status both within the community and outside it. For immigrants, on the other hand, education was less important as a route to status.

Although urban conditions by themselves cannot explain the problems of inner-city education, they remain important elements of our interpretation. For instance, the schools' financial hardships in the 1920s and 1930s shaped their policy in ways that constrained later responses to the challenges faced by black schools. To take another example, the significance of education for black economic and social status helps us understand why racial inequality in schooling led to such widespread anger and mobilization among black Chicagoans. These examples could be multiplied many times. School officials had to reckon with changing political, economic, and demographic conditions in the city; so did teachers.

Yet we cannot understand the troubles of inner-city schooling without considering Chicago's public schools themselves. During the 1920s and 1930s, in three policy domains, school officials took decisive steps that set the institutional stage for later problems in urban education. In the domain of race, they took actions that intensified the rise in school seg-regation and did little to remedy the growing inequality between white and black schools; efforts to improve the climate of race relations in the schools were too modest and came too late. In vocational education, the schools created a two-tiered system in which white students had ready access to selective technical and commercial training, while black stu-dents were concentrated in the lower tier. White vocational students had an incentive to work hard in school; many black students did not. Finally, the schools invested too little in remedial education. Black students, handicapped by poverty and also by the Chicago schools' racial inequal-ity, needed remedial assistance more than other students, but provisions for remedial education were more inadequate in black schools.

The roots of classroom alienation, antagonism, and disorder can be found in school policy decisions made long before the problems of inner-city schools attracted public attention. These policies struck at the foun-dations of authority and engagement, making it much more difficult for inner-city teachers to gain student cooperation in learning. The district's history of segregation and inequality undermined school legitimacy in the eyes of its black students; as a result, inner-city teachers struggled to gain cooperation from children and parents, who had little reason to trust the school. In trying to motivate their students, teachers could offer neither the gratification of growing mastery nor the prospect of economic reward.

Why did this happen? Who was responsible? The most visible actors in this story were the superintendents and other senior administrators of the Chicago Public Schools. Yet the responsibility was shared more widely, because school officials answered to powerful interests who lob-bied to keep property taxes low and protect the racial homogeneity of white neighborhoods. In more limited ways, responsibility extended fur-ther, for instance to the real estate agents who fomented racial hostil-ity and fear, and to teachers and administrators who acquiesced in the miseducation of black children. Indeed, there are few who did not par-ticipate in some way, even if reluctantly or indirectly, in the problems of inner-city schooling—that is the bitter reality of an institution with such deep and extensive roots in our society.

This history suggests why the inequality of urban schools has been so durable. Unlike the segregated schools of the South, the black schools of the North were not unequal because of overt and state-driven action. Chicago's schools were formally race blind; Illinois law prohibited racial exclusion in the schools. Instead, inequality emerged through a myriad of small actions, in both the public and private sectors, in domains from politics to work to housing markets to informal social settings. Taken singly, most of these actions appeared reasonable and legally defensible, and sometimes even well intentioned. Taken together, these actions created a brutally effective system of inequality. The history of Chicago's inner-city schools is a story of damage done by ordinary people taking the path of least resistance.

Implications for History

This account of the Chicago schools speaks to several lines of inquiry in the history of education. First, this work highlights the importance of classroom dynamics and school organization in the history of northern black schooling. With a few exceptions, including work by Joel Perlmann and Michael Homel, studies of black education in the North have given little attention to the educational process itself; this neglect is particularly striking in contrast with the historical research on class and education.[1] The Chicago case suggests that urban black education cannot be subsumed under the history of working-class schooling, but instead has its own distinct trajectory. To explore further this distinctive character, research based on oral history accounts from former students and their parents would be an important contribution. In addition, it may be fruitful to compare classroom dynamics or home-school relations in northern and southern black schools, to see how differences in segregation regimes shaped the character of black schooling.[2] Finally, this book has focused on the African-American experience in this regard, but a growing share of the inner-city population is of Latin American or Caribbean origin. The influence of these distinctive histories on the character of inner-city schooling opens some extremely interesting comparative questions.

This work also recasts the role of science in the history of twentieth-century education. In this context, science is usually equated with the use of intelligence tests for sorting and tracking students, with spurious theories linking race and intelligence, and with a shift from democratic governance to school management by elite professionals. The history of science in education, however, was more varied and contested than we have realized. The Chicago case highlights a neglected current of applied research carried out, in the 1920s, not by university-based academics but by educators in the school system or at the Chicago Normal School. This research received little financial or logistical support from the district, and over time it fell away from the mainstream of social science research. For a short period, however, it had a salutary effect, promoting and enriching teachers' own reflections on the craft of teaching. Given the present-day emphasis on evidence-based reform, it may be instructive to recover this history of applied research in the schools, and to learn more about how teachers participated in and were influenced by this research.

Third, this work engages the historical study of school practices such as social promotion, special education, intelligence testing, curriculum differentiation, vocational education, and tracking. These practices have been blamed for lowering academic expectations and restricting educational opportunity for low-income and minority students. In some ways, the Chicago history is consistent with the now-familiar critiques of these practices. This work suggests two kinds of revisions, however. First, in explaining these practices, historians have written about the influence of educational theories and the politics of class and immigration, but have given less attention to practical factors. The Chicago case highlights the difficulties teachers faced in teaching academically heterogeneous classes, as well as the expense and administrative obstacles associated with alternatives such as curriculum differentiation and tracking. While educational theory and political developments may have made these new practices more palatable, it was the more practical considerations that drove implementation. Second, the Chicago case draws attention to the dual character of these measures. As envisioned by some educators, innovations such as remedial classes and vocational education offered teachers new tools to promote achievement among disadvantaged students. When these measures were implemented, however, their educational goals were compromised to limit cost and minimize disruption to the status quo. As with scientific research on education, school practices such as remedial education, vocational education, and tracking were contested.

Finally, the Chicago history builds on and extends institutional research in education. In early work in this area, the sociologists John Meyer and Brian Rowan wrote that certain kinds of organizations, including schools, tend to seek legitimacy by conforming to institutionalized ideas about what organizations should look like. They noted the tensions created by this performative dimension of organizational life: school staff may be pressed to do things they find unproductive, because their "audience" of parents, taxpayers, and accrediting agencies expects it. David Tyack and Larry Cuban add a historical dimension by chronicling the ways in which teachers resisted or modified policy edicts from above.[3] The Chicago history spotlights the superintendents, central office staff, and other administrators who carried out the mundane tasks—balancing budgets, recruiting teachers, assigning students—of running a big-city public school system. These school managers followed and sometimes participated in ivory tower debates over the ideals and aims of education, but their attention was selective and pragmatic. More showmen than philosophers, they chose ideas that would help them juggle political cross-pressures and satisfy their various constituencies. These school managers were important intermediaries between the educational elites and the teachers; it was through their strategic action that lofty ideas were (or were not) translated into practical reality. This history also highlights the implications of these performances for subordinates in the organization. School managers may have satisfied their external audiences, but they did not always convince those within the organization, who saw at close range the discrepancy between performance and reality. Teachers and students could not hold school officials accountable for their representations of reality, but the slippage between policy talk and institutional practice had an impact nonetheless, alienating and demoralizing them.

History and School Reform

The problems of inner-city schools remain with us today. American schools are marked by profound racial and ethnic differences in student performance. Although the racial gap in school attainment and achievement narrowed during the 1970s and 1980s, progress stalled after 1990.[4] How can history speak to these problems? It cannot provide definitive guidance on which school reforms will work best. What it can do, instead, is illuminate the schools' institutional legacy: the tangle of laws, regulations, practices, political constituencies, and beliefs and expectations which have made inner-city schooling so resistant to change. The following sections consider this institutional legacy in the areas of racial segregation and inequality, vocational education, remedial education, and discipline.

Racial Segregation and Inequality

At an ideological level, Americans affirm equality of opportunity in education, but at the level of practice, there are many incentives to compromise, reflecting the socioeconomic centrality of schools in our society as well as the career incentives they provide to teachers. Parents seek to pass on class advantages to their children; teachers fashion career trajectories through mobility from school to school; localities try to attract affluent residents. For these reasons, many people have had a stake in practices that generate inequality, such as local control and financing, arcane budgetary practices, teacher pay and recruitment arrangements, and the parallel sorting of students by race and class and of teachers by qualifications.

Given the perpetuation of these practices, urban schools remain highly segregated by race and class. Indeed, Chicago's schools became more segregated over the 1990s, even as residential segregation declined. Racial isolation leads to class segregation. In 1999, across all metropolitan areas, the average black child attended a school in which 65 percent of the student body lived at or near the poverty level. These patterns are unlikely to change anytime soon. Indeed, the retreat from court-ordered desegregation and the rise of public schools of choice may intensify segregation.[5] Inequality in school resources also persists. In predominantly low-income or minority schools, teachers and other professional staff have less education and experience. Inner-city students attend school in worse facilities and have less access to textbooks, supplies, libraries, laboratory equipment, and specialized curricula.[6] There have been many efforts to alter these patterns, including racial desegregation, magnet schools, school finance reform, Title I funding for disadvantaged students, and other public programs to supplement the resources of low-income schools. These efforts have ameliorated but not solved the problem of inequality.

We cannot expect to ensure equality, much less tilt school resources toward students who need them most, without modifying the long-accepted mechanisms for allocating resources and staffing to schools. One approach is to reduce the racial and socioeconomic sorting of students. Richard Kahlenberg, for instance, advocates economic desegregation of schools, which may offer a number of educational advantages. While economic desegregation is an important long-term goal, in the short term it will be politically and logistically difficult. A more tractable alternative is to address resource disparities directly through a shift in funding formulas. As Ross Rubenstein and Lawrence Miller point out, inner-city schools are disadvantaged by the oft-used procedure of basing school budgets on average rather than actual teacher salaries. When these schools hire less qualified or less experienced teachers, as so often happens, they cannot use the resulting savings for other purposes. School systems including those in Houston, Seattle, and San Francisco are trying new budgeting procedures that would eliminate this problem. One option is for money to follow students. Another is to allocate funds directly to the school rather than filtering them through the district. In both approaches, funding can be adjusted based on student need, promoting "vertical equity" in which the added challenges faced by disadvantaged students are taken into account.[7]

Even with such a shift in financial support, inner-city schools will still find it difficult to obtain the most important resource a school can have — good teachers and administrators. High rates of staff turnover and shortages of qualified teachers and principals will persist as long as personnel in inner-city schools face more difficult conditions but are paid no more than they can earn in public schools elsewhere. To change this situation, it will be necessary to shift the incentive structure. Salary supplements may help; so may smaller classes, mentoring, status rewards, or other changes that would make inner-city teaching jobs more attractive. The details must be worked out in negotiation with administrators and the teachers' unions, and should be responsive to the felt needs of teachers. But the goal is simple: to shift incentives to attract the strongest teachers to teach in the inner city.

Vocational Education

The institutional model for vocational education is marked by a tension between two goals: meeting the needs of employers and motivating youth by giving high school an explicit connection to the labor market. For a brief time, the schools could do both. As the Chicago case suggests, however, this model is inherently unstable. An attractive vocational program draws expanded enrollments, flooding the market with a less highly selected pool of graduates and jeopardizing the value of the credential. The Chicago Public Schools responded by restricting access to the top-tier vocational courses, creating a nonselective alternative to which it diverted students with lower grades and test scores. Over the last several decades, high-quality vocational education has shifted even further out of reach for inner-city students. Employers demand higher-level cognitive skills even for many blue-collar positions.[8] Much vocational education now takes place in community colleges. Under pressure from the standards movement, high schools have cut back on vocational education. When half of all inner-city students drop out of high school, vocational education in community college is too distant a prospect to motivate them.[9]

Revitalizing vocational education in high school could have broad benefits by giving students an incentive to learn while offering them at least a toehold in the labor market. But if this is to happen, it will require change in our institutional model for vocational education. In their book *The Education Gospel,* Norton Grubb and Marvin Lazerson offer an alternative that could, they write, infuse high school with a new sense of purpose. Their model comes from the career academies and other theme-based high schools which have sprung up in the last couple of decades. The curricula of these schools have an emphasis such as the arts, political science, environmental science, or science and technology. Rather than providing specific job training, they prepare students broadly for labor market entry, college, or the combination of work and postsecondary training that so many young adults pursue. Some schools also link students to part-time jobs or internships, giving youth connections to employers and allowing a more engaging work-based learning experience.[10]

Whether through career academies or another model, it remains imperative to find a new solution to the old tension between the needs of employers and those of disadvantaged students. Certainly, some inner-city students will go on to postsecondary education. For many, however, even completing high school may appear both too difficult and not worthwhile. For them, an enriched vocational education could be a valuable adjunct to academic learning. By providing a more specific and credible set of economic incentives, and a context in which a variety of cognitive skills can be applied and reinforced, vocational education is likely to be particularly compelling for the most economically vulnerable students. To work, the new vocational programs would need to ensure skill acquisition—otherwise employers will not be interested—but must also build in second chances with flexible timing of entry, courses for improving specific skills, and an array of alternative tracks. Whatever these programs look like, we must guard against the tendency, long institutionalized, to serve employers at the expense of the most disadvantaged students.

Remedial Education

At the most general level, the institutional legacy of efforts to address school failure is a pair of strategies for sidestepping the problem. Remediating low achievement is a difficult and expensive undertaking, and the schools have never had the resources to do it right. Instead, they have relied on two different models, both represented historically in the Chicago schools. During the early twentieth century, the schools imposed uniform and relatively inflexible standards; students who could not reach those standards were held back and eventually dropped out. In the second model, the schools adopted reforms such as social promotion, tracking, and special education, which allowed low-achieving students to move through school with others of their age, and sometimes even to graduate. These measures let the schools accommodate heterogeneity in academic achievement within each grade.

With the standards and accountability movements in school reform, including most recently the No Child Left Behind law, many components of this second approach have come under fire. Unfortunately, the resulting reforms could shift us back to the older model of inflexible academic standards and high dropout rates. By setting benchmarks without expanding schools' capacity to raise achievement, the NCLB regulations give schools an incentive to push failing students out so that their low test scores will not jeopardize the school's mandated progress in achievement. While NCLB sets stringent standards for progress in achievement, its monitoring of graduation rates is comparatively lax. NCLB remains symbolically quite important, but it is coupled with too thin an understanding of how schools work. If the problem was simply that teachers and students weren't trying hard enough, then its assessments and incentives might make a difference. Instead, history suggests that problems with motivation arise when teachers and students don't have the right tools and resources to make their efforts effective.

Most of the measures that have been shown to benefit low-achieving students are costly to offer on a large scale. They include smaller classes, a longer school day, summer school, more extensive and higher-quality preschool, and one-on-one tutoring. Unlike the redesign of vocational education, these measures do not require much organizational creativity. What they do require is the determination to protect these investments in the face of significant budgetary pressure. In this context, the advantage we have now is a growing base of knowledge about the efficacy of school reforms. This knowledge can guide policy choices by identifying the measures that are the most cost-effective. It can also promote public support for school reform by demonstrating that such investments do indeed make a difference. The work of the Consortium on Chicago School Research, based at the University of Chicago, is just one example of the rigorous applied research being conducted by scores of researchers. The Chicago schools abandoned their old program of instructional research in the 1930s, having adopted a set of policies that made such research irrelevant. It is a striking and heartening reversal that Chicago researchers are now generating some of the leading work in this field.

Discipline

In the area of discipline, the schools' institutional legacy has two elements. The first is an essentialist view that blames discipline problems on the deficits of individual students or teachers. Thus, students are spoken of as disruptive, unruly, or incorrigible, and teachers as poor disciplinarians. The other element is the reflexive use and acceptance of strict and coercive disciplinary tactics in the inner city. Both elements are evident in the history of Chicago's inner-city schools, and remain part of our lens on urban education today. Media coverage of successful inner-city schools highlights strategies for keeping order, such as school uniforms, highly scripted curricula, or regimented school environments. This framework may leave educators and the public too willing to accept practices that cross the line from strict to abusive, and too unwilling to explore alternatives to punitive measures.[11]

There is no question that discipline problems remain a concern in inner-city schools. These problems are costly, distracting students, disrupting instruction, and driving away good teachers. Problems of discipline are even more salient now that schools are under pressure to raise achievement; teachers, in the inner city and elsewhere, have sometimes bought surface order at the expense of educational goals. In addition, given the context of violence in many inner-city communities, making the school a safe haven may be as critical psychologically as it is educationally. Black and Latino students are more than twice as likely as white students to fear being attacked on the way to and from school or on its premises.[12] Yet the zero-tolerance policies that many districts have adopted may alienate students and imperil their educational future without addressing the deeper problems that classroom disorder signals. As the Harvard Civil Rights Project cautions, many black and Latino students are being diverted into the "school-to-prison pipeline." Almost one in four black male students has been suspended over a four-year period, a rate much higher than for any other category of students. Black students are also more likely than others to be punished for "subjective offenses," such as defiance of authority or disruptive behavior.[13]

In his recent book *Judging School Discipline,* Richard Arum contends that students' rights litigation has made teachers and administrators reluctant to impose disciplinary sanctions. He writes that prostudent legal measures have created an ambiguous legal environment within which teachers enforce school rules without much consistency or confidence.[14] He may very well be correct. Yet the Chicago history shows that discipline problems in inner-city schools predate these broad changes in the legal environment. To explain the breakdown of authority in the schools, we should look beyond the courts to the deficits of urban schooling itself. Addressing problems of authority requires schools to move beyond the old model of addressing discipline problems through rules and sanctions alone. Instead, we must seek a transformation in the social relations of the school.[15]

Poverty, Politics, and School Reform

Some say it is futile to try to reform inner-city schools without addressing poverty and other issues outside the school. In Jean Anyon's memorable phrase, that is like trying to clean the air on one side of a screen door. There is much merit in this position. Racial and class differences in academic achievement appear long before children begin school. After school starts, inner-city children remain at a disadvantage for many reasons, including elevated rates of illness, poor nutrition, residential instability, and neighborhood violence. Even if school quality were equalized, race and class disparities in achievement would persist and perhaps widen as children move through school.[16] Add to that the complexity of fixing the schools compared to, say, expanding the food stamp program or providing free immunizations, and it is easy to understand the appeal of the other side of the screen door.

Yet addressing poverty has its own challenges. Over the last four decades, under quite varied economic and political conditions, poverty rates have fluctuated within a narrow band of about 11 to 15 percent. There is no reason to expect a significant drop in poverty anytime soon.

Quite the reverse: the recent increase in economic inequality is likely to have long-term consequences, making it more difficult for families to escape poverty. Political action to change this situation will take time. As Jean Anyon notes, the struggles for collective bargaining rights, civil rights, and the minimum wage all took years to come to fruition. New movements for economic justice are afoot, but they, too, are likely to face a long struggle given the implications for politics of the recent rise in economic inequality.[17]

In the short term, we need to protect children and youth from the damage poverty does. There is no shortage of ideas and models. Particularly promising are comprehensive programs that address the multidimensional challenges faced by inner-city families. Examples include the Harlem Children's Zone initiative in New York City, which promotes education, child care, health care, violence prevention, and parenting skills within a sixty-square-block area of Harlem. Also attractive are school-based programs, which offer efficient service delivery and help to build a community around the school. Examples include New York City's Beacon Program and the "community schools" in a number of cities.[18]

These programs lack adequate and stable funding, and reach only a small fraction of those who could benefit. Over the past few years, the de-funding of federal community development and social service programs has put many of them in jeopardy. Although local initiatives can generate ideas and mobilize resources from foundations and private partners, a base of flexible and stable federal funding is essential. If we are serious about promoting the education and well-being of the most vulnerable children in our society, we will build a national coalition for measures that revitalize inner-city neighborhoods and support low-income urban families. The political will—in the sense of broad public support for these kinds of initiatives—may already exist. What is needed now is coalition building to mobilize this support and press for action.

Quantitative Evidence

This appendix describes the data sources and methods of analysis for quantitative evidence presented in the book.

Chicago School Enrollment, Expenditures, Teacher Salaries, and Graduates

Chapters 1 and 5 use information on Chicago's public schools drawn from the *Proceedings* volumes published annually by the Chicago Board of Education and available in the Regenstein Library at the University of Chicago.

Average daily membership (fig. 1.2)—A good measure of demand for teachers and classroom space is the average daily membership for the month of October. Average daily membership figures are slightly lower than but correlated with enrollment; membership figures taken in October are not affected by the attrition that took place over the school year. For the sake of comparability, high school membership figures include all students in grades nine through twelve, including those of junior high school age; even at the peak of junior high school enrollment in Chicago, around 1930, only a minority of students in the relevant grades attended junior high.

Per-pupil spending for education (fig. 1.4)—The measure of school spending is drawn from budgets published in the annual *Proceedings* volumes. The Chicago Board of Education had five separate funds—education, building, playground, free textbook, and pension—with a separate tax rate for each. The education fund is the largest, and is the best measure consistently available over time of the resources devoted to classroom instruction, administration, and related support services. To calculate per-pupil spending for education, I deducted debt service from the education fund budget published during the spring in the *Proceedings* volumes, and divided the result by the average daily membership for October of that year, adjusted for the changing mix of elementary and high school students. The membership figure is a weighted total of the numbers of elementary and high school students. The weight for high school students was set at 2.0 in 1900 and 1.25 in 1960, and interpolated for the intervening years; these figures reflect contemporary estimates of the relative cost of educating high school and elementary students. Junior high school students were allocated to elementary or high school based on their grade level. The measure is adjusted for inflation, with all figures expressed in 1960 dollars.

Teachers' minimum and maximum salaries (fig. 1.5)—These figures were derived from the *Proceedings* volumes, which listed salary figures for teachers at each school. They were adjusted for inflation and for the reported pay cuts during the 1930s, as chronicled by Mary Herrick in *Chicago Schools* (pp. 198, 229–30, 292).

Graduates by course of study (figs. 5.1–5.4)—These figures report information on the number of graduates by course of study, and were derived from the *Proceedings*. Each year these volumes listed the names of graduates by school and type of degree. I categorized and counted these graduates based on type of high school (general versus vocational) and type of degree received (general versus vocational, and two-year versus four-year). Students graduated in February, June, and August; I counted only the June graduates, who were the majority. Schools were identified as vocational only if they did not offer a general course of study at all. Graduates were categorized as receiving a general diploma if no specialized course was listed or if the type of degree was science, language, or other nonvocational designations.

IPUMS City Sample

Chapters 1 and 2 use information on the demographic and economic characteristics of blacks and southern/eastern European immigrants in northeastern and midwestern cities. The "city sample" drawn from the Integrated Public Use Microdata Samples includes cases from all central cities in metropolitan areas located in the northeastern and north central (midwestern) regions. In 1940 and 1950, the U.S. Census asked for detailed information, such as educational attainment and earnings, only from individuals on the "sample line." Only sample-line individuals were selected for the 1940 and 1950 analyses; the 1940 analysis sample included only cases in the self-weighting sample.

Ethnicity—Ethnicity was defined on the basis of birthplace, parents' birthplace, and (in the 1910 and 1920 censuses only) mother tongue. Individuals born outside the United States were assigned an ethnicity based on their own birthplace. U.S.-born individuals with one foreign-born parent were assigned an ethnicity based on the birthplace of that parent; if both parents were foreign born, they were assigned an ethnicity based on the father. For first- or second-generation persons in 1910 and 1920, information on mother tongue overrode birthplace information for those speaking Polish, Czech, Slovak, Serbo-Croatian, Slovene, Lithuanian, Other Balto-Slavic, or "Slavic unknown." Countries categorized as part of southern and eastern Europe included Albania, Bulgaria, Czechoslovakia, Estonia, Gibraltar, Greece, Hungary, Italy, Latvia, Lithuania, Malta, Poland, Portugal, Romania, San Marino, Spain, and Yugoslavia; individuals with the nonspecific codes of Central Europe, Eastern Europe, and Baltic States not specified were also included. Germany, Austria, and Russia were specifically excluded except for cases included on the basis of mother tongue information.

Family characteristics—Individuals in the census samples were assigned parent characteristics using information on other household members. For each individual in the sample, the IPUMS identifies whether that person's father or mother lived in the same household and, if so, identifies who are the likely parents within the household. Social relationships such as stepparent or adoptive parent as well as biological relationships are included. For each individual for whom a likely parent lived in the household, the ethnic and socioeconomic characteristics of those likely parents were assigned to that individual. I used IPUMS-constructed variables for the number of siblings (including step- and half-siblings) in the household. Children were classified as living in a two-parent family if a (social or biological) father and a (social or biological) mother both resided in the household.

Public and private school enrollment figures (fig. 1.8)—First, an overall rate of attendance in private elementary school was constructed for every ten years from 1910 to 1960 using enrollment figures in Herrick, *Chicago Schools* (p. 403), and Sanders, *Education of an Urban Minority* (p. 5). (These figures include Catholic school students only.) The 1960 census included a question on public and private school attendance; this information was used to construct race-specific ratios of the rates of private school attendance for black and nonblack children aged seven through thirteen years to the rate of private school attendance for all children in Illinois in 1960. These ratios were applied to the Chicago rates of private school attendance from 1910 to 1960 to estimate the proportions of black and white children attending private school in each of these census years. These estimated rates were applied to population figures for the number of black and nonblack children aged seven through thirteen years in Chicago, 1910 to 1960, to generate the estimates found in figure 1.8. (In 1960 only, population figures are for Illinois central cities rather than Chicago, because the 1960 census does not identify cities. In that year, Chicago accounted for more than 90 percent of central city residents in Illinois. The 1960 proportion of black students in all three categories is inflated by 1.112, the ratio of the percentage of black residents in Chicago to the percentage of black residents in Illinois cities, to adjust for the fact that the 1960 IPUMS sample includes residents of other Illinois cities.)

The resulting estimates of the percentage of black children in Chicago public schools are similar to those found in Havighurst, *Public Schools of Chicago* (p. 54): 6.4 percent in 1930 and 11.0 percent in 1940.

Enrollment rates (fig. 1.9)—The federal decennial census reports school attendance for all persons (in 1950, all sample-line persons) in the age groups specified in figure 1.9, but for several census years the sample size for these age-by-race/ethnic categories is quite small. For more reliable estimates of school enrollment, I used predicted values from a logistic regression predicting school attendance; the analysis was run on a pooled sample including cases from 1900 to 1960 census samples. Variables included were age; age squared; indicators for female sex, black race, foreign birth, southern U.S. birth; dummy variables for census years; and race-year interaction terms. Predictions for youth aged fourteen to fifteen years were based on an analysis including ten- through seventeen-year-olds. Predictions for youth aged sixteen to seventeen years were based on an analysis including fifteen- through seventeen-year-olds. (Analyses using this restricted age range produced estimates that more closely matched the descriptive statistics.) Results using other specifications were not qualitatively different. Table A.1 shows the predicted enrollment rates for city sample youth by place of birth. Figure 1.9 displays a subset of this table.

Students over age for their grade (fig. 1.10)—Figure 1.10 and table A.2 include only children and youth who were coded as attending school. Over-age students were those for whom the difference between age and the number of grades completed was more than 6. Table A.2 shows the

TABLE A.1:   **Enrollment rates, city sample youth by age and place of birth**

	Immigrant (all)	Immigrant (northern born)	Black (all)	Black (northern born)	Black (southern born)
Ages 14–15					
1910	59.6	60.7	74.2	73.5	74.8
1920	69.6	70.7	78.0	76.8	78.7
1940	93.3	93.4	91.1	88.8	91.6
1950	94.9	95.0	93.2	92.6	93.4
1960	95.3	95.4	93.8	92.7	94.1
Ages 16–17					
1910	17.2	18.9	34.0	33.7	35.2
1920	26.4	27.5	35.7	37.2	33.3
1940	69.7	70.0	60.2	62.0	57.3
1950	74.7	75.0	70.1	71.3	66.9
1960	77.1	77.9	70.2	72.0	65.9

Source: IPUMS city sample.

TABLE A.2:   **Percentage over age for grade, city sample students by place of birth**

	Immigrant (all)	Immigrant (northern born)	Black (all)	Black (northern born)	Black (southern born)
Ages 7–9					
1940	16.6	16.7	21.3	20.0	—
1950	26.2	24.9	30.4	29.4	35.9
1960	24.2	20.3	31.9	31.2	36.6
Ages 10–13					
1940	35.2	35.3	40.4	38.2	—
1950	33.5	32.0	49.1	47.3	53.7
1960	34.6	28.2	43.6	41.3	55.6
Ages 14–17					
1940	45.8	45.2	48.1	44.0	—
1950	36.3	34.9	56.2	52.6	67.4
1960	31.3	23.1	52.8	50.4	60.2

Source: IPUMS city sample.

proportion of city sample students who were over age for their grade by age categories and place of birth.

High school graduation rates (fig. 1.11)—Beginning in 1940, the decennial census collected information on years of education completed. High school graduation rates were constructed using pooled samples from 1940, 1950, and 1960 of all individuals born in the United States and outside the South who were at least twenty years old at the relevant census year.

Racial differences in children's family characteristics—Table A.3 shows the difference in family measures for immigrant and black students in 1920, 1940, and 1960 for all children (top panel) and for northern-born children only (bottom panel). Between 1920 and 1960, immigrant children gained ground relative to black children in most measures of their family characteristics. For instance, the racial difference in the proportion of children living in a two-parent household increased between 1920 and 1960 for all children and for northern-born children. Trends between 1920 and 1960 in most other socioeconomic indicators were also unfavorable to black children.

Analysis of racial gap in schooling (fig. 1.12)—The estimates of the percentage point difference in the proportion of sixteen- to seventeen-

TABLE A.3: **Immigrant-black differences in family characteristics, students aged 5–17 years, city sample, 1920–60**

	1920	1940	1960
All children			
In two-parent family	17.2	27.3	27.5
Number of siblings	1.3	0.3	−1.2
Own home	19.6	26.5	22.4
Mother is high school graduate	—	−8.3	−1.5
At least one parent in the labor force	−1.1	3.7	1.2
Parent in white-collar occupation	8.4	8.0	14.5
Mother's occupation score (mean)	11.7	8.7	4.8
Father's occupation score (mean)	3.2	3.7	4.0
Northern-born children			
In two-parent family	16.1	24.8	27.2
Number of siblings	1.3	0.2	−1.3
Own home	17.3	27.7	23.8
Mother is high school graduate	—	−9.0	−1.9
At least one parent in the labor force	−1.7	4.1	1.0
Parent in white-collar occupation	2.3	6.8	15.8
Mother's occupation score (mean)	12.1	8.3	4.9
Father's occupation score (mean)	3.6	3.4	4.4

Source: IPUMS city sample.

year-olds enrolled in school and at the expected grade are based on a series of logistic regressions using census data from 1940, 1950, and 1960. The analyses included all black and southern/eastern European immigrant youth aged fifteen through seventeen years who were born in the United States and outside the South and who lived with at least one parent. The dependent variable was coded 1 if the individual was enrolled in school and if the difference between his or her age and the number of grades completed was no more than 6. The first analysis included age, age squared, and indicator variables for female sex and black race. The second analysis added the number of siblings and indicator variables for two-parent family, no parent in the labor force, and parent in a white-collar job.

White-collar employment by sector (figs. 2.1 and 2.2)—Descriptive statistics for white-collar occupations include adults aged twenty-two through fifty-four years who were in the labor force and reported an occupation in the given year. Private-sector white-collar workers included all employees with a white-collar occupation who were not classified elsewhere. Self-employed white-collar workers were identified using information on class of worker. In 1910 and 1920, public-sector workers included any white-collar employees whose industry was public administration or whose occupation was teacher, postmaster, mail carrier, or inspector or official in public administration. Beginning in 1940, when the class of worker codes became more detailed, class of worker (government) was also used to identify public-sector employees. The independent professions included all workers who, regardless of their industry or class of worker, had one of the following occupations: clergy, lawyer or judge, physicians or surgeon, chiropractor, veterinarian, or dentist.

Economic value of education (figs. 2.7 and 2.8, table 2.2)—Analyses of the economic value of education were based on a series of OLS and logistic regressions predicting the economic outcomes shown in table A.4. Analyses included individuals in the 1940, 1950, and 1960 IPUMS city samples who were aged twenty-two through sixty-four years. All analyses controlled for age, age squared, number of children, and indicator variables for southern birth, foreign birth, a coresident spouse, school attendance, and state of residence. All analyses were run separately by sex. Figures 2.7 and 2.8 were based on regressions which included a series of dummy variables indicating levels of education; these analyses were run separately by racial/ethnic category (black, immigrant, and other white). The results in table 2.2 are based on sex-specific analyses pooling cases

TABLE A.4: **Outcomes for analysis of economic value of education**

Economic outcome	Definition and population
Annual earnings	Total wage and salary earnings for calendar year before the census, logged. Analysis excludes the self-employed and those with zero earnings.
Occupation score	IPUMS-constructed score for occupation based on earnings in 1950 for men with that occupation. Analysis excludes those with no reported occupation.
White-collar occupation	White-collar occupation includes those with professional, managerial, clerical, or sales occupation according to 1950 occupation codes. Analysis excludes those with no reported occupation.
Occupational status	Duncan socioeconomic index, a commonly used measure of occupational status. Analysis excludes those not in the labor force and those with no reported occupation.
Unemployment	In the labor force but not employed (standard census definition). Analysis excludes those not in the labor force.
Labor force	Employed or looking for work. Analysis includes all individuals in age range.
Weeks worked	Weeks worked in the calendar year before the census. In 1940 and 1950, census reports number of weeks. In 1960, when weeks-worked measure was "intervalled," cases were assigned the midpoint of the range. Analysis excludes those with zero weeks of work in the previous year.
Full-time employment	Works 35+ hours in week prior to census. Analysis excludes those not at work in the week before the census.

from all ethnic categories. The independent variables included black race, immigrant status, educational attainment, and interaction terms for black*education and immigrant*education. Using the statistical package STATA, I tested whether the two interaction terms were significantly different from each other at the .05 level of significance.

Readers should note that these are simple analyses which do not take account of a number of factors that might influence labor force participation, earnings, and other economic outcomes. In addition, women who are working outside the home are undoubtedly a selected sample; it is unclear what implications this selection process has for the results.

Some Historical Evidence about Language Styles and Schooling

B eginning in the 1960s with research by William Labov and others, linguists have documented the patterns of African-American Vernacular English, a variant of American English governed by distinctive rules of grammar and pronunciation and with some distinctive vocabulary. Those who use AAVE may do so to a greater or lesser extent, and often shift their usage based on social context.[1] The origins and history of AAVE remain unclear, but some black children in early-twentieth-century Chicago probably recognized and spoke a version of it. The fragmentary evidence available suggests that these children may have been placed at a disadvantage in school by their use of vernacular speech.

References to distinctive language styles among black children in Chicago often cite such speech as characteristic of southern children. For instance, in 1920 Charles Thompson conducted a study of white (mostly Irish and Jewish) and black children at Moseley School in Chicago. On tests of both oral and silent reading, the white and northern-born black children had similar scores, but the southern-born black children were far behind. One reason, Thompson noted, was "the slowness of speech typical of the section of the country from which they came and the general peculiarities of speech which almost invariably result in inaccurate pronunciation." Occasional references to southern black children's "language difficulties" continued throughout the period. For instance, in 1939 a school administrator referred to southern migrants' "completely different vocabulary as to home surroundings and their quite different enunciation and pronunciation."[2] Although use of AAVE was not specific to region, it is likely to have been more common in racially segregated contexts; in the early twentieth century, when northern cities were less segregated than the South, use of AAVE consequently may have been more common among southern-born than northern-born black children. In addition, regional differences in speech may have heightened teachers' awareness of AAVE and led them to associate that style with southern-born black children.

Linguistic studies of black vernacular speech did not begin to appear until the 1960s; before then, there is no indication that teachers viewed AAVE as a legitimate and rule-governed variant of English, or understood the cultural significance of this speech for black children. A *Chicago Schools Journal* article from the 1920s suggests how teachers may have responded to AAVE. In 1924, a committee of teachers at the predominantly black Doolittle School conducted an informal survey of their students' "speech errors," giving examples consistent with African-American Vernacular. To root out these "errors," the Doolittle committee suggested that teachers "emphasize the correct form," using vigilant correction, drills, and class projects, and "create a desire on the part of the pupil to speak correctly at all times in school, at home, on the playground—everywhere."[3] The difficulty with this approach, later research suggests, is that it stigmatizes the home language and pushes students to alter their speech in family and community settings in which Standard English would be considered inappropriate. Indeed, a 1973 study found that incessant correction in school led to greater frequency of use of vernacular speech, as children came to resent this criticism and resist the correction.[4]

As a 1930 master's thesis by Maudelle Bousfield suggests, black students may have been disadvantaged by the Chicago public school system's increasing reliance on standardized tests that were heavily language dependent. Bousfield compared scores from three different intelligence tests which varied in their dependence on language, conducting the tests with two hundred students at Keith School, located in a poor black neighborhood. More than half of the children were southern born, although most had migrated to Chicago before starting school. The most highly language-dependent test, the Otis, was widely used in Chicago's schools. On this test, the Keith students averaged 87.2, significantly below the norm of 100. By contrast, on the Pintner Non-Language Mental

Test, which required no reading at all (students were asked to follow verbal instructions), the Keith students averaged 49.7, almost identical to the national norm of 50.[5]

Chicago educators had some awareness that lack of fluency in English impeded immigrant students' academic progress and lowered their performance on standardized tests. For instance, a 1928 canvass of Chicago school principals (which focused on children of Italian origin) found that most attributed Italian students' lower test scores to the language difference and to poverty; one principal reported that 80 percent of the Italian students at his school tested below the norm but added, "The group intelligence tests are, as you probably know, based to a large extent on reading ability."[6] Perhaps because the differences between standard and vernacular English are more subtle than between English and other languages, educators did not apply the same reasoning to AAVE. As a result, they may have overlooked a disadvantage that many black children faced in school.

Notes

Introduction

1. Clark, *Dark Ghetto;* quotation is from p. 137.

2. For other discussions of social relations in the inner-city schools, see e.g. Larry Cuban, *To Make a Difference: Teaching in the Inner City* (New York: Free Press, 1970); James P. Comer, *School Power: Implications of an Intervention Project* (New York: Free Press, 1980); Jonathan Kozol, *Death at an Early Age: The Destruction of the Hearts and Minds of Negro Children in the Boston Public Schools* (New York: Penguin Group, 1967); Eleanor Leacock, *Teaching and Learning in City Schools: A Comparative Study* (New York: Basic Books, 1969); McDermott, "Social Relations as Contexts for Learning in Schools"; Ogbu, *The Next Generation;* Ray C. Rist, "Student Social Class and Teachers' Expectations: The Self-Fulfilling Prophecy in Ghetto Education," *Harvard Educational Review* 40 (1970): 411–50.

3. This inquiry falls within the tradition of sociological research that traces inequality to social relations rather than to individual attributes; for instance, Charles Tilly, *Durable Inequality* (Berkeley and Los Angeles: University of California Press, 1998).

4. Among them: Wilson, *The Truly Disadvantaged;* Michael B. Katz, *The "Underclass" Debate: Views from History* (Princeton, NJ: Princeton University Press, 1993); Sugrue, *Origins of the Urban Crisis;* Massey and Denton, *American Apartheid;* Hirsch, *Making the Second Ghetto.*

5. See Mirel, *Rise and Fall;* Anyon, *Ghetto Schooling;* Emanuel Tobier, "Schooling in New York City: The Socioeconomic Context," in *City Schools: Lessons from New York,* ed. Diane Ravitch and Joseph P. Viteritti (Baltimore, MD: Johns Hopkins University Press, 2000); Rury, "Race, Space, and the Politics of Chicago's Public Schools."

6. On the growing awareness of discrimination during the early twentieth century, see Grossman, *Land of Hope.* On changes in inner-city communities,

see Wilson, *The Truly Disadvantaged;* Elijah Anderson, *Streetwise: Race, Class, and Change in an Urban Community* (Chicago: University of Chicago Press, 1990); Lieberson, *Piece of the Pie,* 328–34, 354–59. Also see Smith, "Native Blacks and Foreign Whites." On the economic woes of black workers in northern cities during the postwar period, see e.g. Sugrue, *Origins of the Urban Crisis.*

7. The oppositional culture argument is grounded theoretically in work by the anthropologists John U. Ogbu and Signithia Fordham; see e.g. Ogbu, *The Next Generation;* Fordham and Ogbu, "Black Students' School Success"; Fordham, *Blacked Out: Dilemmas of Race, Identity, and Success at Capital High.* (Chicago: University of Chicago Press, 1996). Alejandro Portes has developed a similar line of analysis; see for instance Alejandro Portes and Julia Sensenbrenner, "Embeddedness and Immigration: Notes on the Social Determinants of Economic Action," *American Journal of Sociology* 98 (1993): 1320–50; Portes and Zhou, "The New Second Generation." The discussion of oppositional culture is echoed in many recent accounts of inner-city life, including Elijah Anderson, *Code of the Street: Decency, Violence, and the Moral Life of the Inner City* (New York: W.W. Norton), and is integrated into a historical discussion of segregation by Massey and Denton, *American Apartheid.* It should be noted that Ogbu consistently framed oppositional culture as characteristic of all African Americans and Latinos, not just those in inner-city communities. For another perspective, see Carter, *Keepin' It Real;* Mark Gould, "Race and Theory: Culture, Poverty and Adaptation to Discrimination in Wilson and Ogbu," *Sociological Theory* 17:171–200.

8. On the differentiated high school curriculum, see for instance Fass, *Outside In,* 36–72; Kliebard, *Struggle for the American Curriculum.* For dilution of the academic curriculum, see Angus and Mirel, *Failed Promise of the American High School,* 71–101; Diane Ravitch, *The Troubled Crusade: American Education, 1945–1980* (New York: Basic Books, 1985), 43–80; it is a central theme of Ravitch's more recent *Left Back.* For discussion of low expectations, see e.g. Ronald Edmonds, "Effective Schools for the Urban Poor," *Educational Leadership* 37 (1979): 15–24; Foster, *Black Teachers on Teaching;* Ronald F. Ferguson reviews the literature on teachers' expectations in "Teachers' Perceptions and Expectations and the Black-White Test Score Gap," in *The Black-White Test Score Gap,* ed. Christopher Jencks and Meredith Phillips (Washington, DC: Brookings, 1998). There is a voluminous social science literature on the effects of tracking; for a critical review, see Tom Loveless, *The Tracking Wars: State Reform Meets School Policy* (Washington, DC: Brookings, 1999). On academic core curriculum, see e.g. Anthony S. Bryk, Valerie Lee, and Peter Holland, *Catholic Schools and the Common Good* (Cambridge, MA: Harvard University Press, 1993); James M. Braddock and Barbara Schneider, "Opportunities to Learn: Prospects and Pitfalls of a Common Core Curriculum," *Sociology of Education* (1996): 66–81.

9. David B. Tyack, "Public School Reform: Policy Talk and Institutional Practice," *American Journal of Education* 100 (1991): 1–19; also see Tyack and Cuban, *Tinkering toward Utopia.*

10. For a caution against giving too much attention to the narrative of Chicago, see Marvin Lazerson, "If All the World Were Chicago: American Education in the Twentieth Century," *History of Education Quarterly* 24:165–79. Although comparison with other cities is far beyond the scope of this book, recent case studies of schools in other cities balance this portrait and provide a starting point for comparison; see e.g. Anyon's *Ghetto Schooling* (Newark), Mirel's *Rise and Fall* (Detroit), Angus and Mirel's *Failed Promise of the American High School* (Grand Rapids, Michigan), and Dougherty's *More Than One Struggle* (Milwaukee).

11. Clark's *Dark Ghetto* suggests that the critical period falls between the 1930s and the early 1960s. In the early 1930s, Clark wrote, the academic achievement of black students in Harlem was not very different from that of white students in New York City. Yet by the early 1960s, when he led the Harlem Youth Study on which *Dark Ghetto* was based, the achievement gap had widened. As he pointed out, something changed between the 1930s and the early 1960s.

12. As other research has found, Jewish and non-Jewish immigrants were quite different in their backgrounds, economic strategies, cultural orientations to education, and patterns of school enrollment and attainment. See e.g. Perlmann, *Ethnic Differences;* also note contrasts in Ewa Morawska's *For Bread with Butter* and her *Insecure Prosperity* (Princeton, NJ: Princeton University Press, 1996), which examine non-Jewish and Jewish immigrants, respectively, from eastern Europe.

13. IPUMS has recently released a small "beta test" version of the 1930 microdata. The full dataset is expected to be available late in 2007.

Chapter One

1. This chapter relies heavily on data from the IPUMS, which provides consistent data for the decennial census between 1850 and 2000 with the exception of 1930. For most of these years, the number of Chicago residents in the IPUMS samples was too small to provide reliable estimates for black and immigrant schooling patterns. Thus, most analyses presented here use the "city sample," which includes residents of all central cities in the Northeast and Midwest. Appendix A contains details of the census sample and analyses.

2. Berry et al., *Chicago,* 2–11; Rast, *Remaking Chicago.* On the importance of transportation to Chicago's economy, see also Lewis Mandell, *Industrial Location Decisions: Detroit Compared with Atlanta and Chicago* (New York: Praeger Publishers, 1975), 35.

3. Slayton, *Back of the Yards,* 228; Rast, *Remaking Chicago,* 25–27, 66, 88; on the industrial parks, Berry et al., *Chicago,* 36.

4. On the minimum wage, see Ralph E. Smith and Bruce Vavrichek, "The Minimum Wage: Its Relation to Incomes and Poverty," *Monthly Labor Review* (June 1987): 24–30. In 1960 dollars, the city's tax revenues were $86,626,000 in 1948 and $148,153,000 in 1960; see *City and County Data Book* (Washington, DC: Bureau of the Census, 1949), 531; *City and County Data Book* (Washington, DC: Bureau of the Census, 1962), 504.

5. High school students were more costly to educate because high school teachers were paid more and their classes were smaller than their elementary school counterparts; see Herrick, *Chicago Schools,* 140.

6. On technological change, see Hogan, *Class and Reform,* 56–57. On credentials requirements, see chapter 5 of the present text. Chicago Board of Education, *Annual Report* (1913), 170, 285; Wild, "Special Divisions of the Chicago School System"; Tropea, "Bureaucratic Order and Special Children."

7. The state's Child Labor Law of 1903 required work permits for 14- to 15-year-olds leaving school and forbade workers under the age of sixteen years from operating heavy machinery or working more than eight hours a day. The Board of Education could now fine parents who did not send their children to school; fines ranged from $5 to $20. In 1904–5, the Compulsory Education Department sent more than 4,000 warnings to parents, and brought 451 parents into municipal court. On evasion of compulsory education laws, see e.g. Theresa Wolfson, "Why, When, and How Children Leave School," *The American Child* 1 (1919): 59–64. Accounts of evasion are also commonplace in oral history accounts. For additional regulations, see Chicago Board of Education, *Annual Report* (1913), 287; Chicago Board of Education, *Annual Report* (1918), 176–78; Strayer et al., *Survey of the Schools of Chicago,* vol. 1, 335.

8. Herrick, *Chicago Schools,* 180–81, 287–89. In 1960 dollars, my estimates of per-pupil state aid are $15.39 in 1900 and $13.97 in 1930.

9. Ibid., 141–42, 180–82.

10. Peterson, *Politics of School Reform,* 157–60; Herrick, *Chicago Schools,* 101–2, 179–90, 222.

11. See Wrigley, *Class Politics and Public Schools,* 200–260, on the politics of this period.

12. Herrick, *Chicago Schools,* 286–90.

13. Rury, "Race, Space, and the Politics of Chicago's Public Schools"; Herrick, *Chicago Schools,* 277–78.

14. On teachers' salaries, see Herrick, *Chicago Schools,* 198, 229–30, 292. The happy state of the school budget also allowed Superintendent Benjamin Willis a generous salary, which, according to *Time* magazine, made him the fourth most highly paid public official in the country; see "The Education of Big Ben," *Time,* August 30, 1963.

15. Because some teachers taught special small classes (special education, vocational education, or specialized subjects) or had other duties, most regular classes were larger than these figures indicate; Herrick, *Chicago Schools,* 140–41, 155–56, 225, 286; Peterson, *Politics of School Reform,* 157.

16. For excellent histories of the Great Migration and of ghetto formation in northern cities, see e.g. Peter Gottlieb, *Making Their Own Way: Southern Blacks' Migration to Pittsburgh, 1916–1930* (Urbana: University of Illinois Press, 1987); Grossman, *Land of Hope;* Kenneth Kusmer, *A Ghetto Takes Shape: Black Cleveland, 1870–1930* (Urbana: University of Illinois Press, 1976); Spear, *Black Chicago;* Joe William Trotter Jr., *Black Milwaukee: The Making of an Industrial Proletariat, 1915–45* (Urbana: University of Illinois Press, 1985). On suburbanization, see Hirsch, *Making the Second Ghetto;* Jackson, *Crabgrass Frontiers,* 190–219.

17. Sanders, *Education of an Urban Minority,* 4–5, 76, 164–69, 187–93; enrollment figures from Sanders were compared with Herrick's figures for public school enrollments in *Chicago Schools,* 403.

18. Sanders, *Education of an Urban Minority,* 203–23.

19. On the 1950s, see Mark J. Stern, "Poverty and Family Composition since 1940," in *The "Underclass" Debate: Views from History,* ed. Michael B. Katz (Princeton, NJ: Princeton University Press, 1993): 220–53. On benefits, also see chapter 2 of the present text.

20. Estimating trends in social indicators for public school students only is difficult because we have no information on the social characteristics of private school students prior to 1960. Public school students in 1960 were more disadvantaged than students overall; in 1960, the poverty rate was 9 percent among private school students, compared with 22 percent in the public schools. Although the presence of black students increased in the public schools, even more than in city schools overall, this change in racial composition was more than offset by the significant decline in poverty during the 1940s and 1950s. Poverty rates decreased significantly over this period among both white and black families, and by any reasonable estimate this shift far outweighed the rising proportion of black students in the public schools. If we use national poverty rates from Gerald David Jaynes and Robin M. Williams's *A Common Destiny: Blacks and American Society* (Washington, DC: National Academy Press, 1989), for instance, the poverty rate among public school students would have fallen from 53 percent in 1939 to 29 percent in 1959. Even using figures for northern populations, however, which show a more moderate drop in black and white poverty overall, the estimated poverty rates among public school students still fall, from 39 percent in 1939 to 26 percent in 1959.

21. For contemporary evidence, see e.g. Abbott and Breckinridge, *Truancy and Non-Attendance in the Chicago Schools;* Gertrude H. Britton, *An Intensive Study of the Causes of Truancy in Eight Chicago Public Schools including*

a Home Investigation of Eight Hundred Truant Children (Chicago: Hollister, 1906).

22. Chicago Commission on Race Relations, *Negro in Chicago*, 257–60, 271. Figures for percentage of students over age are averages for six black schools and twelve immigrant schools; failure rates are based on five black schools and eight immigrant schools. In the six black schools, the proportion of black students ranged from 70 percent to 93 percent. No information is available on the composition of the schools attended "mainly" by immigrants; Bousfield, "A Study of the Intelligence and School Achievement of Negro Children," 9. For Lieberson's discussion of this question, see *Piece of the Pie*, 233.

23. Lieberson, in *Piece of the Pie*, 200–206, used a different measure (a net difference index) and a slightly different mix of nationalities, but his results do not differ qualitatively.

24. William Henry Burton, "The Nature and Amount of Civic Information Possessed by Chicago Children of Sixth Grade Level" (Ph.D. diss., University of Chicago, 1924); Gertrude Whipple, "An Analytical Study of the Reading Achievement of Three Different Types of Pupils," (master's thesis, University of Chicago, 1927); Fanny Segalla, "Writing Vocabularies of Negro and White Children," *School Review* 42 (1934): 772–79; U.S. Immigration Commission, *The Children of Immigrants in Schools* (Washington, D.C., 1911), 2:554–57; Chicago Board of Education, *Annual Report* (1926), 102–4.

25. Havighurst, *Public Schools of Chicago*, 208–9.

26. See appendix A for details.

27. Measures of socioeconomic status were number of siblings and indicators for two-parent family, a parent in the labor force, and a parent with a white-collar occupation. Lieberson examined this question more than twenty years ago, with a wide range of evidence although without the IPUMS data, and came to much the same conclusion; see *Piece of the Pie*, 173–99.

Chapter Two

1. Lieberson, *Piece of the Pie*, 328–34, 354–59. Also see Smith, "Native Blacks and Foreign Whites."

2. Interview with Theodore Sajewski, OHP, 38. Interview with Avignone, IC, 45–46. Anthony Sorrentino, "It's an Inside Job," manuscript autobiography, Anthony Sorrentino papers, 1974, Chicago History Museum, p. 53.

3. Interview with Josephine Piegzik, OHP, 25. Interview with Florence Roselli, IC, 106–7. Jeannette Merk Gariss, "A Study of Women Clerical Workers in Chicago" (master's thesis, University of Chicago, 1942), 70–71.

4. Interview with Leonard Giuliano, IC, 67–69.

5. Wright, "Industrial Condition of Negroes in Chicago," 1, 12–15. On early twentieth-century opportunities for educated blacks, see Chicago Commis-

sion on Race Relations, *Negro in Chicago,* 391, 393; Drake and Cayton, *Black Metropolis,* 256–59. On nonprofits, see Bowles, "Opportunities for the Educated Colored Woman." Drake and Cayton discuss passing for white for economic reasons in *Black Metropolis,* 159–71.

6. Chicago Commission on Race Relations, *Negro in Chicago,* 380–83. On the opposition of white employees, see Washington, "Reconstruction and the Colored Woman," 4.

7. Chicago Urban League, *Annual Report,* 1937, pt. 2, sec. 1, 4. On the boycotts, see St. Clair Drake, "Churches and Voluntary Associations in the Chicago Negro Community," Report of Official Project 465–54–3–386 (Chicago: WPA, District 3, 1940), 247–54. On progress in white-collar jobs, Hyde Park–Kenwood Conference of Churches and Synagogues, "Negro Problems of the Community to the West," 23.

8. John A. Davis, "Nondiscrimination in the Federal Services," *Annals of the American Academy of Political and Social Science* 244 (March 1946): 65–74. Paul Burstein, *Discrimination, Jobs, and Politics: The Struggle for Equal Employment Opportunity in the United States Since the New Deal* (Chicago: University of Chicago, 1985), 7–9. On the antidiscrimination law in Illinois, which finally passed in 1961, see Drake and Cayton, *Black Metropolis,* xlviii. On workforce integration, see *A Fair Chance for All Americans,* Cantwell, Box 30, Folder 4; and President's Committee on Government Contracts, *Five Years of Progress, 1953–1958,* 6, 10, Cantwell, Box 30, Folder 4. For the speech by Berry, see "The Negroes' Role in the New Era," May 22, 1956, Cantwell, Box 29, Folder 7.

9. On the discriminatory job orders, see Drake and Cayton, *Black Metropolis,* xlvii. Albert H. Miller, "Negro in the North," *The Ave Maria—Catholic Home Weekly,* January 24, 1959, p. 6, Cantwell, Box 30, Folder 5.

10. For references to black government workers in supervisory roles, see Chicago Commission on Race Relations, *Negro in Chicago,* 375; Hyde Park–Kenwood Council of Churches and Synagogues, "Negro Problems of the Community to the West," 23–27.

11. Gosnell, *Negro Politicians,* 304, 318. On black representation in postal service, see Drake and Cayton, *Black Metropolis,* 295. Herrick, "Negro Employees," 41.

12. Gosnell, *Negro Politicians,* 231, 307. On racial discrimination, patronage, and other irregularities in civil service hiring, see discussions in Herrick, "Negro Employees"; Gosnell, *Negro Politicians;* Mayor's Committee on Race Relations, *City Planning in Race Relations,* 45–46. On the limited African-American benefits from the political machine in Chicago, see also Grimshaw, *Bitter Fruit.*

13. On segregation and government jobs for black professionals, see e.g. Jack Dougherty, "'That's when we were marching for jobs': Black Teachers and the Early Civil Rights Movement in Milwaukee," *History of Education Quarterly* 38 (1998): 121–41; Gosnell, *Negro Politicians,* 287–93. For the Siberia reference:

"The World's Fastest Mail Sorter," *Opportunity* (1923): 19. See also Frank T. Cherry, "Southern In-migrant Negroes in North Lawndale, Chicago 1949–59: A Study of Internal Migration and Adjustment," (Ph.D. diss., University of Chicago, 1965), 14. Faw, "Vocational Interests of Chicago Negro and White Junior and Senior Boys," 92.

14. On Polish employment in the public sector, see Kantowicz, *Polish-American Politics in Chicago*, 180–82.

15. See Cohen, *Making a New Deal*, 106–20, on ethnic businesses and the rise of chain stores.

16. Wright, "Industrial Condition of Negroes in Chicago," 18. Harold Lloyd Sheppard, "Conflicting Business Associations in Chicago's Black Belt" (master's thesis, University of Chicago, 1945), 19.

17. See e.g. Faw, "Vocational Interests of Chicago Negro and White Junior and Senior Boys."

18. Hale, "Negro Lawyer in Chicago," 66–67. Chicago Commission on Human Relations, "A Resolution concerning Alleged Discrimination against Negro Physicians in Chicago Hospitals," Cantwell, Box 31, Folder 1.

19. Charles S. Johnson, *The Negro College Graduate* (New York: Negro Universities Press, 1938), p. 14–18. Hyde Park–Kenwood Council of Churches and Synagogues, "Negro Problems of the Community to the West," 14. Also see Lieberson, *Piece of the Pie*, 331–32, on the declining proportion of black professionals.

20. There were returns to education even in manual occupations. Workers who spoke English tended to earn more, as did—in some instances—those with more education. However, credentials requirements were less common in blue-collar and service occupations, and the economic rewards of education less substantial.

21. See Beth Stevens, *Complementing the Welfare State: The Development of Private Pension, Health Insurance, and Other Employee Benefits in the United States* (Geneva: International Labour Organization, 1986), 13–20; Sanford M. Jacoby, *Modern Manors: Welfare Capitalism since the New Deal* (Princeton, NJ: Princeton University Press, 1998), 11–34; also see Cohen, *Making a New Deal*, 162–83. On early internal labor markets, see also William A. Sundstrom, "Internal Labor Markets before World War I: On-the-Job Training and Employee Promotion," *Explorations in Economic History* 25 (1988): 424–45; for later developments, see Jacoby, *Employing Bureaucracy*, 154–57, 171–205; David M. Gordon, Richard Edwards, and Michael Reich, *Segmented Work, Divided Workers: The Historical Transformation of Labor in the United States* (New York: Cambridge University Press, 1982), 162–227.

22. Cohen, *Making a New Deal*, 292–321; Jacoby, *Employing Bureaucracy*, 232–50, 262–69.

23. Paul Albert Joray, "The Temporary Industrial Labor Service Market in the Chicago and St. Louis Metropolitan Areas," (Ph.D. diss., University of Illinois, Champaign-Urbana), 34–46.

24. Grace Abbott, "The Chicago Employment Agency and the Immigrant Worker," *American Journal of Sociology* 14 (1908): 290–92. For black workers' low representation in manufacturing, Lieberson, *Piece of the Pie*, 313–19; also see Bowen, "Colored People of Chicago," 117–19.

25. On strikebreaking, Spero and Harris, *The Black Worker*, 264–68; Pacyga, *Polish Immigrants and Industrial Chicago*, 174–80.

26. For discussion of immigrant networks, see e.g. John Bodnar, Roger Simon, and Michael P. Weber, *Lives of Their Own: Blacks, Italians, and Poles in Pittsburgh, 1900–1960* (Urbana: University of Illinois Press, 1982), 56–59; Model, "Ethnic Niche and the Structure of Opportunity," 140–41; Slayton, *Back of the Yards*, 87; also see Roger Waldinger, *Still the Promised City? African-American and New Immigrants in Postindustrial New York* (Cambridge, MA: Harvard University Press, 1996), chap. 1. Anecdotal accounts of network-based recruitment are ubiquitous in oral histories and documentary sources. In a 1920s survey of working-class households, 15 percent of employed children of immigrants worked for the same firm as one of their parents, and 8 percent of employed black children did so as well; author's tabulations from the Cost of Living Survey, collected in 1925 for study by Leila Houghteling, *The Income and Standard of Living of Unskilled Laborers in Chicago* (Chicago: University of Chicago Press, 1927); survey schedules are in Special Collections, University of Chicago Libraries. Hereafter cited as "Houghteling survey." Perhaps half of youth jobs were found through networks: Larcomb, "Survey of Free Junior Placement in Chicago," 31; Ernest L. Talbert, *Opportunities in School and Industry for Children of the Stockyards District* (Chicago: University of Chicago Press, 1912), 22. Despite the adoption of more formalized employment procedures, informal recruitment, often through foremen, remained common; see Jacoby, *Employing Bureaucracy*, 161–63; Albert Rees and George Schulz, *Workers and Wages in an Urban Labor Market* (Chicago: University of Chicago Press, 1970); Roy W. Kelly, *Hiring the Worker* (Boston, 1918). Quotation from Nelson, "Study of an Isolated Industrial Community," 79–80.

27. See Chicago Commission on Race Relations, *Negro in Chicago*, 359–85; Grossman, *Land of Hope*, 181–207; Whatley, "Getting a Foot in the Door"; Washington, "Reconstruction and the Colored Woman."

28. Chicago Commission on Race Relations, *Negro in Chicago*, 364–67, 385–91; Alma Herbst, *The Negro in the Slaughtering and Meat Packing Industry in Chicago* (New York: Arno & The New York Times, 1971); Grossman, *Land of Hope*, 206–7, quotation from p. 196; Washington, "Reconstruction and the Colored Woman," 6. Also see Lieberson, *Piece of the Pie*, 335–39. Wage discrimination, in which black and white workers in the same jobs were paid different wages, was probably unusual, in part because of the scrutiny of white workers themselves. On pay disparities, see Whatley, "Getting a Foot in the Door"; Spero and Harris, *The Black Worker*, 174–77. Chicago Commission on Race Relations, *Negro in Chicago*, 365; cf. 398–99.

29. On the CIO, see Cohen, *Making a New Deal*, 292–301. Drake and Cayton, *Black Metropolis*, 250–52; Oscar D. Hutton Jr., "The Negro Worker and the Labor Unions in Chicago" (master's thesis, University of Chicago, 1939), 52–55. "All Clad in Shining Armor . . . With Dirty Underwear!" (Chicago: Chicago Urban League, 1942), CAP, Box 21, Folder 4. Chicago Urban League, *Annual Report*, (Chicago: Chicago Urban League, 1938), pt. 2, sec. 1, 10. See Maloney, "Wage Compression and Wage Inequality between Black and White Males in the United States, 1940–1960."

30. Model, "Ethnic Niche and the Structure of Opportunity." See also Palmore, "Introduction of Negroes," 51–52, on turnover and the role of white informal cliques in resisting integration. For an interpretation which emphasizes employer incentives, see Whatley, "Getting a Foot in the Door."

31. Palmore, "Introduction of Negroes," 15–16, 27, 34–35.

32. Chicago Urban League, "The Dynamics of Job Changing: A Case Study of Employment Conditions for Black Workers in the Chicago Labor Market," Report Number Two in the Chicago Urban League's Studies of the Labor Market (Chicago: Chicago Urban League, n.d.). See also Sugrue, *Origins of the Urban Crisis*, 125–52. For other discussions of declining relative employment and labor market status, see Gerald D. Jaynes, "The Labor Market Status of Black Americans: 1939–1985," *Journal of Economic Perspectives* 4:9–24; Robert S. Fairlie and William A. Sundstrom, "The Emergence, Persistence, and Recent Widening of the Racial Unemployment Gap," *Industrial and Labor Relations Review* 52 (1999): 252–70; Model, "Ethnic Niche and the Structure of Opportunity."

33. On wage compression, see Claudia Goldin and Robert Margo, "The Great Compression: The Wage Structure in the United States at Mid-Century," *Quarterly Journal of Economics* 107 (1992): 1–34; Maloney, "Wage Compression and Wage Inequality between Black and White Males in the United States, 1940–1960."

34. The analyses were conducted using years of education (as a continuous variable) as well as with a series of dummy variables indicating levels of schooling. Figure 2.7 is based on the latter. Results of the two types of models were consistent.

35. The family budgets available from the Houghteling survey show that for many home owners, rental income was a significant share of total household income. Some schedules, collected in 1925, also detail a number of transactions in which immigrant families sold at a significantly higher price than they had originally paid for the residence.

36. Abram L. Harris, *The Negro as Capitalist* (Philadelphia: The American Academy of Political and Social Science, 1936), 144–48. On race and housing in the postwar period, see Jackson, *Crabgrass Frontiers*. For discussions of race and homeownership, see Dalton Conley, *Being Black, Living in the Red: Race, Wealth, and Social Policy in America* (Berkeley and Los Angeles: University of California Press, 1999); Melvin Oliver and Tom Shapiro, *Black*

Wealth/White Wealth: A New Perspective on Racial Inequality (New York: Routledge, 1995).

37. Merrill, "A Report concerning the Plans of 596 Children on Leaving the Eighth Grade"; Faw, "Vocational Interests of Chicago Negro and White Junior and Senior Boys," 92; Schwartz, "Vocational Ambitions of Two Groups of Negro Girls," 31, 33, 86. Also see Julia Hermione Lorenz, "The Reading Achievements and Deficiencies of Ninth Grade Negro Pupils," (master's thesis, University of Chicago, 1937), 12, 33. Focus group, Former Residents of the Woodlawn Community, August 4, 1993, Center for the Study of Urban Inequality, University of Chicago. Chicago Urban League, "Proposed Project in Guidance for Negroes in Chicago," Cantwell, Box 29, Folder 7, dated mid-1950s by internal evidence. Bowen, "Colored People of Chicago," 117–19.

Chapter Three

1. See for instance Fordham and Ogbu, "Black Students' School Success"; Portes and Zhou, "The New Second Generation." Massey and Denton, in *American Apartheid,* 167–70, link the emergence of oppositional culture to the rise of segregation in northern cities in the 1920s.

2. On immigrant elites, see e.g. Bodnar, *Transplanted,* 117–43; Morawska, *For Bread with Butter,* 222–65. Also see Joseph Wierczerzak, "Pre- and Proto-Ethnics: Poles in the United States before the Immigration 'After Bread,'" *The Polish Review* 21 (1976): 7–38. For examples of immigrant elite concerns about Americans' opinions, see Thomas Capek, *The Czech (Bohemian) Community in New York* (New York: America's Making, Inc., 1921), 259–60; Schiavo, *Italians in Chicago.* On African-American elites in Chicago, including their concern about white opinion, see Spear, *Black Chicago,* 51–89; Grossman, *Land of Hope,* 129–40; Drake and Cayton, *Black Metropolis,* 526–64; also see Shaw, *What a Woman Ought to Be and Do,* 74.

3. Judge Francis Borrelli, "'Little Italy' Raises Big Men for Chicago," *Chicago Herald and Examiner,* October 20, 1927. Black Women Oral History Project, "Interview with Alfreda Duster" (Schlesinger Library, Radcliffe College, 1978), 23. Harris, "Professional Negroes in Chicago," 47–48.

4. CFLPS: *Lietuva,* June 8, 1917; *Dziennik Zwiazkowy,* June 16, 1908. Also see Bodnar, *Transplanted,* 139–40.

5. For concerns about denationalization and efforts to maintain home-country culture, see e.g. Fainhauz, *Lithuanians in Multi-Ethnic Chicago,* 27–32; Schiavo, *Italians in Chicago,* 69–71; Eugene Ray McCarthy, "The Bohemians in Chicago and Their Benevolent Societies: 1875–1946" (master's thesis, University of Chicago, 1950), 11–12, 67–69; issues of *The New American,* a monthly magazine of the Polish Students and Alumni Association of America (available in Regenstein Library, University of Chicago).

6. Grossman, *Land of Hope*, 146–52. Helen Sayre, "Making Over Poor Workers," *Opportunity* 1 (1923): 17–18. "Set September 12 As 'Hold Job' Drive Week," *Chicago Defender*, clipping in CAP, Box 30, Folder 3.

7. CFLPS: *Denni Hlasel*, February 9, 1916; on educational organizations see *Denni Hlasel*, September 20, 1906, and July 27, 1911; *Lietuva*, October 16, 1908; *Bulletin of Italo-American National Union*, August 1931, March 1936. Also see Fainhauz, *Lithuanians in Multi-Ethnic Chicago*, 158–60.

8. CFLPS: *Denni Hlasel*, September 11, 1915; *Dziennik Zwiazkowy*, June 29, 1917; *L'Italia*, September 16, 1893; *Dziennik Zwiazkowy*, June 16, 1909; *Polonia*, August 28, 1919. Also see Hogan, *Class and Reform*, 129–33.

9. CFLPS: *Narod Polski*, June 29, 1921; see also *Narod Polski*, October 5, 1910. For discussion of the secular-clerical divide among Polish immigrants, see John J. Bukowczyk, *And My Children Did Not Know Me: A History of the Polish-Americans* (Bloomington: Indiana University Press, 1987), 45–48; Parot, *Polish Catholics in Chicago, 1850–1920*, 161–65; Edward R. Kantowicz, "Polish Chicago: Survival through Solidarity," in *Ethnic Chicago*, ed. Melvin G. Holli and Peter d'A. Jones, rev. ed., 223–24 (Grand Rapids, MI: William B. Eerdmans Publishing Company, 1984); among other immigrant groups, see Morawska, *For Bread with Butter*, 173–74; Andrew T. Kopan, "Greek Survival in Chicago: The Role of Ethnic Education, 1890–1980," in *Ethnic Chicago*, ed. Holli and Jones, 45–50; Horak, "Assimilation of Czechs in Chicago," 52–53.

10. On the division between supporters of W. E. B. Du Bois and Booker T. Washington among black Chicagoans, see Spear, *Black Chicago*, 79–84. Washington Intercollegiate Club of Chicago, *Wonder Book;* Drake and Cayton, *Black Metropolis*, 393–95, 515–16, 536–37; Shaw, *What A Woman Ought to Be and Do;* Paula Giddings, *In Search of Sisterhood: Delta Sigma Theta and the Challenge of the Black Sorority Movement* (New York: Morrow, 1988).

11. Grossman, *Land of Hope*, 147, 250–51. Washington Intercollegiate Club of Chicago, *Wonder Book,* 125. The children's page quotation is from the *Chicago Defender,* September 19, 1925, pt. 2, p. 2.

12. See e.g. Hogan, *Class and Reform,* 52–79. For contemporary discusions see Abbott and Breckinridge, *Truancy and Nonattendance in the Chicago Schools;* Sophonisba P. Breckinridge, *Family Welfare Work in a Metropolitan Community: Selected Case Records* (Chicago: University of Chicago Press, 1924).

13. Interview with Julia Matiashek, OHP, 21–22. On class sorting, see Zunz, *Changing Face of Inequality*, 340–51; Thomas Sugrue, "The Structures of Urban Poverty: The Reorganization of Space and Work in Three Periods of American History," in *The "Underclass" Debate*, ed. Michael B. Katz, 85–117 (Princeton, NJ: Princeton University Press, 1993); Nelli, *Italians in Chicago*, 203–11; Kantowicz, *Polish-American Politics in Chicago*, 23–26; Julius John Ozog, "A Study of Polish Home Ownership in Chicago" (master's thesis, University of Chicago, 1942).

14. Interview with Frank Bertucci, IC, 29; also see Nelli, *Italians in Chicago*, 235. In *The Transplanted*, 138–42, Bodnar emphasizes the continuing involvement of ethnic elites in working-class communities, but the people he highlights are clerics and political leaders.

15. Josef Chalasinski, "Parish and Parochial School among Polish Immigrants in America," CAP, Box 33, Folder 2, 9. Kantowicz, *Polish-American Politics in Chicago*, 26. See also Kornblum, *Blue-Collar Community*, 22–26; Lopata, *Polish Americans*, 61–62.

16. Gaetano DeFilippis, "Social Life in an Immigrant Community," 39, Burgess Box 130, Folder 2. See also interview with Julia Matiashek, OHP, 7–8; Antanas J. Van Reenan, *Lithuanian Diaspora: Konigsberg to Chicago* (New York: University Press of America, 1990), 65; Zand, *Polish Folkways in America*, 32.

17. CFLPS: *Dziennik Zwiazkowy*, 1922. Zand, *Polish Folkways in America*, 41–42. Gaetano DeFilippis, "Social Life in an Immigrant Community," 40, Burgess, Box 130, Folder 2. Also see Horak, "Assimilation of Czechs in Chicago," 117; Lopata, *Polish Americans*, 123–28.

18. See e.g. Coleman, "Social Capital in the Creation of Human Capital."

19. On the character of immigrant neighborhoods, see Gans, *Urban Villagers*, 36–41; Slayton *Back of the Yards*, 110–12; Kornblum, *Blue-Collar Community*, 21–29. For rates of home ownership, see chapter 2. As McGreevy notes in *Parish Boundaries*, 19, Catholic priests encouraged their parishioners to buy homes. In the 1925 Houghteling survey, 83 percent of the immigrant workers at the West Side McCormick tractor plant lived within a mile of the factory, as did all of those at a Far South Side International Harvester plant. On walking to work, Kornblum, *Blue-Collar Community*, 71. On taverns: among others, Slayton, *Back of the Yards*, 101–3. Cf. Zunz, *Changing Face of nequality*, 181–84.

20. On the fraternals, Dominic Candeloro, "Suburban Italians: Chicago Heights, 1890–1975," in *Ethnic Chicago*, ed. Holli and Jones, 239–68; Bodnar, *Transplanted*, 123–30; Slayton, *Back of the Yards*, 99; Myron Kuropas, "Ukrainian Chicago: The Making of a Nationality Group in America," in *Ethnic Chicago*, 169–213; Nelli, *Italians in Chicago*, 173–74. Also see Cohen, *Making a New Deal*, 144–47; Kornblum, *Blue-Collar Community*, 129–31, 191–202. On the parish: Slayton, *Back of the Yards*, 97–99; McGreevy, *Parish Boundaries*, 13–20; Nelson, "Study of an Isolated Industrial Community," 19–20; Giese, *Revolution in the City*, 50, 114–15. References to the role of the parish in the lives of Catholic immigrants, especially those from eastern Europe, are ubiquitous in oral histories, memoirs, and community studies.

21. Josef Chalasinski, "Parish and Parochial School among Polish Immigrants in America," CAP, Box 33, Folder 2. Kornblum, *Blue-Collar Community*, 69–70. Also see Emily Balch, *Our Slavic Fellow Citizens* (New York: Charities Publications Committee, 1910), 60. On the concern with character and moral-

ity in immigrant communities and the role of education in the status order, see also Slayton, *Back of the Yards,* 113; Morawska, *For Bread with Butter,* 245–48; Lopata, *Polish Americans.* For discussion of the relative "portability" of status characteristics such as income and education and status based in a specific place and primary group, see Elijah Anderson, *A Place on the Corner: A Study of Black Street Corner Men* (Chicago: University of Chicago Press, 1981), 31–53.

22. For instance, see Pacyga, *Polish Immigrants and Industrial Chicago,* 168–97, 238–57; Cohen, *Making a New Deal,* 292–321. One sign of the increasing legitimacy of labor is the inclusion of union contingents in municipal parades.

23. Kantowicz, *Polish-American Politics in Chicago,* 151–61.

24. Sanders, *Education of an Urban Minority,* 43–71, 121–31; Parot, *Polish Catholics in Chicago 1850–1920,* 142–60; S. M. Liguori, CSFN, "Polish American Sisterhoods and Schools to 1919," *Polish American Studies* 13 (1956): 72–76.

25. Harriet Clark Cade, "Statistics of Chicago Relief Agencies" (master's thesis, University of Chicago, 1927), 36, 89, 143. Also see Cohen, *Making a New Deal,* 57–64. Raymond E. Nelson and Edwin H. Sutherland, "The Problem of Constructing a Community Delinquency Index," circa 1933, Burgess, Box 138, Folder 6, 16, 18, 28. For the Chicago Area Project, see Steven Schlossman and Michael Sedlak, *The Chicago Area Project Revisited* (Santa Monica, CA: Rand, 1983).

26. Matthew Frye Jacobson, *Whiteness of a Different Color: European Immigrants and the Alchemy of Race* (Cambridge, MA: Harvard University Press, 1998). On white ethnic resistance and the response to it, see Hirsch, *Making the Second Ghetto,* 197–210.

27. On the changing character of the black elite, see Spear, *Black Chicago,* 71–89; Grossman, *Land of Hope,* 129–30; also Bart Landry, *The New Black Middle Class* (Berkeley and Los Angeles: University of California Press, 1987).

28. Drake and Cayton, *Black Metropolis,* 545–46, 660. Harris, "Professional Negroes in Chicago," 98. Also see "Effect of the Depression . . . Harrison, Proprietor of the Grand Hotel," 3, Burgess, Box 133, Folder 1. On the Colored Big Brothers, see "Colored Big Brothers of Chicago, Inc.," CAP, Box 30, Folder 7. In black schools in 1930, as chapter 4 discusses, about one-third of the teachers were black; around 1950, about half were. On the Chicago Urban League and the YMCA, see Grossman, *Land of Hope,* 141–43.

29. Drake and Cayton, *Black Metropolis,* 521, 531–36.

30. Ibid., 606–7, 688–710. In 1961, Drake and Cayton observed that the social clubs were as popular and widespread then as during the late 1930s, when they had conducted their earlier research; see the epilogue to the 1961 edition of *Black Metropolis,* xxii. Ehrenhalt, *Lost City,* 153–54, reports on these clubs in the 1950s, and estimates more than two thousand clubs.

31. Hale, "Negro Lawyer," 40. Harris, "Professional Negroes in Chicago," 69, 81. "Why Hoodlums?" *Chicago Defender,* September 4, 1943, CAP, Box 30, Folder 3. The historically black colleges, many of them church affiliated, incul-

cated a conservative dress and demeanor that clashed with the folk traditions of the African-American working class, which included styles of dress and display that the elite regarded as gaudy and offensive; Shaw, *What a Woman Ought to Be and Do,* 81–90; White and White, *Stylin',* 91–106.

32. Drake and Cayton, *Black Metropolis,* 521. See also Geneva Smitherman, *Black Talk: Words and Phrases from the Hood to the Amen Corner* (Boston: Houghton Mifflin, 1994). Shack, "Social Change in an Isolated Negro Community," 34. Smitherman defines *haincty* as "unpleasant, contentious; picky and petty"; *Miss Ann* is a derisive term for a white woman, but can also refer to "an uppity-acting Black woman, especially one who 'acts white' "; *moriney* is a term for an African American with a light, reddish complexion; *Black Talk,* 48, 130, 162.

33. Hale, "Negro Lawyer," 148. "Effect on Families . . . Visited in Company with Mrs. Bradburn, Truant Officer for the Colman and Farren Schools," case 4, Burgess, Box 133, Folder 1.

34. Drake and Cayton, *Black Metropolis,* 576–81, quotation is from p. 580; Kathryn M. Neckerman, "Divided Households: Extended Kin in Working-Class Chicago, 1924," *Social Science History* 19 (1995): 371–98. Also see Harvey W. Zorbaugh, *The Gold Coast and the Slum: A Sociological Study of Chicago's Near North Side* (Chicago: University of Chicago Press, 1929), 148, for a survey of the residential stability of black families in Chicago. Author's tabulations from the 1925 Cost of Living Survey. A similar difference appears in the 1940 U.S. Census. For middle-class enclaves, see "Former Residents of the Woodlawn Community, Focus Group," August 4, 1993; focus group conducted for "Communities in Transition," a project of the Center for the Study of Urban Inequality, University of Chicago. Also see description of Lilydale in Pardee, "A Study of the Functions of Associations in a Small Negro Community in Chicago."

35. In the 1925 Cost of Living Survey, almost no black men lived within a mile of their workplace, and black families spent 50 percent more on public transportation than immigrant families did. On the journey to work, see also Kornblum, *Blue-Collar Community,* 71, who finds that 91 percent of black workers at a South Side steel mill lived outside the community. Spear, *Black Chicago,* 93; Drake and Cayton, *Black Metropolis,* 612; Cohen, *Making a New Deal,* 148; Grossman, *Land of Hope,* 159.

36. On Chicago's "Stroll," White and White, *Stylin',* 225–32; Drake and Cayton, *Black Metropolis,* 603, 380. The black community on the West Side of Chicago, home to about 10 percent of the city's African-American population, has received little research attention; for an exception see Christopher Randolph Reed, "Beyond Chicago's Black Metropolis: A History of the West Side's First Century," *Journal of the Illinois State Historical Society* 92 (1999): 119–49. Drake and Cayton, *Black Metropolis,* 400. On the *Defender*'s continuing influence in the 1950s, and on the "Mayor of Bronzeville," see Ehrenhalt, *Lost City,* 148, 150–51.

37. On redemption and backsliding, see for instance Drake and Cayton, *Black Metropolis,* 615–17. On the permeability of boundaries between sacred and secular, consider Clarence Taylor, *The Black Churches of Brooklyn* (New York: Columbia University Press, 1994), 78–98; White and White, *Stylin',* 173–79. On the policy kings, Drake and Cayton, *Black Metropolis,* 524–25. On the problem of prostitution near middle-class buildings, see "Effect of the Depression . . . as Reflected upon Tenants in the Michigan Boulevard Garden Apartments in an Interview with Mr. Robert Taylor," Burgess, Box 133, Folder 1.

38. For the early period, see the discussions in Barrett, *Work and Community in the Jungle,* 188–239; Grossman, *Land of Hope,* 208–45. For the 1930s, see Cohen, *Making a New Deal,* 333–49.

39. On Thompson's administration, see Gosnell, *Negro Politicians,* 37–62. Grimshaw, *Bitter Fruit,* 47–114.

40. Drake and Cayton, *Black Metropolis,* 412–14.

41. E. Franklin Frazier, "Some Effects of the Depression on the Negro in Northern Cities," *Science and Society* 11 (1938): 489–99. Philip Jackson, "Black Charity in Progressive Era Chicago," *Social Service Review* 52 (1978): 400–417. Shack, "Social Change in an Isolated Negro Community," 45.

Chapter Four

1. Homel, *Down from Equality,* 2–6; Chicago Commission on Race Relations, *The Negro in Chicago,* 242.

2. Spear, *Black Chicago,* 22–23, 44–45; Grossman, *Land of Hope,* 253–55; Homel, *Down from Equality,* 7–14, 42–46. Chicago Commission on Race Relations, *The Negro in Chicago,* 245–56, quotations from pp. 245, 249.

3. See Herrick, *Chicago Schools,* 134, 267, and Homel, *Down from Equality,* 157, on school board representation. For numbers of black teachers, Homel, *Down from Equality,* 28. See Gosnell, *Negro Politicians,* 281–93, on discrimination in public school employment.

4. For contemporary evidence on educators' views of class segregation as undemocratic, see e.g. W. C. Bagley, "The Unit versus the Dual System of Vocational Education," *Educational Bi-Monthly* 9 (1915): 191–92; for more general discussion, see Wrigley, *Class Politics and Public Schools,* 78–87. Chicago Commission on Race Relations, *The Negro in Chicago,* 255.

5. Chicago Commission on Race Relations, *The Negro in Chicago,* 252–55; quotation is from p. 245. Spear, *Black Chicago,* 45–46. Homel, *Down from Equality,* 10–12.

6. Thomas Lee Philpott, *The Slum and the Ghetto: Neighborhood Deterioration and Middle-Class Reform* (New York: Oxford University Press, 1978), 115–45 on racial change in Chicago neighborhoods and 162–80 for discussion of the violence that often accompanied it; William M. Tuttle Jr., *Race Riot: Chi-*

cago in the Red Summer of 1919 (New York: Atheneum, 1970), documents the 1919 riot; William Julius Wilson, *The Declining Significance of Race: Blacks and Changing American Institutions*, 2nd ed. (Chicago: University of Chicago Press, 1980), 70–76, and Barrett, *Work and Community in the Jungle*, 219–24, discuss competition and racial tensions. On restrictive covenants, see Drake and Cayton, *Black Metropolis*, 179–84.

7. For racial composition of the schools, see Homel, *Down from Equality*, 2–6, 10–12; Chicago Commission on Race Relations, *The Negro in Chicago*, 242; Herrick, "Negro Employees," 92–105. Chicago Commission on Race Relations, *The Negro in Chicago*, 242; Homel, *Down from Equality*, 30–31, 34–42, 48–52.

8. On immigrants, see for instance Gosnell, *Black Politicians*, 291–92; Drake and Cayton, *Black Metropolis*, 180–82. Zorbaugh, *The Gold Coast and the Slum*, 148–49. Homel, *Down from Equality*, 36–40; as Grossman, *Land of Hope*, 118, describes, Wentworth was a hotly contested dividing line between the Black Belt and the predominantly Irish neighborhood immediately to the west. Chicago Commission on Race Relations, *The Negro in Chicago*, 254–56.

9. On the racial composition of Phillips High School, see Washington Intercollegiate Club of Chicago, *Wonder Book*, 45. On Englewood, Herrick, "Negro Employees," 29–30.

10. Homel, *Down from Equality*, 28–34; Washington Intercollegiate Club of Chicago, *Wonder Book*. For concern about the employment of black teachers, see also Jack Dougherty's case study of Milwaukee, *More Than One Struggle*.

11. Grossman, *Land of Hope*, 174. On the segregation and dismissal of civic service employees, see Henry Blumenthal, "Woodrow Wilson and the Race Question," *Journal of Negro History* 48 (1963): 6–7. Other moves toward segregation were regularly chronicled in *The Crisis* during the 1910s.

12. On the families of Englewood students, see Herrick, "Negro Employees," 29. On resistance to school segregation, see Homel, *Down from Equality*, 41–53.

13. Homel, *Down from Equality*, 152–56.

14. On racial inequality before 1930, see Peterson, *Politics of School Reform*, 78–80; Chicago Commission on Race Relations, *Negro in Chicago*, 243–44; Homel, *Down from Equality*, 63–70.

15. On restrictive covenants, Drake and Cayton, *Black Metropolis*, 179–84. Hyde Park–Kenwood Council of Churches and Synagogues, "Negro Problems of the Community to the West," 16, on the enrollment increase. Homel, *Down from Equality*, 175–76, discusses school officials' refusal to permit black students to transfer to white schools.

16. Homel, *Down from Equality*, 58–87 (on portables as "dog houses," see p. 75); Hyde Park–Kenwood Council of Churches and Synagogues, "Negro Problems of the Community to the West," 16–17.

17. On teachers in inner-city schools, see Gosnell, *Negro Politicians*, 287. Chicago Teachers College, "Report of the Curriculum Revision Committee," 59–67. Quotation from Hyde Park–Kenwood Council of Churches and Syna-

gogues, "Negro Problems of the Community to the West," 16. Homel, *Down from Equality*, 67−69.

18. Homel, *Down from Equality*, 134−45. For description of the Lilydale neighborhood, Pardee, "A Study of the Functions of Associations in a Small Negro Community in Chicago." For the school episode, see Homel, *Down from Equality*, 166−69.

19. Hyde Park–Kenwood Council of Churches and Synagogues, "Negro Problems of the Community to the West," 17. For discussions of black political and electoral participation during the 1920s and early 1930s, see Gosnell, *Negro Politicians*. Grimshaw, *Bitter Fruit*, continues this historical account after the 1930s, and discusses what he calls the "code of silence." On Bousfield, see Homel, *Down from Equality*, 162−64. "Dr. Bousfield Refuses Aid in School Fight," *Chicago Defender*, November 15, 1941.

20. For discussion of these organizations, see Hirsch, *Making the Second Ghetto*, 42−44; McGreevy, *Parish Boundaries*, 55−78. For their positions on school overcrowding, see Hyde Park–Kenwood Council of Churches and Synagogues, "Negro Problems of the Community to the West"; for the Chicago Teachers Union, see "Education for Better Intercultural Group Relations," 1945, CTU, Box 26, Folder 4; Chicago Council Against Racial and Religious Discrimination, "Proposed Statement of Objectives," September 15, 1943, CTU, Box 26, Folder 4. The National Education Association also spoke out against overcrowding in Chicago's public schools; see Harold Baron, "History of Chicago School Segregation to 1953," *Integrated Education* 1 (1963): 19.

21. Mayor's Committee on Race Relations, *City Planning in Race Relations*, 22, 30, 63. A copy of the pamphlet, "A 1944 Message about Chicago's Schools," can be found in Wirth, Box 21, Folder 2.

22. Mayor's Committee on Race Relations, *City Planning in Race Relations*, 29.

23. For discussion of the end of the McCahey-Johnson administration and of the new superintendent, Herold C. Hunt, see Herrick, *Chicago Schools*, 272−80. On the Committee to End Segregation in the Public Schools of Illinois, see Waitstill H. Sharp to Mary Herrick, December 13, 1950, and Committee to End Segregation in the Public Schools of Illinois, August 10, 1950, both in CSC, Box 10, Folder 3.

24. Chicago Commission on Human Relations, *Report*, 1945, 16−18.

25. Herrick, *Chicago Schools*, 284−85. Some documents concerning the activities of the Technical Committee can be found in Wirth, Boxes 21−22. Minutes of the Meeting of the Committee on Education, Training, and Research in Race Relations, the University of Chicago, January 27, 1950, p. 3, Wirth, Box 21, Folder 2.

26. On the response of the black community, see Louis Wirth to Herold Hunt, January 29, 1952, Wirth, Box 21, Folder 3. Amerman, "Impact of Intergroup Relations," 120−21. Minutes of the Meeting of the Technical Committee on the Chicago Public Schools, June 14, 1948, Wirth, Box 21, Folder 2, p. 2. On parent opposition to redistricting, see Minutes of the Meeting of the Technical Commit-

tee on the Chicago Public Schools, March 3, 1952, Wirth, Box 21, Folder 4. Louis Wirth to Herold Hunt, January 29, 1952, Wirth, Box 21, Folder 3.

27. Helen E. Amerman to Louis Wirth, May 28, 1951, Wirth Box 22, Folder 10. "Memorandum on Conferences of Mr. Campbell and Miss Amerman with Drs. Rogers and Lubera and Miss Stanek Regarding the Elementary School Redistricting Study, and the Events Preceding These Conferences," Wirth, Box 21, Folder 4.

28. Leonard Z. Breen to Louis Wirth, February 4, 1952, Wirth, Box 21, Folder 3.

29. Minutes of the Meeting of the Technical Committee on the Chicago Public Schools, March 3, 1952, Wirth, Box 21, Folder 4. On Hunt's departure, see Herrick, *Chicago Schools,* 296–300.

30. Hirsch, *Making the Second Ghetto,* 212–59. Figures calculated from Chicago Fact Book Consortium, *Local Community Fact Book: Chicago Metropolitan Area* (Chicago: Chicago Review Press, 1984). Changes in enrollment calculated from figures in Homel, *Down from Equality,* 81, and "Here's School-by-School Breakdown on Racial Head Count," *Chicago American,* October 14, 1964, CTU, Box 26, Folder 4.

31. On Willis's building campaign, Herrick, *Chicago Schools,* 309; Chicago Board of Education, *Annual Report,* 1963. "Here's School-by-School Breakdown on Racial Head Count," *Chicago American,* October 14, 1964, CTU, Box 26, Folder 4.

32. Amerman, "Impact of Intergroup Relations," 150–51. Chicago Branch, NAACP, "De Facto Segregation in the Chicago Public Schools."

33. On numbers of teachers, Herrick, *Chicago Schools,* 406. The new teacher assignment procedure is described in Chicago Board of Education, *Annual Report,* 1963, 37. For evidence about the relative desirability of black and white schools, see Graham et al., "An Investigation of the Chicago School Redistricting Program," 272; John A. Winget, "Teacher Inter-School Mobility Aspirations: Elementary Teachers, Chicago Public School System, 1947–48" (Ph.D. diss., University of Chicago, 1952). On substitutes, see Chicago Teachers Union, untitled document on school discipline, dated 1961 by internal evidence, CTU, Box 22, Folder 4.

34. On the NAACP research, Christopher Robert Reed, *The Chicago NAACP and the Rise of Black Professional Leadership, 1910–1966* (Bloomington: Indiana University Press, 1957), 175–77. Chicago Branch, NAACP, "De Facto Segregation in the Chicago Public Schools." For examples from the *Defender,* see "Says Most 100,000 Negro Students in State Attend Jim Crow Schools," *Chicago Defender,* September 10, 1955; "Claim Jim Crow Schools Here Outstrip Arkansas," *Chicago Defender,* October 5, 1957. Willis's response can be found in "Jones Blasts Segregation in Chicago Public Schools," *Chicago Defender,* September 27, 1958.

35. Mrs. Green's husband had been a protégé of Mayor Edward Kelly; see Grimshaw, *Bitter Fruit,* 105, 136. On the NAACP takeover, see Ehrenhalt, *Lost City,* 186. "Mrs. Green Defends Willis: 'Supreme Effort,' Says Lone Negro Board Member," *Chicago Defender,* April 7, 1962. On the graduation ceremony,

see "Mrs. Green Booed, Picketed at Dunbar H. S. Graduation," *Chicago Sun-Times,* June 20, 1963. See Nicholas Lemann, *The Promised Land: The Great Migration and How It Changed America* (New York: Alfred A. Knopf, 1991), 234, on the boycott.

36. On intercultural education, see Michael Olneck, "The Recurring Dream: Symbolism and Ideology in Intercultural and Multicultural Education," *American Journal of Education* 98 (1990): 147–74.

37. The new curriculum is documented in Chicago Teachers College, "Report of the Curriculum Revision Committee"; quotations are from pp. 164, 184, 199; research for the report was the dissertation project of John Bartky, appointed as head of Chicago Teachers College in 1938. Also see Jules Karlin and George J. Steiner, "Future Teachers Serve Their Community," *Chicago Schools Journal* 24 (1943): 68–74; Jules Karlin, *Chicago: Backgrounds of Education* (Chicago: Werkman's Book House, 1940).

38. William H. Johnson, "Teaching Americanism in the Chicago Public Schools," *Chicago Schools Journal* 22 (1940): 97–103. On the National Conference of Christians and Jews, see Edward G. Olsen, "A Quarter-Century of Service to American Schools," *Chicago Schools Journal* 34 (1953): 112–16. Intercultural education was extensively discussed in the *Chicago Schools Journal;* for instance see Mary G. Lusson, "A Working Program in Americanism in the Chicago Public Schools," *Chicago Schools Journal* 27 (1945): 10–13; Don C. Rogers, "Human Relations in the Chicago Public Schools," *Chicago Schools Journal* 29 (1947): 13; Amerman, "The Impact of Intergroup Relations," 203–9. On the black history curriculum, Mavis B. Mixon, "Teachers on a New Frontier," *Chicago Schools Journal* 24 (1942): 17–22. For other discussion of these activities, see Helen Bridgeman, Memorandum to Mr. Wirth, February 24, 1950, Wirth, Box 21, Folder 2; L. K. Bishop, "Education for Democracy," *Chicago Schools Journal* 31 (1949): 136–38.

39. On the psychological foundations of intercultural education, see William Van Til and George W. Denemark, "Review of Intercultural Education," CSC, Box 9, Folder 4, circa 1950. See also chapter 3 on ethnic elites. Clara Ingram Judson, "America, A Tapestry," *Chicago Schools Journal* 31 (1950): 161–64; "Stories of National Customs by Students in Kelly High School," from "The Kelly Community, A Survey by Students of the Thomas Kelly High School," 1938, CAP, Box 57, Folder 7.

40. Sema Williams Herman, "Sowing the Seed of Democracy," *Chicago Schools Journal* 28 (1946): 13, 14. On Senn High School, see Henrietta Hafemann, "Vitalizing Intercultural Relations," *Chicago Schools Journal* 28 (1947): 57. The survey results, entitled "What Do I Think?," are in CSC, Box 8, Folder 1, dated March 1949.

41. Marian Lovrien, "Studying an Urban Community," *Chicago Schools Journal* 31 (1950): 169–70.

42. Mayor's Committee on Race Relations, *City Planning in Race Relations*, 52.

43. Herold C. Hunt, "Chicago's Intercultural Relations Program," *Chicago Schools Journal* 31 (1949): 115. V. Johnson, "Teachers' Conceptions of Pupil-Discipline," 115.

44. See "Intercultural Education," WCFL radio talk show by Leo Shapiro of the Chicago Anti-Defamation League, and "Brotherhood—Pattern for Peace," WCFL radio talk show by Ethel Alpenfels of the National Conference of Christians and Jews, transcripts in CTU, Box 26, Folder 4. On the PTA discussion group, see "Report of Interviews with Dr. Pierce, Miss Stannick, Miss Herrick, Board of Education, Department of Curriculum Studies, and Mrs. Saperstien, Chicago Branch of the PTA, January 9, 10, 1950, Submitted by Helen Bridgeman," Wirth, Box 21, Folder 2.

45. On the controversy over Hunt's curriculum, see Herrick, *Chicago Schools,* 294–96. The PTA discussion group episode can be tracked through the Wirth papers; from Box 21, Folder 2, see "Report of Interviews with Dr. Pierce, Miss Stannick, Miss Herrick, Board of Education, Department of Curriculum Studies, and Mrs. Saperstien, Chicago Branch of the PTA, January 9, 10, 1950, Submitted by Helen Bridgeman"; Mary Herrick to Louis Wirth, January 17, 1950; "Memorandum to Mr. Wirth, Chairman, Technical Committee from Helen Bridgeman, Secretary of the Technical Committee," February 24, 1950.

46. Gordon Allport, *The Nature of Prejudice* (Reading, MA: Addison-Wesley, 1954). William Van Til and George W. Denemark, "Review of Intercultural Education," CSC, Box 9, Folder 4, circa 1950; also see descriptions of shop floor integration of the time. Louis Wirth to Representative Charles J. Jenkins, January 25, 1951, Wirth, Box 21, Folder 3. Herrick, *Chicago Schools,* 284–85. On the Companion Plan, see Amerman, "Impact of Intergroup Relations," 223. Also see "Du Sable Entertained at School," *Schurz Times,* November 23, 1950, vol. 27, no. 5, p. 7, in CSC, Box 10, Folder 3.

47. "Minutes, Workshop on Human Relations," December 15, 1950, CSC, Box 10, Folder 3, quotations from pp. 5–6. Chicago Branch, NAACP, "De Facto Segregation in the Chicago Public Schools."

48. For differences in white attitudes about integration based on the age of the child, see Alvin E. Winder, "White Attitudes towards Negro-White Interaction in an Area of Changing Racial Composition," (Ph.D. diss., University of Chicago, 1952). Also see Chicago Commission on Race Relations, *The Negro in Chicago,* 245–56. Also notable is the difference between the process of school integration and the cautious and incremental efforts at shop floor integration during the 1940s and 1950s. Chicago Branch, NAACP, "De Facto Segregation in the Chicago Public Schools," 93.

49. Becker, "Role and Career Problems," 75. "Report to Earl Johnson on the January 10, 1950, Meeting of the Committee on Human Relations, of the Cur-

riculum Council of the Chicago Public Schools," memo by Helen Bridgeman, Wirth, Box 21, Folder 2.

50. On the race of teachers in racially mixed and predominantly black schools, see Graham et al., "An Investigation of the Chicago School Redistricting Program," 297. Quotation from Schwartz, "Vocational Aspirations of Two Groups of Negro Girls," 71. Herrick, "Negro Employees," 29–30, and Homel, *Down from Equality,* 110, discuss relations between black students and white teachers and administrators at Englewood in the 1920s and 1930s. On the elementary school, see V. Johnson, "Teachers' Conceptions of Pupil-Discipline," 118. For other examples of insensitivity in mixed schools, see for instance Rosen, "The Story of a School That 'Changed' Successfully," 216–17.

51. "Mixed Schools in the Minority," *Chicago Defender,* September 21, 1957; Giese, *Revolution in the City,* 27 (emphasis in the original). "Racial Tension Flares at Fenger," *Chicago Defender,* March 23, 1957, p. 3. "Cops Smash New School Riot Here," *Chicago Defender,* October 4, 1958, p. 3.

52. On language courses, Chicago Board of Education, *Annual Report,* 1912, 113. Also see e.g. CFLPS: *Denni Hlasel,* January 19, 1913, January 16, 1916; *Mens Italica,* April 1929.

53. Chicago Branch, NAACP, "De Facto Segregation in the Chicago Public Schools," 89.

54. Hirsch, *Making the Second Ghetto,* 171–211. On these pressures in the Catholic Church, see especially McGreevy, *Parish Boundaries,* 79–110. In the unions, Cohen, *Making a New Deal,* 333–49, outlines elite positions, and Palmore, "Introduction of Negroes," 17–18, shows these were not universally shared among the rank and file.

Chapter Five

1. Suloway, "Chicago's High School Curriculums." On early manual training in Chicago, see Hogan, *Class and Reform,* 153–57. On the meaning of manual training, see Kliebard, *Struggle for the American Curriculum,* 128–33.

2. On the growth of clerical employment, see Mrazek, "Development of Commercial Education," 12; also Hogan, *Class and Reform,* 141–42. Claudia Goldin, *Understanding the Gender Gap: An Economic History of American Women* (New York: Oxford University Press, 1990), 106–7, 160–71, and Lisa M. Fine, *The Souls of the Skyscraper: Female Clerical Workers in Chicago, 1870–1930* (Philadelphia: Temple University Press, 1990), 77–103, discuss the shift to female clerical employment, the age and marriage bars, and the effect of standardization. On the mechanization of clerical work and standardization of clerical skills, Mrazek, "Development of Commercial Education," 17–19. On testing, Larcomb, "Survey of Free Junior Placement in Chicago," 72–76.

3. *State Occupational Legislation: A Marketing Laws Survey Publication* (Washington, DC: U.S. Department of Commerce, 1942), 382–83; *Occupational Licensing Legislation in the States* (Chicago: Council of State Governments, 1952), 78–80. For examples of training programs, see the discussions in Anne S. Davis, "A Study of Opportunities for Home Economists in Food Preparation," Occupation Studies no. 11 (Chicago: Chicago Vocational Guidance Bureau, 1926), and Anne S. Davis, "A Study of Mechanical Dentistry," Occupation Studies no. 9 (Chicago: Chicago Vocational Guidance Bureau, 1926).

4. On business education, see e.g. Michael Sedlak and Harold F. Williamson, *The Evolution of Management Education: A History of the Northwestern University J. L. Kellogg School of Management 1908–1983* (Urbana: University of Illinois Press, 1983).

5. Kliebard, *Schooled to Work*, 26–44; Krug, *Shaping of the American High School, 1880–1920*, 217–24. For developments in Chicago, see Wrigley, *Class Politics and Public Schools*, 48–54, 60–65.

6. Hogan, *Class and Reform*, 152–54; Wrigley, *Class Politics and Public Schools*, 50; Peebles, "History of Armour Institute of Technology," 5–14; Lelon, "Emergence of Roosevelt College," 130–31; Royster, "Graduates of the Pullman Free School of Manual Training," 3; Mrazek, "Development of Commercial Education," 31; Sanders, *Education of an Urban Minority*, 162–66. Also see Jacoby, *Employing Bureaucracy*, 68–69, on the emergence of corporation schools between 1900 and 1915. On the curricula of private schools, see Peebles, "History of Armour Institute of Technology," 53–56. Dunn, "Central Y.M.C.A. Schools of Chicago," 96–100, 218. Mrazek, "Development of Commercial Education," 131–33.

7. On certificate-based admissions, see Krug, *Shaping of the American High School, 1880–1920*, 151–54; Clyde Bowman Furst, *College Entrance Requirements* (New York: Educational Record, 1927). For admissions standards at Chicago-area colleges, see Chauncey Boucher, *The Chicago College Plan* (Chicago: University of Chicago Press, 1935), 276–77; Harold Francis Williamson and Payson S. Wild, *Northwestern University: A History, 1850–1975* (Evanston, IL: Northwestern University, 1976), 111. For the secondary-school programs at Chicago's private-sector schools, see Dunn, "Central Y.M.C.A. Schools of Chicago," 96–112, 136, 233–36; Royster, "Graduates of the Pullman Free School of Manual Training," 4; Peebles, "History of Armour Institute of Technology," 13. Also see Lelon, "Emergence of Roosevelt College," 130–31.

8. Enrollment figures are from Sanders, *Education of an Urban Minority*, 13; Herrick, *Chicago Schools*, 403; Mrazek, "Development of Commercial Education," 93; Dunn, "Central Y.M.C.A. Schools of Chicago," 164. The estimate of business college enrollment is likely to be on the high side; it is drawn from the City Club's 1912 *Report on Vocational Training in Chicago and Other Cities*, whose purpose was to urge the establishment of public school vocational education.

9. Kliebard, *Struggle for the American Curriculum*, 89–152; Ravitch, *Left Back*, 51–87. For a skeptical account of Thorndike's research, see Ravitch, *Left Back*, 64–69. The Douglas Commission is discussed in e.g. Kliebard's *Schooled to Work*, 33–35.

10. Hogan, *Class and Reform*, 159–61; Herrick, *Chicago Schools*, 117; Kliebard, *Schooled to Work*, 68–69. For examples of contemporary discussions, see Abbott and Breckinridge, *Truancy and Nonattendance in the Chicago Schools;* between 1900 and 1920, W. Lester Bodine, who served as director of compulsory education in the Chicago schools for some forty years, often reported in the schools' annual reports on efforts aimed at youth aged fourteen to years; see e.g. Chicago Board of Education, *Annual Report,* 1910, 32–34; Chicago Board of Education, *Annual Report,* 1915, 142–44.

11. Chicago Board of Education, *Annual Report,* 1902, 61–62. Chicago Board of Education, *Annual Report,* 1903, 13–16. Strayer et al., *Survey of the Schools of Chicago,* 3:208–14, 221–23; Albert W. Evans and J. O. Groves, "Technical Training for the High School Youth," *Chicago Schools Journal* 18 (1936): 31–32. The board had offered commercial courses sporadically before, including at its manual training school; see Hogan, *Class and Reform,* 158. For the curricula of the vocational schools, see for instance *Industrial and Commercial Education in Relation to Conditions in the City of Chicago* (Chicago: Chicago Association of Commerce), 57–59, which describes the technical curriculum at Lane; Mrazek, "Development of Commercial Education," 117–22, describes the commercial courses.

12. For discussion of the two-year programs, see Chicago Board of Education, *Annual Report,* 1912, 107–8; Mrazek, "Development of Commercial Education," 143. Business English is mentioned in Chicago Board of Education, *Annual Report,* 1915, 87, and occasionally in the board's *Proceedings* volumes. On the continuation schools, see e.g. Mortenson, "Report of the Superintendent of Schools"; Nona Goodwin, "Socializing Influences in a Part–Time School for Girls," *Chicago Schools Journal* 5 (1922): 4–9; Mrazek, "Development of Commercial Education," 121–22. On Washburne, see Strayer et al., *Survey of the Schools of Chicago,* 3:219–20.

13. On manual training, Chicago Board of Education, *Annual Report,* 1902, 51; Chicago Board of Education, *Annual Report,* 1905, 119; Chicago Board of Education, *Annual Report,* 1909, 146–47; Strayer et al., *Survey of the Schools of Chicago,* 3:224–25. On the industrial schools, see Chicago Board of Education, *Annual Report,* 1915, 85–86. Cf. Hogan, *Class and Reform,* 168–69. On time spent in manual training see e.g. "Manual Arts Work of the Upper Grade Boys at the Haines Practice School," *Educational BiMonthly* 9: 114–24.

14. "Lots of machinery": see Chicago Board of Education, *Annual Report,* 1912, p. 112. "Alfred G. Lane Technical School, September 17, 1934, Dedication," Chicago schools (public) files, Chicago History Museum. For early demand for

the commercial programs, see Chicago Board of Education, *Annual Report,* 1902, 61. For other discussion, see Chicago Board of Education, *Annual Report,* 1906, 125–26. Here, nonvocational degrees include "general" as well as "science" or "language." Vocational degrees included normal college preparatory, pharmacy, architecture, art, household arts, and all technical and commercial courses of study; technical and commercial courses accounted for the vast majority.

15. On Tilden students: Marston, "Shop Mathematics versus Algebra," 428. For the value of vocational training, see Cromwell, "Value of Trade Training Given in Hammond Technical-Vocational School," 16; W. Johnson, "A Suggested Program of Vocational Guidance"; Nathan, "Occupational Training and Employment of Commercial Graduates of Hirsch High School"; Royster, "Graduates of the Pullman Free School of Manual Training."

16. Fass, *Outside In,* 44–54, 61–63. Kliebard, *Schooled to Work,* 163–71. Although vocational guidance was becoming institutionalized, the emphasis was on scientific matching of applicants to jobs, not on guiding choice of school curriculum; see Jacoby, *Employing Bureaucracy,* 65–97. W. Johnson, "A Suggested Program of Vocational Guidance." Marie S. Ross, "The Use of Intelligence Tests in Our Schools," *Chicago Schools Journal* 5 (1922): 152–53; Central Council of High School Teachers, "Aspects of Vocational Guidance," *Chicago Schools Journal* 4 (1921): 86–91. For the platform of the National Vocational Guidance Association, see "The Principles of Vocational Guidance," *Chicago Schools Journal* 3 (1921): 298–302. See Wrigley, *Class Politics and Public Schools,* 173, on the demonstration.

17. On Chicago's Bureau, see Hogan, *Class and Reform,* 183–84; Anne S. Davis, "Report of the Bureau of Vocational Supervision from April 1 to October 1, 1914," *Educational BiMonthly* 9 (1915): 200–207; Arthur W. Waltz, "Vocational Education and the Vocational Guidance Bureau," *Chicago Schools Journal* 7 (1925): 161–67. Strayer et al., *Survey of the Schools of Chicago,* 2:204–9 documents infrequent testing and spotty record keeping around 1930; similarly, the *Chicago Schools Journal* reported only sporadic and unsystematic testing throughout the 1920s.

18. Frank A. Fucik, "Advice to High School Freshmen," *Chicago Schools Journal* 5 (1923): 400–401. On student choice of vocational curricula, also see Chicago Board of Education, *Annual Report,* 1912, 110–11. Strayer et al., *Survey of the Schools of Chicago,* 3:122–23. According to Strayer, in 1931 there were only 33 vocational advisors for all the city's 27 junior high schools and 24 high schools; in 1932 the number fell to 19. Also see Strayer et al., *Survey of the Schools of Chicago,* 2:197–204, on the inadequacy of career guidance in the Chicago schools. On students' limited access to guidance in curriculum selection during the 1930s, see also David B. Tyack, Robert Lowe, and Elisabeth Hansot, *Public Schools in Hard Times: The Great Depression and Recent Years* (Cambridge, MA: Harvard University Press, 1984), 162–63.

19. For figures on Catholic and public secondary school enrollment, see Sanders, *Education of an Urban Minority*, 13, and Herrick, *Chicago Schools*, 403. Peebles, "History of Armour Institute of Technology," 35. The Association Institute dropped its elementary school program in 1928. Although it continued to offer high-school-level training, enrollment in its commercial and technical high school programs fell during the 1920s and the Institute began to emphasize college-level courses; see Dunn, "Central Y.M.C.A. Schools of Chicago," 181–88. On the decline in private business colleges, see Federation of Women High School Teachers, "High School Education in Chicago," May 1934, Chicago History Museum. On Medill, see Mrazek, "Development of Commercial Education," 122.

20. Wrigley, *Class Politics and Public Schools*, 177–80. Strayer et al., *Survey of the Schools of Chicago*, 3:15. This interpretation is indebted to two historical accounts: David F. Labaree, *The Making of an American High School: The Credentials Market and the Central High School of Philadelphia, 1838–1939* (New Haven, CT: Yale University Press, 1988), which examines how educators at Philadelphia's Central High School sought to protect the economic value of its credentials, and Brint and Karabel's *Diverted Dream*, which shows educational institutions—in this case community colleges—as competing for training markets. Also see Randall Collins, *The Credential Society: An Historical Sociology of Education and Stratification* (New York: Academic Press, 1979).

21. Anne Davis, "Opportunities of Employment" (Chicago: School of Civics and Philanthropy, University of Chicago, 1911), 37–38. *A Study of Beginning Office Positions for Young Women*, Occupational Studies no. 5 (Chicago: Vocational Guidance Bureau, Office of the Superintendent, 1927), 13–14. See Carey, "Training in an All-Commercial High School," 171, on dissatisfaction with the four-year commercial graduates. Nathan, "Occupational Training and Employment of Commercial Graduates of Hirsch High School," 49–54, quotation from p. 54.

22. Lemann, *The Big Test*, 20–23. The Carnegie Foundation is quoted in W. Lloyd Sprouse, "The Development of College Admissions," *The Encyclopedia of Educational Research* (New York: MacMillan, 1950), 262. On the University of Chicago, see Pupa, "Manual for High School Principals on College Entrance Procedures," 56–57. Peebles, "History of Armour Institute of Technology," 136–37. For expressions of concern or changes in admissions policies at other Chicago-area schools, see Kearney and Moore, *A History: Chicago State University, 1867–1979*, 46–47; Dunn, "Central Y.M.C.A. Schools of Chicago," 248, 258–60; J. M. McCallister, "Reading Ability of Junior College Freshmen," *Chicago Schools Journal* 18 (1936): 24–26.

23. Chicago Board of Education, *Annual Report*, 1938, 126–27. Mrazek, "Development of Commercial Education," 126. Angus and Mirel, in *Failed Promise of the American High School*, 71–76, write that during the 1930s and 1940s, educators began to de-emphasize vocational education, believing that

many high school students were incapable of serious vocational training, and that many jobs did not require it.

24. On the selective vocational schools, see Havighurst, *Public Schools of Chicago,* 247–50, who reports that CVS, Dunbar, Flower, Jones, Prosser, and Richards had entrance criteria beyond the elementary school diploma. It is not clear when Lane became selective, but Donald R. Moore and Suzanne Davenport, "The New Improved Sorting Machine" (Madison, WI: National Center on Effective Secondary Schools, 1988), 58, 65, 233, referred to Lane as an exam school of long standing. For discussion of Jones, see Mrazek, "Development of Commercial Education," 127; Carey, "Training in an All-Commercial High School." On the admissions standards planned for the new CVS, see Chicago Board of Education, *Annual Report,* 1941, 497–99. On distributive education, see Havighurst, *Public Schools of Chicago,* 254–55.

25. On the Upper Vocational Centers, see W. Johnson, "New Opportunities for 'Slow Learners.'" Chicago Board of Education, *Annual Report,* 1941, 478–83. Havighurst, *Public Schools of Chicago,* 259.

26. Chicago Board of Education, *Annual Report,* 1937, 105.

27. On the University of Chicago, Pupa, "Manual for High School Principals on College Entrance Procedures," 56. Also see Robert M. Hutchins, "The State of the University: A Twenty-Year Report" (Chicago: University of Chicago, 1949), 7–8. For a general discussion of the adoption of the SAT and other college admission tests, see Lemann, *The Big Test,* 83–95. On the Illinois Plan, Pupa, "Manual for High School Principals on College Entrance Procedures," 53–57. On the University of Illinois, "News in Education," *Chicago Schools Journal* 38 (1956): 106. On the changing admissions policies at the Chicago Teachers College, see "News," *Chicago Schools Journal* 31 (1950): 237–38; "News," *Chicago Schools Journal* 33 (1952): 166; Raymond M. Cook, "A Five-Year Report," *Chicago Schools Journal* 34 (1953): 193–202; "News in Education," *Chicago Schools Journal* 39 (1957): 164.

28. Lester J. Schloerb, "Occupational Research," *Chicago Schools Journal* 20 (1939): 157. For enrollment figures, see Herrick, *Chicago Schools,* 403.

29. Chicago Board of Education, *Annual Report,* 1941, 175, 192–97, quotation from pp. 192–93. Brint and Karabel, *The Diverted Dream,* 7, 59–61. There are parallels with the process of "cooling out" that Burton Clark described in "The Cooling-Out Function in Higher Education," in *Education, Economy, and Society: A Reader in the Sociology of Education,* ed. A. H. Halsey, J. E. Floud, and C. A. Anderson, 513–21 (New York: Free Press, 1961).

30. Chicago Board of Education, *Annual Report,* 1941, 168–85. W. Johnson, "Our Schools, 1938–1939," 8. Quotation from William H. Johnson, "Parent Interview Day in the Chicago Public Schools," *Chicago Schools Journal* 28 (1946): 8.

31. Black Women Oral History Project, "Interview with Alfreda Duster" (Schlesinger Library, Radcliffe College, 1978), 5.

32. On scholarships, see Sybel Loughead and Katherine F. White, "A Survey of Scholarship Funds Available in Chicago," *Chicago Schools Journal* 8 (1925): 136–41. On the ethnic societies, see chapter 3 of the present text. Washington Intercollegiate Club of Chicago, *Wonder Book,* 13, 19, 38. Among the honor students feted in the *Wonder Book,* 29, are two winners of scholarships from Alpha Kappa Alpha and Delta Sigma Theta, a winner of a history scholarship from Hyde Park High School, and a winner of a "Morgan Park scholarship to Armour [a technical college]." For the 1909 figures, see U.S. Immigration Commission, *Children of Immigrants in Schools* (Washington, DC, 1911), 5:729–822.

33. Count of graduates from annual Chicago Board of Education *Proceedings* volumes. Also see Merrill, "A Report concerning the Plans of 596 Children on Leaving the Eighth Grade." For a similar finding, see Angus and Mirel, *Failed Promise of the American High School,* 90–92.

34. On the racial composition of Tilden in 1930, see Herrick, "Negro Employees."

35. Although some local educators believed that "Negro children took academic work because they thought it gave them better social standing" (Chicago Commission on Race Relations, *Negro in Chicago,* 269–70), the balance of evidence suggests that the job market was the more important factor. Even black elites were receptive to the idea of vocational training; see e.g. W. E. B. Du Bois and Augustus Dill, *The College-Bred Negro American* (Atlanta: The Atlanta University Press, 1910), 82–85. Bowen, "Colored People of Chicago," 117, 119. On opportunities for educated blacks around 1920, see also Chicago Commission on Race Relations, *Negro in Chicago,* 391–93; Bowles, "Opportunities for the Educated Colored Woman," 8–10. On the interest in commercial training, see e.g. A. Albertine Wetter, "A Glimpse into an Unusual Night School," *Chicago Schools Journal* 4 (1921): 132–34. Cromwell, "Value of Trade Training Given in Hammond Technical-Vocational School," 48.

36. "Wanted: More Negro Apprentices at Washburne Trade School," Chicago Area Chapter, Negro American Labor Council, June 1961, in CORE, Box 1, Folder 2.

37. Homel, *Down from Equality,* 119–22; Report of the National Conference of Negro Organizations, circa 1940–41, Gaines, Box 2; Chicago Board of Education, *Annual Report,* 1941, 169.

38. On the board's original intentions, see Homel, *Down from Equality,* 122. In June 1955, Dunbar was the only vocational or trade school with graduates in brick masonry, painting and decorating, shoe rebuilding, and tailoring; all of these were fields in which black men were represented at or near their proportion in the labor force in 1950. For information on enrollment and dropout rates at Dunbar, see "A Cursory Analysis of Membership Figures of Dunbar Trade School from 1943 through 1950," prepared by Ernestine V. Oldham, Wirth, Box 22, Folder 2. For information about Clifford Campbell and Dunbar, see

Kermit Holt, "Dunbar Chief Opens Way to Skilled Jobs," *Chicago Tribune*, July 15, 1951; Roi Ottley, "Dunbar Opens New Horizons for Negro," *Chicago Tribune*, November 29, 1953; Clifford Campbell, "The Dunbar Trade School: An Educational Experience in Human Engineering," all in the "Dunbar Vocational High School" file, Chicago History Museum. Havighurst, *Public Schools of Chicago*, 250.

39. Replogle, "Problems Encountered by Senior High School Students," 32, 49–50. Gudatis autobiography, Burgess, Box 134, Folder 5.

40. Replogle, "Problems Encountered by Senior High School Students," 32.

Chapter Six

1. "Our Little Tragedies," *Chicago Schools Journal* 5 (1923): 204–5. (The article is written anonymously by "a teacher.") Teachers expressed their views of the curriculum in a 1908 canvass of Chicago educators, summarized in Chicago Board of Education, *Annual Report,* 1908, 81–147; a number of teachers cited in this canvass noted the pressure to promote students who had not mastered the material; see Chicago Board of Education, *Annual Report,* 1908, 81, 83, 85, 88, 91.

2. For concern about grade retention and failure among educators in general, see e.g. David Tyack, *The One Best System: A History of American Urban Education* (Cambridge, MA: Harvard University Press, 1974), 199–203; Kliebard, *Struggle for the American Curriculum,* 102–4. For views of efficiency and grade retention among Chicago educators, see e.g. Weck, "Elimination of Waste in Education"; William J. Bogan, "Is the High School Part of the Public School System?" *Chicago Schools Journal* 10 (1928): 286; Wavrinek, "The Failing Pupil"; Wight, "Bureau of Standards and Statistics"; Willard N. Clute, "Promoting the Dull Pupil," *Chicago Schools Journal* 4 (1922): 389–90.

3. Chicago Board of Education, *Annual Report,* 1908, 81–147; see also Mary F. Willard, "Practical and Practicable Checks on the Elimination of Pupils," *Chicago Schools Journal* 3 (1920): 114–17; Wavrinek, "The Failing Pupil," 296. For discussions of mid- to late-nineteenth-century views, see Steven A. Gelb, "'Not Simply Bad and Incorrigible': Science, Morality, and Intellectual Deficiency," *History of Education Quarterly* 29, no. 3 (1989): 359–79; Barbara Finkelstein, *Governing the Young: Teacher Behavior in Popular Primary Schools in Nineteenth-Century United States* (New York: Falmer Press, 1989), 106–8.

4. Chicago Board of Education, "Report on Underfed Children," *Proceedings,* October 21, 1908. Mrs. Robert McMurdy, "School Children's Aid Society," *Chicago Schools Journal* 11 (1928): 95–97.

5. On the industrial course, Hogan, *Class and Reform,* 168–69; Chicago Board of Education, *Annual Report,* 1912, 102–3; Chicago Board of Education, *Annual Report,* 1915, 85. For discussion of the ungraded rooms, see Chi-

cago Board of Education, *Annual Report,* 1913, 170, 285; Wild, "Special Divisions of the Chicago School System"; Tropea, "Bureaucratic Order and Special Children." William Hedges, "A Year of Prevocational Work," *Educational Bi-Monthly* 7 (1913): 191–202, provides a review of the prevocational curriculum at Jackson School, which included physiology, nature study, and elementary physics as well as sewing, cooking, and mechanical drawing.

6. On the educational progress of "subnormal" children, see Chicago Board of Education, *Annual Report,* 1918, 51. On progress in the industrial and prevocational classes, ibid., 53. Quotations are from Chicago Board of Education, *Annual Report,* 1915, 86.

7. Chicago Board of Education, "Report of the Director of Special Schools for the School Year 1922–23," Special Collections, Columbia Teachers College.

8. Wavrinek, "The Failing Pupil," 295.

9. The *Chicago Schools Journal* was usually published monthly during the school year (less often during the 1930s, reflecting budget constraints), and included feature articles, summaries of books and articles, current events in the Chicago schools, a short "Questions & Answers" section, and sometimes summaries of reports issued by committees of teachers and administrators. During the late 1930s and early 1940s, it is likely the magazine's content was strongly influenced by the viewpoint of Superintendent William Johnson, who also was a frequent contributor to the magazine. The *Journal* was not overtly critical of any superintendent, although it did acknowledge some contemporary controversies over education. Contributors included central office administrators, school principals, teachers, and Chicago Normal School instructors. On occasion the *Journal* included articles by educators in other cities, but the focus was on Chicago.

10. For discussion of achievement testing in the Chicago schools, see Keener, "The Cleveland Survey Arithmetic Test," 336–40; Keener, "Ability in the Fundamentals of Arithmetic in Grade 5-B," 309; E. E. Keener, "Silent Reading Ability in 4-A Grade," *Chicago Schools Journal* 6 (1923): 51–53; Wight, "Bureau of Standards and Statistics," 123; E. E. Keener, "Spelling in the Chicago Schools," *Chicago Schools Journal* 7 (1925): 291–94. On intelligence testing, see Richards, "Reliability of Mental Tests"; Keener, "A Mental Ability Test in First Year High School." In 1932, George Strayer's research found that some schools did no standardized testing; in others, testing was "haphazard and sporadic"; see Strayer et al., *Survey of the Schools of Chicago,* 2:12–13, 108–9; Strayer et al., *Survey of the Schools of Chicago,* 3:69. For statistical training for teachers, see for instance Geyer, "Can We Depend upon the Results of Group Intelligence Tests? [I]"

11. Tobin, "Classification in 6-A and After," 131. On Ray School, see Rape, "What Mental Tests Mean to the Class-Room Teacher," 18.

12. Bartholf's letter was quoted in "News of the Chicago Schools," *Chicago Schools Journal* 8 (1925): 149; also see Prinsen, "Failure Prevention at Mayfair

Branch," 58. Judith R. Raftery, "Missing the Mark: Intelligence Testing in Los Angeles Public Schools, 1922–32," *History of Education Quarterly* 28 (1988): 73–93, also notes skepticism about intelligence testing among public school educators.

13. Richards, "Reliability of Mental Tests," 372. Schiavo, *Italians in Chicago,* 111–13. The review of Carl Brigham's book is found in *Chicago Schools Journal* 6 (1923): 78; it was written by Denton Geyer, an expert on educational measurement at the Chicago Normal School; see also "Periodicals," *Chicago Schools Journal* 5 (1922): 37.

14. On teachers' reflection on test results, see Wight, "Bureau of Standards and Statistics," 122–23. For other discussions of test results and their interpretation, see Keener, "The Cleveland Survey Arithmetic Test," 342–43; E. E. Keener, "Statistical Methods for the Class Room Teacher," *Chicago Schools Journal* 5 (1922): 108–10; E. E. Keener, "Improving the Technique of Instruction," *Chicago Schools Journal* 5 (1923): 168. For the test-retest studies, see E. E. Keener, "Improving Instruction in Silent Reading," *Chicago Schools Journal* 7 (1924), 62; Keener, "Ability in the Fundamentals of Arithmetic in Grade 5-B," 309–11.

15. On measured teaching, see Wight, "Bureau of Standards and Statistics," 123–24; "News of the Chicago Schools," *Chicago Schools Journal* 5 (1923): 377–78. For the Corkery remedial class, see Catherine F. Lynch, "Corrective Practice with a Slow Group in Silent Reading," *Chicago Schools Journal* 6 (1924): 305–8. For a similar account, see Corretta Williams and Merrill McCabe, "Improvement of Reading Ability in a Fourth Grade Class," *Chicago Schools Journal* 6 (1923): 54–56.

16. There was methodological progress over the decade; see E. E. Keener, "How to Study in High School," *Chicago Schools Journal* 11 (1929): 167–69, which describes a randomized experiment used to test the efficacy of instruction in study skills.

17. Levitt, "Opportunity Walks Right In," 205. Also see Bixler, "High School Problem Cases"; Morse, "Reducing Failures at Harrison Technical High School"; H. W. Sumner, "Health and Home Factors in Non-Promotions," *Chicago Schools Journal* 9 (1926): 101–3.

18. See e.g. McCoy, "Individual Differences in Junior High Schools"; Gonnelly, "Development of the Junior High School in Chicago"; Prinsen, "Failure Prevention at Mayfair Branch"; Morse, "Reducing Failures at Harrison Technical High School"; Strayer et al., *Survey of the Schools of Chicago,* 3:66. Marston, "Shop Mathematics versus Algebra."

19. Quotation from Anna F. Carpenter, "Oral English in the Elementary School," *Chicago Schools Journal* 4 (1921): 29. On the English Center, see also James Fleming Hosic, "Chicago English Centers," *Chicago Schools Journal* 1 (1918): 9–10; Katherine M. Parker, "The Aftermath of the English Drive,"

Chicago Schools Journal 5 (1923): 188–89; Jane E. Miles, "New Light on Teaching Primary Reading," *Chicago Schools Journal* 5 (1923): 283–85.

20. For instance, Laughlin, "Measuring School Efficiency"; Weck, "Elimination of Waste in Education." For a perceptive discussion relating curriculum differentiation and homogeneous grouping to the social efficiency and Progressive movements, see Fass, *Outside In,* 38–72.

21. For minimum essentials at the national level, see Kliebard, *Struggle for the American Curriculum,* 161–62. For Chicago, see Chicago High School Teachers, "Syllabus of a Course in French for High Schools, Presenting Minimum Essentials for Each Grade," *Chicago Schools Journal* 4 (1921): 134–36; Sophia C. Camenisch, "Minimum Essentials in High School English," *Chicago Schools Journal* 4 (1922): 211–15. For minimum essentials in instruction for slow learners, see Morse, "Reducing Failures at Harrison Technical High School," 26. Also see Tobin, "Classification in 6-A and After"; "Curriculum Making in Chicago—II," *Chicago Schools Journal* 9 (1927): 210–15. For discussion of the curriculum revision, see "News for Chicago Schools," *Chicago Schools Journal* 13 (1930): 85–86.

22. On the Dalton Plan, see e.g. Tyack and Cuban, *Tinkering toward Utopia,* 94–97. On individualized education in Chicago, see James E. McDade, "Individualizing Education," *Chicago Schools Journal* 8 (1926): 216–17; James H. Henry, "Individual Advancement and Instruction under Chicago Conditions," *Chicago Schools Journal* 8 (1925): 100–103; Eston V. Tubbs, "The Bureau of Curriculum," *Chicago Schools Journal* 11 (1929): 179; James McDade, "Questions on Individual Learning," *Chicago Schools Journal* 11 (1929): 281–83.

23. In today's parlance, homogeneous grouping usually concerns instructional groups within the classroom; in early twentieth-century Chicago, it usually referred to sorting students between classes. For the *Journal's* support of homogeneous grouping, see "Questions and Answers," *Chicago Schools Journal* 3 (1921): 248; "Questions and Answers," *Chicago Schools Journal* 4 (1921): 149–50; "Questions and Answers," *Chicago Schools Journal* 4 (1922): 401; Geyer, "Can We Depend upon the Results of Group Intelligence Tests? [I]." See also Wight, "Bureau of Standards and Statistics." For accounts of other cities, see "General Education News," *Chicago Schools Journal* 4 (1921): 75–77; Denton Geyer, "Can We Depend upon the Results of Group Intelligence Tests? [II]" *Chicago Schools Journal* 4 (1922): 245–53; Ella Luedemann, "Outline of Methods of Dealing with Gifted Children," *Chicago Schools Journal* 5 (1923): 388–90.

24. On homogeneous grouping in the junior high schools, see Keener, "Homogeneous Classification of Junior High School Pupils." See Gonnelly, "Development of the Junior High School in Chicago"; also see "News of Chicago Schools," *Chicago Schools Journal* 7 (1924): 107. On the acceleration scheme, see McCoy, "Individual Differences in Junior High Schools." For experiments with grouping, see for instance Richards, "Reliability of Mental Tests"; Rape, "What Mental Tests Mean to the Class-Room Teacher." Although there was some grouping in high schools, both de facto because of student self-selection into ac-

ademic and vocational curricula and as a result of limited efforts at grouping students, contemporary accounts indicate that Chicago high school students were not comprehensively and systematically tracked by test score. "Cities Reporting the Use of Homogeneous Groups, the Winnetka Technique and the Dalton Plan," *City School Leaflet,* no. 22 (Washington, DC: U.S. Bureau of Education, December 1926), reports that Chicago grouped secondary students homogeneously. But the reports of local educators indicate that systematic grouping was limited to students in junior high school and did not extend to the senior high schools; see Gonnelly, "Articulation between Junior and Senior High Schools"; McCoy, "Individual Differences in Junior High Schools"; Joint Committee Report on Articulation, "Junior-Senior High Adjustment Problems."

25. "Why Teachers Are Leaving the Profession," *Chicago Schools Journal* 3 (1920): 86–87; contrast with "Questions and Answers," *Chicago Schools Journal* 4 (1921): 38. School administrators argued that intelligence testing could protect teachers' ratings, because those working with low-intelligence students wouldn't be expected to move through the curriculum as quickly; see Laughlin, "Measuring School Efficiency," 129–31. Wrigley, *Class Politics and Public Schools,* 167–74, describes labor opposition to testing and tracking.

26. From the review of Charles W. Odell, *The Use of Intelligence Tests as a Basis of School Organization and Instruction* (Urbana: University of Illinois, 1922) by Denton Geyer, "Recent Books on Intelligence Tests," *Chicago Schools Journal* 5 (1923): 341–44. Keener, "Homogeneous Classification of Junior High School Pupils." Cf. Gonnelly, "Articulation between Junior and Senior High Schools." On the value for low-achieving students, see Rape, "What Mental Tests Mean to the Class-Room Teacher," 18–19. See also Richards, "Reliability of Mental Tests"; Keener, "Homogeneous Classification in Junior High Schools"; Fredrik L. Gjesdahl, "Type Adjustments to Individual Differences," *Chicago Schools Journal* 8 (1925): 92–95; Tobin, "Classification in 6-A and After." "Questions and Answers," *Chicago Schools Journal* 4 (1921): 38. Morse, "Reducing Failures at Harrison Technical High School."

27. Mortenson, "Report of the Superintendent of Schools," 69. Chicago Board of Education, "Report of the Director of Special Schools for the School Year 1922–23," Special Collections, Columbia Teachers College, 17–26. Also see Levitt, "Opportunity Walks Right In." On the ungraded rooms in black schools, see Chicago Commission on Race Relations, *Negro in Chicago,* 267.

28. Prinsen, "Failure Prevention at Mayfair Branch," 58. On McAndrew, see Wrigley, *Class Politics and Public Schools,* 157–61. Morse, "Reducing Failures at Harrison Technical High School," 19.

29. On testing, see Strayer et al., *Survey of the Schools of Chicago,* 2:12–13, 108–9; 3:69. For the complexity of scheduling in today's large urban high schools, see Brian DeLany, "Allocation, Choice, and Stratification within High Schools: How the Sorting Machine Works," *American Journal of Education* 99 (1991): 181–207. Richards, "Reliability of Mental Tests," 373. Strayer et al., *Survey of*

the Schools of Chicago, 2:194–95, describes the limited homogeneous grouping that Chicago high schools conducted, only within curricula, not across them. On differences in average test scores across the high school courses of study, see Richards, "Reliability of Mental Tests"; Keener, "A Mental Ability Test in First Year High School."

30. "Curriculum Making in Chicago—III," *Chicago Schools Journal* 9 (1927): 325–29; Eston V. Tubbs, "Our New Courses of Study," *Chicago Schools Journal* 13 (1930): 85–86. On the 1933 budget cuts, Herrick, *Chicago Schools,* 210.

31. Cohler, "Promotions: A Pragmatist's Viewpoint," 18. "Individual Differences: A Report by the Chicago Regional White House Conference Committee," *Chicago Schools Journal* 14 (1931): 153–56; Charlotte C. Rowe, "Individual Instruction in General Science," *Chicago Schools Journal* 15 (1933): 23, 25.

32. On Johnson, see Herrick, *Chicago Schools,* 224–25, 237–38.

33. Cohler, "Promotions: A Pragmatist's Viewpoint," 18–19. Lyle H. Wolf and Raymond M. Cook, "Elementary Principals' Conference Groups, II," *Chicago Schools Journal* 18 (1937): 179. Also see Vernon L. Bowyer, "An Ideal Elementary School," *Chicago Schools Journal* 18 (1936): 70–73; Cohler, "Primary Reading Program." Until the 1930s, although chronological age was a factor in elementary promotion decisions, teachers' judgment of academic achievement was more important; see Strayer et al., *Survey of the Schools of Chicago,* 2:5, 22. For opposition to social promotion, see W. H. Comstock, "The Ethics of Promotion," *Chicago Schools Journal* 9 (1927): 343–44. Also see Joint Committee Report on Articulation, "Junior High-Senior High Adjustment Problems," 118. On the 1C classes, W. Johnson, "Our Schools, 1938–1939," 1–2; Fallon, "The Pre-Reading Program"; Chicago Board of Education, *Annual Report,* 1941, 27–34.

34. Ray A. Bixler, "Evaluating and Reporting Pupil Progress," *Chicago Schools Journal* 19 (1937): 14. W. Johnson, "The Status of the Chicago School System for the Year 1936–1937," 3. For high school, Chicago Board of Education, *Annual Report* 1937, 109. Also see W. Johnson, "In-Service Education in Developmental Reading," for the rise in emphasis on nonacademic criteria. On the 1947 change in report cards, see William A. Pollak, "Time for Another Change in Report Cards?" *Chicago Schools Journal* 41 (1959): 114.

35. William H. Johnson, "Educational Policies for 1936–1937," *Chicago Schools Journal* 18 (1936): 2. For the two-track plan, see Chicago Board of Education, *Annual Report,* 1938, 84–86. On individualized instruction, see Chicago Board of Education, *Annual Report,* 1939, 43; Chicago Board of Education, *Annual Report,* 1941, 132–35, 143–47. For a reference to ability grouping, see Cohler, "Primary Reading Program." On the experience curriculum, Turner C. Chandler, "Trends in Elementary English," *Chicago Schools Journal* 18 (1937): 122.

36. Chicago Board of Education, *Annual Report,* 1937, 103–6. General Science had been advocated in the 1920s as suitable particularly for likely dropouts and for the non-college-bound; see J. E. Teder, "General Science in the Second-

ary Schools," *Chicago Schools Journal* 7 (1924):·53–59. On course enrollments see Strayer et al., *Survey of the Schools of Chicago,* 3:57–60; Chicago Board of Education, *Annual Report,* 1940, 384–93. By the late 1940s, some Chicago educators viewed high school academic standards as too low; see Butler Laughlin, "High School Reorganization," *Chicago Schools Journal* 30 (1949): 300–303. A 1950s study found that one of eight high school graduates had taken no mathematics at all, and more than half took neither physics nor chemistry. A committee of local educators recommended tougher graduation requirements; see Suloway, "Chicago's High School Curriculums"; "News in Education," *Chicago Schools Journal* 38 (1956): 102–7. The new requirements included four years of English and a total of three years of science or math courses; see Clay Gowran, "Students Like Science, High School Survey Indicates," *Chicago Tribune,* February 16, 1958.

37. Chicago Board of Education, *Annual Report,* 1937, 107; Chicago Board of Education, *Annual Report,* 1939, 130. On the perceived urgency of differentiation, see Chicago Board of Education, *Annual Report,* 1940, 119–20.

38. Chicago Board of Education, *Annual Report,* 1941, 185–89, 232, 237. Chicago Board of Education, *Annual Report,* 1963, 11. Havighurst, *Public Schools of Chicago,* 221. On advanced placement, see Rast, "Building a Program for the Heterogeneous High School"; "News in Education," *Chicago Schools Journal* 41 (1961): 330–31. On the novelty of the minimum essentials mathematics, see Chicago Board of Education, *Annual Report,* 1939, 108–9.

39. Chicago Board of Education, *Annual Report,* 1937, 97–98; Chicago Board of Education, *Annual Report,* 1938, 129. On the new testing program, see Chicago Board of Education, *Annual Report,* 1939, 42. Richard M. Page, "Division of Child Study Golden Anniversary," *Chicago Schools Journal* 30 (1949): 303–5. For the WPA Adjustment Project; see Chicago Board of Education, *Annual Report,* 1940, 228–30, 330–31.

40. Ryan, "Getting Down to Cases." William H. Johnson, "Individualized Methods of Learning," *Chicago Schools Journal* 20 (1939): 206. Also, on pupil management: "News," *Chicago Schools Journal* 18 (1937): 132. Cohler, "Remedial Reading Plan," 29, 32. On remedial classes, see Chicago Board of Education, *Annual Report,* 1937, 107. Also see Hicks, "Procedures of an Adjustment Teacher."

41. Chicago Board of Education, *Annual Report,* 1941, 183. Cohler, "Remedial Reading Plan." On phasing out English R, see Hicks, "Procedures of an Adjustment Teacher."

42. W. Johnson, "The Status of the Chicago School System for the Year 1936–1937"; Chicago Board of Education, *Annual Report,* 1937: 98; Chicago Board of Education, *Annual Report,* 1941, 477. Also see Francis Whalen, "An Ungraded Room," *Chicago Schools Journal* 19 (1938): 216–17; Bernardine G. Schmidt, "Vocational Guidance for the Mentally Deficient," *Chicago Schools Journal* 25 (1943): 25–30; Jacqueline White Baskin, "Vitalizing School Experi-

ences, I," *Chicago Schools Journal* 33 (1952): 138–45 and "Vitalizing Schools Experiences, II," *Chicago Schools Journal* 33 (1952): 187–93. Cf. Strayer et al., *Survey of the Schools of Chicago,* 2:97–98. On the Lower Vocational Centers, see W. Johnson, "New Opportunities for 'Slow Learners.'" Also see Barry M. Franklin, *From "Backwardness" to "At-Risk": Childhood Learning Difficulties and the Contradictions of School Reform* (Albany: SUNY Press, 1994).

43. On school-based research, see e.g. William H. Johnson, "The Eight Point Program in Chicago High Schools," *Chicago Schools Journal* 22 (1940): 1–9. The quotation is from W. Johnson, "In-Service Education in Developmental Reading," 55. (The exception was a pet project of Johnson's, "non-oral reading." Johnson had championed this technique for teaching reading, and the schools sponsored a large-scale evaluation study; the project was quietly dropped when an outside evaluation showed little effect. See Chicago Board of Education, *Annual Report,* 1937, 34–36; Chicago Board of Education, *Annual Report,* 1939, 41.)

44. Kearney, *A History: Chicago State University, 1867–1979,* describes the unsupportive environment for research at Chicago Teachers College (later renamed as Illinois State University). Also see Woodie T. White Jr., "The Decline of the Classroom and the Chicago Study of Education, 1909–1929," *American Journal of Education* 90 (1982): 144–74; Ellen Condliffe Lagemann, *An Elusive Science: The Troubling History of Education Research* (Chicago: University of Chicago Press, 2001).

45. The study is described in Frances A. Mullen, "Washington and Chicago Cooperate in Research," *Chicago Schools Journal* 38 (1957): 274; Mullen and Itkin, "Special Classes for the Mentally Handicapped." The study's matched-pair design compared academic progress among children on the educable-mentally-handicapped waiting list (who remained in the regular classes) and those placed in EMH classes; critics noted that placement of wait-listed children might reflect unusual academic or behavioral problems.

46. On language styles, see appendix B.

47. Bernard, "Homogeneous Grouping for Reading Instruction"; quotation from Rosen, "Story of a School That 'Changed' Successfully," 220.

48. See Adaline G. Bourke, "A Success Story in the Sixth Grade: Techniques Used to Teach Reading to a Defeated Boy," *Chicago Schools Journal* 40 (1959): 373–77; Betty Whamond Quenon, "Suggestions for the Improvement of Cumulative Records," *Chicago Schools Journal* 39 (1958): 209. W. Gloria Williams, "Teaching Language Arts on a Divisional Basis," *Chicago Schools Journal* 39 (1958): 146.

49. Gorman, "Character Education under Difficulties," 118. Jacqueline White Baskin, "Teaching Reading to Older Mentally Handicapped Pupils," *Chicago Schools Journal* 39 (1958): 152–58; Frances A. Mullen, "Research on the Education of the Mentally Handicapped," *Chicago Schools Journal* 41 (1959): 119–22.

50. Mullen and Itkin, "Special Classes for the Mentally Handicapped," 262; "Workshop on Human Relations," December 15, 1950, pp. 2, 12, 13, CSC, Box 10, Folder 3; Chicago Teachers Union, "Report on Retaining and Recruiting Teachers for High Transiency Schools," June 1, 1960, CTU, Box 34, Folder 8; Havighurst, *Public Schools of Chicago,* 186–98.

51. On the high representation of ungraded and 1C classes in predominantly black schools, see W. Johnson, "New Opportunities for 'Slow Learners.'" Becker, "Role and Career Problems," 54, 55. Havighurst, *Public Schools of Chicago,* 207–15. V. Johnson, "Teachers' Conceptions of Pupil-Discipline," 108.

52. "Workshop," December 15, 1950, CSC, Box 10, Folder 3, 13. V. Johnson, "Teachers' Conceptions of Pupil-Discipline," 108. "News in Education," *Chicago Schools Journal* 39 (1958): 37.

53. Havighurst, *Public Schools of Chicago,* 212, 216, 252–59, 267.

54. "A 'Basic Program' in Junior College," *Integrated Education* 1 (1963): 27.

55. "Seniors Offer Ideas for Improving DuSable," *DuSable Dial,* May 1959, CSC, Box 28, Folder 2.

56. Summers and Walden, "Adjusting Disabled Readers."

57. Wilhelmina G. Williams, "Remedial Reading on a Three-Track Plan," *Chicago Schools Journal* 20 (1938): 65–66. Also see Mary E. Williamson, "A Project in Socialized Free Reading," *Chicago Schools Journal* 19 (1937): 73–76.

58. Bernard, "Homogeneous Grouping for Reading Instruction," 138, 139. For school-level intensification of ability grouping, also see Rast, "Building a Program for the Heterogeneous High School"; Rosen, "Story of a School that 'Changed' Successfully."

59. Summers and Walden, "Adjusting Disabled Readers," 145.

60. Joseph J. Connery, "Experimenting with Upper Grade Centers," *Chicago Schools Journal* 38 (1956): 73. Figures on race and UGCs from "Here's School-by-School Breakdown on Racial Head Count," *Chicago American,* October 4, 1964. On the "continuous development plan," see Albert A. Briggs, "A Non-Graded Approach to the Primary Grades," *Chicago Schools Journal* 42 (1961): 175–79; Chicago Board of Education, *Annual Report,* 1962, n.p. Helen L. Quinn, "Developing a Program for the Master Teacher," *Chicago Schools Journal* 38 (1956): 25; on the summer schools and the special service teachers, see Chicago Board of Education, *Annual Report,* 1963, 12, 14. See also Zoralyn V. Solario, "The Role of the Master Teacher Is a Varied One," *Chicago Schools Journal* 38 (1956): 29–31.

Chapter Seven

1. On the social context of classroom interaction, see Philip Jackson, *Life in Classrooms* (New York: Holt, Rinehart, Winston, 1968), and Robert Dreeben,

On What is Learned in School (Reading, MA: Addison-Wesley, 1968). Engagement and its obverse, alienation, have received much attention from educational psychologists and sociologists of education, and a thorough and systematic review is far beyond the scope of this chapter. For a sampling, see Fred M. Newmann, "Reducing Student Alienation in High Schools: Implications of Theory," *Harvard Education Review* 51 (1981): 546–64; Jeremy D. Finn, *School Engagement and Students at Risk* (Washington, DC: NCES, 1993); Yair, "Educational Battlefields in America"; Ames, "Classrooms: Goals, Structures, and Student Motivation."

2. For empirical research linking engagement to academic success, see for instance Jeremy D. Finn and Donald A. Rock, "Academic Success among Students at Risk for School Failure," *Journal of Applied Psychology* 82 (1997): 221–34; James P. Connell, Margaret Beale Spencer, and J. Lawrence Aber, "Educational Risk and Resilience in African-American Youth: Context, Self, Action, and Outcomes in School," *Child Development* 65 (1994): 493–503. On engagement and learning, see also Fred M. Newmann, Helen M. Marks, and Adam Gamoran, "Authentic Pedagogy and Student Performance," *American Journal of Education* 104 (1996): 280–312; Phyllis C. Blumenfeld, "Classroom Learning and Motivation: Clarifying and Expanding Goal Theory," *Journal of Educational Psychology* 84 (1992): 272–81.

3. Frederick Erickson, "Transformation and School Success: The Politics and Culture of Educational Achievement," *Anthropology and Education Quarterly* 18 (1987): 335–56, 344. Metz, *Classrooms and Corridors*, 26–32; McDermott, "Social Relations as Contexts for Learning in Schools." On negotiations over work and order, see Arthur G. Powell, Eleanor Farrar, and David K. Cohen, *The Shopping Mall High School: Winners and Losers in the Educational Marketplace* (Boston: Houghton Mifflin, 1986), 66–117; also Hugh Mehan, *Learning Lessons: Social Organization in the Classroom* (Cambridge, MA: Harvard University Press, 1979).

4. Metz, *Classrooms and Corridors*, 154–57. Although Metz makes these points in a discussion of discipline in the school at large, they apply also to the classroom.

5. On authority without institutional backing, see Ann Swidler, *Organization without Authority: Dilemmas of Social Order in Free Schools* (Cambridge, MA: Harvard University Press, 1980), 55–82; Gerald Grant, *The World We Created at Hamilton High* (Cambridge, MA: Harvard University Press, 1990), 162–65. A classic discussion of legitimacy and schools, from which I adapt, is Meyer and Rowan, "Institutionalized Organizations." Coleman, "Social Capital in the Creation of Human Capital." Also see Anthony Bryk and Barbara Schneider, *Trust in Schools: A Core Resource for Improvement* (New York: Russell Sage Foundation, 2002).

6. Owenby, "Factors That Govern a Teacher's Desire to Be Assigned to a Difficult School," CTU, Box 26, Folder 4. On the prohibition against corporal

punishment, see Herrick, *Chicago Schools,* 52. For another discussion of discipline during this time, see Kate Rousmaniere, *City Teachers: Teaching and School Reform in Historical Perspective* (New York: Teachers College Press, 1997), 120–26. In her interviews with teachers in New York City, Rousmaniere learned that the rule against corporal punishment was unevenly enforced; scattered anecdotal evidence for Chicago suggests the same.

7. Chicago Board of Education, *Annual Report,* 1913, 285. Chicago Board of Education, *Annual Report,* 1918, 76–77. Wild, "Special Divisions of the Chicago School System," 10. Also see Tropea, "Bureaucratic Order and Special Children"; Strayer et al., *Survey of the Schools of Chicago,* 1:346–50.

8. For contemporary discussions of character education, see Charles E. Germane and Edith Gayton Germane, *Character Education* (New York: Silver, Burdett and Company, 1929). Henry C. McKown, *Character Education* (New York: McGraw-Hill Book Company, Inc., 1935); William E. Stark, *Every Teacher's Problems* (New York: American Book Company, 1922). Also see Stephen M. Yulish, *The Search for a Civic Religion: A History of the Character Education Movement in America, 1890–1935* (Lanham, MD: University Press of America, 1980). For the student's complaint, see Paul Cressey, "Report on Summer's Work with the Juvenile Protective Association of Chicago," Burgess, Box 129, Folder 5, p. 43.

9. Olice Winter, "The Modern High School," *Chicago Schools Journal* 15 (1933): 103. Carroll Edgar Brown, "The Language of Command," *Chicago Schools Journal* 14 (1932): 223–24. See also Sleezer, "Change in Methods of Teaching."

10. Quotation from Committee on Morals and Civics, Principals' Club, "Ethical Training: Not a New Duty," *Chicago Schools Journal* 4 (1921): 15–16. Chicago Board of Education, "Education for Citizenship," report prepared by the Committee on Civic Education of the Superintendent's Advisory Council of the Chicago Public Schools, Special Collections, Columbia Teachers College. Grace Newcomb, "We Adjust Ourselves to Junior High," *Chicago Schools Journal* 11 (1928–29): 94–95. Also see Anna E. Harmon, "Orienting First Graders," *Chicago Schools Journal* 22 (1940): 10–13. Quotation from Gorman, "Character Education under Difficulties," 120. On student activities, see Thomas W. Gutkowski, "Student Initiative and the Origins of the High School Extracurriculum: Chicago, 1880–1915," *History of Education Quarterly* 28 (1988): 49–72.

11. Sleezer, "Change in Methods of Teaching," 56–57. Wagenschein, "'Reality Shock,'" 55. Quotation from William L. Bodine, "Truant Officers Assume a New Role," *Chicago Schools Journal* 20 (1939): 110. "Preliminary Training at Montefiore Special School," Chicago Schools (public) files, Chicago History Museum.

12. "Truancy Program of the Chicago Area Project: Resume and Comments on the Activities of the Six Special Truant Officers, from October 1939, to June, 1940," CAP, Box 54, Folder 4, p. 23. For references to corporal punishment in

Chicago's public schools around 1940, see e.g. "Montefiore School Cases," Burgess, Box 127, Folder 8. Reference to "dummy room" is in "Meeting of the Truant Officers," Friday, April 12, 1940, CAP, Box 27, Folder 6, p. 4. Wagenschein, "'Reality Shock,'" 53.

13. Yair, "Educational Battlefields in America." Ames, "Classrooms: Goals, Structures, and Student Motivation." Jere Brophy, Martin Nystrand, and Adam Gamoran, "Instructional Discourse, Student Achievement, and Literature Achievement," *Research in the Teaching of English* 25 (1991): 261–90.

14. Ames, "Classrooms: Goals, Structures, and Student Motivation." James H. Block, "Making School Learning Activities Playlike; Flow and Mastery Learning," *The Elementary School Journal* 85 (1984): 65–75. On attribution see e.g. Carol Dweck, *Self-Theories: Their Role in Motivation, Personality, and Development* (Philadelphia: Taylor and Francis, 1999). On evasion, see Donald A. Hansen, "Lesson Evading and Lesson Dissembling: Ego Strategies in the Classroom," *American Journal of Education* 97 (1989): 184–208.

15. I. L. Roberts, "The Swift Continuation School," *Chicago Schools Journal* 6 (1923): 57–61; quotation is from p. 59. "An Interview in the First Person with a Young Delinquent at the Cook County Juvenile Detention Home," January 25, 1933, conducted by Joseph D. Lohman for Sociology 264, Burgess, Box 133, Folder 2.

16. Quotation from Ryan, "Getting Down to Cases," 126. Also see Gorman, "Character Education under Difficulties," 119. Bixler, "High School Problem Cases," 142.

17. Becker, "Role and Career Problems," 102.

18. Chicago Commission on Race Relations, *Negro in Chicago*, 247, 256, 265. For indirect evidence, see also Owenby, "Factors that Govern a Teacher's Desire to Be Assigned to a Difficult School," CTU, Box 26, Folder 4. Ione Mack, in her study of black female students in Chicago, reports impudent behavior provoked by a teacher's dictatorial treatment, but adds, "However, in many cases of relationship between Negro students and white teacher there were not the slightest traces of impudence." See Ione Margaret Mack, "The Factor of Race in the Religious Education of the Negro High School Girl" (master's thesis, University of Chicago, 1927), 71. Both black and immigrant youth were overrepresented among students sent to the special schools. In 1931, for instance, some 40 percent were black and half were Polish or Italian; see Chicago Board of Education, "Report of the Committee on the Nervous and Unstable Child," October 1931, Special Collections, Columbia Teachers College.

19. First and third quotations from Becker, "Role and Career Problems," 207, 48. Second quotation from V. Johnson, "Teachers' Conceptions of Pupil-Discipline," 114. Mary Herrick, "Experiment with Core Classes for Slow Learners at DuSable High School," CSC, Box 28, Folder 2, dated 1956. Chicago Teachers College, "Report of the Curriculum Revision Committee," 59.

20. Chicago Teachers College, "Report of the Curriculum Revision Committee," 60. Figures on assaults from "Disposition of Court Cases between April 1, 1955–February 28, 1961," CTU, Box 22, Folder 4.

21. Herrick, "Experiment with Core Classes for Slow Learners at DuSable High School," CSC Box 28, Folder 2. Similarly, in Chicago Teachers College, "Report of the Curriculum Revision Committee," 60, see the reference to the "mob spirit" of the runaway classroom.

22. Quotation from Wagenschein, "'Reality Shock,'" 61. Also see V. Johnson, "Teachers' Conceptions of Pupil-Discipline," 88, 108, 112–13. On teachers' attitudes, including the use of racial epithets in class, see for instance V. Johnson, "Teachers' Conceptions of Pupil-Discipline," 112. On racially mixed schools, see chapter 4.

23. Summers and Walden, "Adjusting Disabled Readers," 146 (emphasis in the original), 147, 148–49.

24. Quotations about Campbell from Roi Ottley, "Dunbar Opens New Horizons for Negro," *Chicago Tribune,* November 29, 1953, in clipping files for Dunbar Trade School, Chicago History Museum. For accounts of the incident, see Clifford J. Campbell to Dr. Hobart H. Sommers, February 26, 1952, Wirth, Box 22, Folder 2, and other materials in the same folder. Quotations from 2–3, 4.

25. "Minutes, Workshop on Human Relations, December 15, 1950," CSC, Box 10, Folder 3.

26. Gorman, "Character Education under Difficulties." Quotations from "Minutes, Workshop on Human Relations, December 15, 1950," CSC, Box 10, Folder 3, p. 7.

27. Becker, "Role and Career Problems," 209, observed that teachers in lower-class schools who had ties to the community had an advantage in maintaining discipline. "Effect of the Depression on Families in the Area between 46th and 54th, Michigan Avenue and the New York Central Tracks, Visited in Company with Mrs. Bradburn, Truant Officer for the Colman and Farren Schools," Burgess, Box 133, Folder 1. See "The Effect of the Depression as Reported by Margaret Bradburn," Burgess, Box 133, Folder 1, pp. 5, 8, for the foiled robbery attempt and for teachers' fears. For other evidence that teachers had become more fearful in inner-city neighborhoods, see Owenby, "Factors That Govern a Teacher's Desire to Be Assigned to a Difficult School," CTU, Box 26, Folder 4. V. Johnson, "Teachers' Conceptions of Pupil-Discipline," 116.

28. Chicago Commission on Race Relations, *Negro in Chicago,* 247, 250–51, quotation from p. 256.

29. V. Johnson, "Teachers' Conceptions of Pupil-Discipline," 115, 83; see p. 109 for a contrasting view. Chicago Teachers College, "Report of the Curriculum Revision Committee," 32. Also see Wagenschein, "'Reality Shock,'" 83; Becker, "Role and Career Problems," 108–9; Gorman, "Character Education under Difficulties."

30. V. Johnson, "Teachers' Conceptions of Pupil-Discipline," 107; Wagenschein, "'Reality Shock,'" 34, 51–52. In her interviews at a white school with parents of "moderate means," Johnson also heard that "the principal explains to incoming teachers—especially those who come from Negro schools, where they have been accustomed to shouting at the children, and executing a strong discipline—that, at School 'C,' strict discipline is not maintained"; see "Teachers' Conceptions of Pupil-Discipline," 121–22.

31. Becker, "Role and Career Problems," 70, 136–37.

32. There was school-to-school variation in the extent to which principals supported teachers; see Homel, *Down from Equality,* 107, for a 1934 incident in which a teacher was transferred for using corporal punishment. Chicago Teachers Union, "Report on Discipline," August 10, 1954; Chicago Teachers Union, "Chicago Teachers Union's Position on Discipline in the Schools," March 28, 1960; John M. Fewkes to Benjamin C. Willis, April 27, 1961; all three items in CTU, Box 22, Folder 4.

33. In addition to the evidence cited below, see for instance Homel, *Down from Equality,* 106–7. Quotations are from Becker, "Role and Career Problems," 73, 54. Interview with Leroy Lovelace in Foster, *Black Teachers on Teaching,* 47–48. See also Prudence Carter's discussion of tough teachers in "Balancing 'Acts': Issues of Identity and Cultural Resistance in the Social and Educational Behaviors of Minority Youth" (Ph.D. diss., Columbia University, 1999), 92–93.

34. Becker, "Role and Career Problems." On the missionary impulse, also see Wagenschein, "'Reality Shock,'" 72. V. Johnson, "Teachers' Conceptions of Pupil-Discipline," 119.

35. Horak, "Assimilation of Czechs in Chicago," 50–51. See for instance the dismissive comment, in a 1930s school staff discussion at a South Chicago school, that "most peasants beat all of their children routinely." Joe Barczak Staff Discussion, 11/17/32, in Burgess, Box 133, Folder 7.

36. Case 11, Ralph Buglio, in "Effect of the Depression on Families in the Area between 46th and 54th, Michigan Avenue and the New York Central Tracks, Visited in Company with Mrs. Bradburn, Truant Officer for the Colman and Farren Schools," Burgess, Box 133, Folder 1, p. 20.

37. Chicago Teachers College, "Report of the Curriculum Revision Committee," 37–40. "Montefiore School Cases," Burgess, Box 127, Folder 8. Schlossman and Sedlak, "Chicago Area Project Revisited," 29–31. Also see the comments by Robert L. Reinsch, "Minutes, Workshop on Human Relations," December 15, 1950, CSC, Box 10, Folder 3, p. 3. Gans, *Urban Villagers,* 66, reported that Italian youth in Boston's North End, despite their negative attitude toward the school, did not misbehave inside school. In *The Social Background of the Italo-American School Child: A Study of the Southern Italian Family Mores and Their Effect on the School Situation in Italy and America,* ed. Francesco Cordasco (Leiden: E. J. Brill, 1967), Leonard Covello wrote that Italian-American

students were alienated from the school, but manifested their disaffection mostly via truancy and school dropout. Also see Nelson, "Study of an Isolated Industrial Community," 212–13. Likewise, if the discussions of working-class (as opposed to "slum" or "underprivileged") children can be taken as primarily about white ethnic children, then teachers saw few problems of discipline in this group. The conspicuous discipline problems, most agreed, were presented by slum children on the one hand and privileged (and spoiled) children on the other; see Becker, "Role and Career Problems," 66–68.

38. Wagenschein, "'Reality Shock,'" 64. Interview with Nick Zaranti, IC, 10–11.

39. Becker, "Role and Career Problems," 52, 95.

40. Some might question whether the teachers quoted in this chapter might have exaggerated reports of classroom disorder in accord with their own racial and ethnic biases. Certainly, teachers' accounts reflected their own preconceptions, but the observations were too consistent across too many observers for there to be no underlying reality. Also of note: much of the interview material was collected by researchers associated with Louis Wirth and other faculty on the University of Chicago's Committee on Education, Training and Research in Race Relations. The work of this committee, as reflected in the archival record, is characterized by an unflinching descriptive realism about race relations in inner-city schools and by a commitment to civil rights and racial equality. Inevitably, faculty and students on this committee shared to some extent the racial preconceptions of their time, yet their association with this committee both reflected and promoted a critical consciousness as they carried out their research. Beyond these specific points about the credibility of the evidence, I am convinced that we can read these reports as useful evidence on classroom relations without accepting teachers' own preconceptions or their attributions of blame. See Robin D. G. Kelley's *Race Rebels: Culture, Politics, and the Black Working Class* (New York: Free Press, 1994), which reframes southern whites' complaints about the work ethic and public behavior of working-class African Americans, mining these accounts for insights about race relations in the South.

Conclusion

1. To date, most such research has taken one of two approaches. The first seeks to explain racial and ethnic differences in education, often by adjudicating between structural factors such as discrimination and cultural factors such as ethnic traditions. For examples, see Joel Perlmann, *Ethnic Differences: Schooling and Social Structure among the Irish, Italians, Jews and Blacks in an American City, 1880–1935* (Cambridge: Cambridge University Press, 1988); Lieberson, *Piece of the Pie;* Claudia Goldin, "Family Strategies and the Family Economy

in the Late Nineteenth Century: The Role of Secondary Workers," in *Philadelphia: Work, Space, Family and Group Experience in the Nineteenth Century*, ed. Theodore Hershberg (New York: Oxford University Press, 1981), 277–310. For the debate between structural and cultural explanations, see e.g. Stephen Steinberg, *The Ethnic Myth: Race, Ethnicity, and Class in America* (Boston: Beacon Press, 1981); Thomas Sowell, *Ethnic America: A History* (New York: Basic Books, 1981). The second offers a political narrative of the emergence of segregation and inequality in the northern schools. Examples include Homel, *Down from Equality;* Judy Jolley Mohraz, *The Separate Problem: Case Studies of Black Education in the North, 1900–1930* (Westport, CT: Greenwood Press, 1979); Vincent P. Franklin, *The Education of Black Philadelphia: The Social and Educational History of a Minority Community, 1900–1950* (Philadelphia: University of Pennsylvania Press, 1979); Dougherty, *More Than One Struggle*, as well as sections of many other histories.

　　2. See for instance Vanessa Siddle Walker, *Their Highest Potential: An African American School Community in the Segregated South* (Chapel Hill: University of North Carolina Press, 1996).

　　3. Meyer and Rowan, "Institutionalized Organizations." Tyack and Cuban, *Tinkering toward Utopia;* David Tyack, *Seeking Common Ground: Public Schools in a Diverse Society* (Cambridge, MA: Harvard University Press, 2003).

　　4. Derek Neal, "Why Has Black-White Skill Convergence Stopped?" NBER Working Paper 11090, 2005.

　　5. John R. Logan, "Choosing Segregation: Racial Imbalance in American Public Schools, 1990–2000," Lewis Mumford Center for Comparative Urban and Regional Research, 2002, http://mumford1.dyndns.org/cen2000/SchoolPop/SPReport/SPDownload.pdf. Charles T. Clotfelter, *After Brown: The Rise and Retreat of School Desegregation* (Princeton, NJ: Princeton University Press, 2004); Jonathan Kozol, *The Shame of the Nation: The Restoration of Apartheid Schooling in America* (New York: Crown, 2005).

　　6. Phillips and Chin, "School Inequality: What Do We Know?" On school budgeting procedures, see Rubenstein and Miller, "Allocating Resources within a Big City School District." The relevance of books, supplies, and lab equipment is obvious; for evidence that the physical design and condition of the school building may affect teacher retention and student learning, see Jack Buckley, Mark Schneider, and Yi Shang, *The Effects of School Facility Quality on Teacher Retention in Urban School Districts* (Washington, DC: National Clearinghouse for Educational Facilities, 2004).

　　7. Ross Rubenstein and Lawrence Miller, "Allocating Resources within a Big City School District: New York City after *Campaign for Fiscal Equity v. New York*," Policy Brief no. 31, Center for Policy Research, Maxwell School, Syracuse University, 2005.

　　8. Harry J. Holzer, *What Employers Want: Job Prospects for Less-Educated Workers* (New York: Russell Sage Foundation, 1997).

9. Kevin Dougherty, *The Contradictory College: The Conflicting Origins, Impacts, and Futures of the Community College* (Albany: SUNY Press, 1994); Grubb and Lazerson, *The Education Gospel,* 45–49.

10. Grubb and Lazerson, *The Education Gospel,* 51–54. On work-based learning, see Thomas R. Bailey, Katherine L. Hughes, and David Thornton Moore, *Working Knowledge: Work-Based Learning and Education Reform* (New York: Routledge Falmer, 2004).

11. Advancement Project and The Civil Rights Project, "Opportunities Suspended."

12. In "School Inequality: What Do We Know?" pp. 506–7, Philips and Chin report that 6 percent of teachers have been assaulted in schools whose student body is composed of less than 5 percent minorities, while 11 percent of teachers have ever been assaulted in schools with a minority proportion of 50 percent or more.

13. Advancement Project and The Civil Rights Project, "Opportunities Suspended." On the subject of subjective offences: Prudence Carter writes that African-American and Latino youth signal group identity through display of "Black cultural capital," including styles of language, dress, and interaction. This cultural capital may be misunderstood by teachers who believe it signals disrespect. Carter, *Keepin' It Real,* 67–69. Also see Pedro A. Noguera, "The Trouble with Black Boys: The Impact of Social and Cultural Forces on the Academic Achievement of African American Males," *Urban Education* 38 (2003): 431–50.

14. Richard Arum, *Judging School Discipline: Crisis of Moral Authority* (Cambridge, MA: Harvard University Press, 2003).

15. Harvard Civil Rights Project, "Opportunities Suspended," 31–39.

16. See e.g. Anyon, *Ghetto Schooling;* Noguera, *City Schools and the American Dream;* Richard Rothstein, *Class and School: Using Social, Economic, and Educational Reform to Close the Black-White Achievement Gap* (Washington, DC: Economic Policy Institute, 2004). On the achievement gap among young children, see Valerie E. Lee and David T. Burkam, *Inequality at the Starting Gate* (Washington, DC: Economic Policy Institute, 2002).

17. Neckerman, ed., *Social Inequality* (New York: Russell Sage Foundation, 2004). Jean Anyon, *Radical Possibilities: Public Policy, Urban Education, and a New Social Movement* (New York: Routledge, 2005).

18. See for instance Noguera, *City Schools and the American Dream,* pp. 40–41.

Appendix B

1. See Beryl Bailey, "A New Perspective on American Negro Dialectology," *American Speech* 11 (1965): 171–77; John L. Dillard, *Black English: Its History and Usage in the United States* (New York: Random House, 1972); William

Labov, *Language in the Inner City* (Philadelphia: University of Pennsylvania Press, 1972); John Baugh, *Black Street Speech: Its History, Structure, and Survival* (Austin: University of Texas Press, 1983); and Theresa Perry and Lisa Delpit, *The Real Ebonics Debate: Power, Language and the Education of African-American Children* (Boston: Beacon Press, 1998).

2. Thompson, "Reading Accomplishments of Colored and White Children," 36. Thompson noted on p. 56 that southern children tended to "elide the letter 'r' and final consonants preceded by a sibilant; and to abbreviate by elision such words as al'most." For the administrator's comment, see Fallon, "The Pre-Reading Program," p. 11. For other references to distinctive language styles or language difficulties among black children, see also Dean W. S. Gray, "Working Problems in Reading," *Chicago Schools Journal* 12 (1930): 190–92; W. Gloria Williams, "Pitfalls in Teaching Foreign Languages: Some Unsolved Problems in the Elementary School Program," *Chicago Schools Journal* 42 (1960): 26–29; Chicago Board of Education, *Annual Report,* 1963, 13; Havighurst, *Public Schools of Chicago,* p. 57.

3. Irene McEnroe, "Errors in Speech," *Chicago Schools Journal* 7 (1924): 135–37, quotations from p. 137. Examples in the article include "He done it," "We was tardy," "I puts it in my desk," "My name Mary Smith," "These are mines," "hisself," "mens," "I didn't do nothing."

4. The study is cited in Frederick Erickson, "Transformation and School Success."

5. Bousfield, "A Study of the Intelligence and School Achievement of Negro Children," 6, 70, 75.

6. Schiavo, *The Italians in Chicago,* 111. Also see Denton Geyer's brief and dismissive review of Carl Brigham's infamous book about race, ethnicity, and intelligence; the review is in *Chicago Schools Journal* 6 (1923): 78; as well as "Periodicals," *Chicago Schools Journal* 5 (1922): 37; "Periodicals," *Chicago Schools Journal* 7 (1924): 111.

Selected Bibliography

I list here all printed sources (including dissertations and theses) that I have cited more than once in the notes. For published sources cited only once, and for manuscript materials, the notes give the full publication information. Listed below are the manuscript collections consulted; abbreviations used in the notes are listed on the left.

Manuscript Collections

Burgess	Papers of Ernest W. Burgess, Special Collections, Regenstein Library, University of Chicago
Cantwell	Papers of Daniel Cantwell, Chicago History Museum (formerly the Chicago Historical Society), Chicago
CAP	Chicago Area Project, Chicago History Museum
CFLPS	Chicago Foreign Language Press Survey, Special Collections, Regenstein Library
CORE	Congress on Racial Equality, Chicago History Museum
CSC	Chicago Schools Committee, Chicago History Museum
CTU	Chicago Teachers Union, Chicago History Museum
Gaines	Papers of Irene McCoy Gaines, Chicago History Museum
IC	The Italians in Chicago, Balch Institute, Philadelphia
OHP	Oral History of Polonia, Chicago History Museum
Wirth	Papers of Louis Wirth, Special Collections, Regenstein Library

Note: Around 1935, students of Ernest Burgess, a University of Chicago sociologist, conducted a number of interviews of community members in the part of the South Side black community bounded by Forty-seventh Street, Fifty-first Street, South Park, and the New York Central tracks. The geographic boundaries of the area surveyed are included in the names of these documents, but are omitted from the note references to save space.

Printed Sources

Abbott, Edith, and Sophonisba P. Breckinridge. 1917. *Truancy and Non-Attendance in the Chicago Schools: A Study of the Social Aspects of the Compulsory Education and Child Labor Legislation of Illinois.* Chicago: University of Chicago Press.

Advancement Project and The Civil Rights Project. 2000. "Opportunities Suspended: The Devastating Consequences of Zero Tolerance and School Discipline Policies." Report from a National Summit on Zero Tolerance, Washington, DC, June 15–16.

Amerman, Helen Ely. 1954. "The Impact of Intergroup Relations on Non-Segregated Urban Public Education." Ph.D. diss., University of Chicago.

Ames, C. 1992. "Classrooms: Goals, Structures, and Student Motivation." *Journal of Educational Psychology* 84:261–71.

Angus, David L., and Jeffrey E. Mirel. 1999. *The Failed Promise of the American High School, 1890–1995.* New York: Teachers College Press.

Anyon, Jean. 1997. *Ghetto Schooling: A Political Economy of Urban Educational Reform.* New York: Teachers College Press.

Barrett, James. 1987. *Work and Community in the Jungle: Chicago's Packinghouse Workers 1894–1922.* Urbana: University of Illinois Press.

Becker, Howard S. 1951. "Role and Career Problems of the Chicago Public School Teacher." Ph.D. diss., University of Chicago.

Bernard, Mary J. 1958. "Homogeneous Grouping for Reading Instruction." *Chicago Schools Journal* 40:135–39.

Berry, Brian J. L., coord., and Irving Cutler et al. 1976. *Chicago: Transformations of an Urban System.* Cambridge, MA: Ballinger Publishing Co.

Bixler, Ray A. 1930. "High School Problem Cases." *Chicago Schools Journal* 13:141–43.

Bodnar, John. 1985. *The Transplanted: A History of Immigrants in Urban America.* Bloomington: Indiana University Press.

Bousfield, Maudelle Brown. 1931. "A Study of the Intelligence and School Achievement of Negro Children." Master's thesis, University of Chicago.

Bowen, Louise deKoven. 1913. "The Colored People of Chicago: Where Their Opportunity Is Choked—Where Open." *Survey* (November 1): 117–20.

Bowles, Eva D. 1923. "Opportunities for the Educated Colored Woman." *Opportunity* 1:8–10.

Brint, Steven, and Jerome Karabel. 1989. *The Diverted Dream: Community Colleges and the Promise of Educational Opportunity in America, 1900–1985.* New York: Oxford University Press.

Carey, Clarence B. 1948. "Training in an All-Commercial High School." *Chicago Schools Journal* 29:170–75.

Carter, Prudence L. 2005. *Keepin' It Real: School Success beyond Black and White.* New York: Oxford University Press.

Chicago Branch, NAACP. 1958. "De Facto Segregation in the Chicago Public Schools." *The Crisis* (February): 87–93, 126–27.

Chicago Commission on Race Relations. 1922. *The Negro in Chicago.* Chicago: University of Chicago Press.

Chicago Teachers College. [ca. 1940]. "Report of the Curriculum Revision Committee—A Teacher Training Program for Underprivileged Urban Committees." Chicago.

Clark, Kenneth. 1965. *Dark Ghetto: Dilemmas of Social Power.* New York: Harper & Row.

Cohen, Lizabeth. 1990. *Making a New Deal: Industrial Workers in Chicago, 1919–1939.* Cambridge: Cambridge University Press.

Cohler, Milton J. 1931. "Promotions: A Pragmatist's Viewpoint." *Chicago Schools Journal* 14:18–19.

———. 1937a. "Primary Reading Program." *Chicago Schools Journal* 18:124–28.

———. 1937b. "Remedial Reading Plan." *Chicago Schools Journal* 19:29–34.

Coleman, James S. 1988. "Social Capital in the Creation of Human Capital." *American Journal of Sociology* 94:S95–S121.

Cromwell, Eskin Emil. 1934. "Value of Trade Training Given in Hammond Technical-Vocational School as Indicated by Reports from 150 Former Students." Master's thesis, University of Chicago.

Dougherty, Jack. 2004. *More Than One Struggle: The Evolution of Black School Reform in Milwaukee.* Chapel Hill: University of North Carolina Press.

Drake, St. Clair, and Horace R. Cayton. [1945] 1962. *Black Metropolis: A Study of Negro Life in a Northern City.* Rev. ed. New York: Harper & Row.

Dunn, Frederick Roger. 1940. "The Central Y.M.C.A. Schools of Chicago: A Study in Urban History." Ph.D. diss., University of Chicago.

Ehrenhalt, Alan. 1995. *The Lost City: Discovering the Forgotten Virtues of Community in the Chicago of the 1950s.* New York: Basic Books.

Fainhauz, David. 1977. *Lithuanians in Multi-Ethnic Chicago until World War II.* Chicago: Lithuanian Library Press, Inc., and Loyola University Press.

Fallon, Minnie E. 1939. "The Pre-Reading Program." *Chicago Schools Journal* 21:10–21.

Fass, Paula. 1989. *Outside In: Minorities and the Transformation of American Education.* New York: Oxford University Press.

Faw, Volney. 1948. "Vocational Interests of Chicago Negro and White Junior and Senior Boys." Ph.D. diss., University of Chicago.

Fordham, Signithia, and John U. Ogbu. 1986. "Black Students' School Success: Coping with the Burden of 'Acting White.'" *Urban Review* 18:176–206.

Foster, Michele. 1997. *Black Teachers on Teaching.* New York: New Press.

Gans, Herbert J. 1962. *The Urban Villagers: Group and Class in the Life of Italian-Americans.* New York: Free Press.

Geyer, Denton. 1922. "Can We Depend upon the Results of Group Intelligence Tests? [I]" *Chicago Schools Journal* 4:203–10.

Giese, Vincent. 1961. *Revolution in the City.* Notre Dame, IN: Fides Publishers.

Gonnelly, Joseph F. 1929. "Development of the Junior High School in Chicago." *Chicago Schools Journal* 12:46–50.

———. 1932. "Articulation between Junior and Senior High Schools." *Chicago Schools Journal* 14:195–98.

Gorman, Susan L. 1939. "Character Education under Difficulties." *Chicago Schools Journal* 20:117–22.

Gosnell, Harold F. 1935. *Negro Politicians: The Rise of Negro Politics in Chicago.* Chicago: University of Chicago Press.

Graham, Polly, Ruth Weaver Halpern, Muriel Herson, and Irene Landkof Jerison. 1952. "An Investigation of the Chicago School Redistricting Program." Master's thesis, University of Chicago.

Grimshaw, William J. 1992. *Bitter Fruit: Black Politics and the Chicago Machine, 1931–1991.* Chicago: University of Chicago Press.

Grossman, James R. 1989. *Land of Hope: Chicago, Black Southerners, and the Great Migration.* Chicago: University of Chicago Press.

Grubb, W. Norton, and Marvin Lazerson. 2004. *The Education Gospel: The Economic Power of Schooling.* Cambridge, MA: Harvard University Press.

Hale, William Henri. 1949. "The Career Development of the Negro Lawyer in Chicago." Ph.D. diss., University of Chicago.

Harris, Ethel Ramsey. 1937. "A Study of Voluntary Social Activity among the Professional Negroes in Chicago." Master's thesis, University of Chicago.

Havighurst, Robert J. 1964. *The Public Schools of Chicago: A Survey for the Board of Education of the City of Chicago.* Chicago: Chicago Board of Education.

Herrick, Mary J. 1931. "Negro Employees of the Chicago Board of Education." Master's thesis, University of Chicago, 1931.

———. 1971. *The Chicago Schools: A Social and Political History.* Beverly Hills, CA: Sage Publications.

Hicks, Thelma F. 1941. "Procedures of an Adjustment Teacher." *Chicago Schools Journal* 22:157–65.

Hirsch, Arnold R. 1983. *Making the Second Ghetto: Race and Housing in Chicago, 1940–1960.* Cambridge: Cambridge University Press.

Hogan, David John. 1985. *Class and Reform: School and Society in Chicago, 1880–1930.* Philadelphia: University of Pennsylvania Press.

Homel, Michael W. 1982. *Down from Equality: Black Chicagoans and the Public Schools: 1920–41.* Urbana: University of Illinois Press.

Horak, Jakub. 1928. "Assimilation of Czechs in Chicago." Ph.D. diss., University of Chicago.

Hyde Park–Kenwood Council of Churches and Synagogues, Commission on Intercommunity Relationships. 1940. "The Negro Problems of the Community to the West." Chicago.

Jackson, Kenneth T. 1985. *Crabgrass Frontiers: The Suburbanization of the United States.* New York: Oxford University Press.

Jacoby, Sanford M. 1985. *Employing Bureaucracy: Managers, Unions, and the Transformation of Work in American Industry, 1900–1945.* New York: Columbia University Press.

Johnson, Virginia Lucille. 1951. "Teachers' Conceptions of Pupil-Discipline." Master's thesis, University of Chicago.

Johnson, William H. 1924. "A Suggested Program of Vocational Guidance." *Chicago Schools Journal* 7:47–50.

——. 1937. "The Status of the Chicago School System for the Year 1936–1937." *Chicago Schools Journal* 19:1–10.

——. 1939. "New Opportunities for 'Slow Learners.'" *Chicago Schools Journal* 20:153–56.

——. 1939. "Our Schools, 1938–1939." *Chicago Schools Journal* 21:1–10.

——. 1945. "In-Service Education in Developmental Reading." *Chicago Schools Journal* 26:49–57.

Joint Committee Report on Articulation. 1930. "Junior High-Senior High Adjustment Problems." *Chicago Schools Journal* 13:114–22.

Kantowicz, Edward R. 1975. *Polish-American Politics in Chicago: 1880–1940.* Chicago: University of Chicago Press.

Katznelson, Ira, and Margaret Weir. 1985. *Schooling for All: Race, Class, and the Democratic Ideal.* New York: Basic Books.

Kearney, Edmund W., and Maynard E. Moore. 1979. *A History: Chicago State University, 1867–1979.* Chicago: Chicago State University.

Keener, E. E. 1922. "The Cleveland Survey Arithmetic Test in Grade 5-B in Chicago." *Chicago Schools Journal* 4:336–44.

——. 1923. "Ability in the Fundamentals of Arithmetic in Grade 5-B." *Chicago Schools Journal* 5:309–11.

——. 1924. "A Mental Ability Test in First Year High School." *Chicago Schools Journal* 6:374–77.

——. 1926. "Homogeneous Classification of Junior High School Pupils." *Chicago Schools Journal* 9:51–55.

Kliebard, Herbert M. 1995. *The Struggle for the American Curriculum, 1893–1958.* 2nd ed. New York: Routledge.

——. 1999. *Schooled to Work: Vocationalism and the American Curriculum, 1876–1946.* New York: Teachers College Press.

Kornblum, William. 1974. *Blue-Collar Community.* Chicago: University of Chicago Press.

Krug, Edward. 1964. *The Shaping of the American High School, 1880–1920.* Vol. 1. Madison: University of Wisconsin Press.

Larcomb, Charles Murello. 1921. "Survey of Free Junior Placement in Chicago." Master's thesis, University of Chicago.

Laughlin, Butler. 1926. "Measuring School Efficiency." *Chicago Schools Journal* 9: 129–30.

Lareau, Annette. 2003. *Unequal Childhoods: Class, Race, and Family Life.* Berkeley and Los Angeles: University of California Press.

Laughlin, Butler. 1926. "Measuring School Efficiency." *Chicago Schools Journal* 9:129–30.

Lelon, Thomas Charles. 1973. "The Emergence of Roosevelt College of Chicago: A Search for an Ideal." Ph.D. diss., University of Chicago.

Lemann, Nicholas. 1999. *The Big Test: The Secret History of the American Meritocracy.* New York: Farrar, Straus & Giroux.

Levitt, Emma. 1930. "Opportunity Walks Right In: An Account of an Opportunity Room Conducted at the Yates School." *Chicago Schools Journal* 12:205–7.

Lieberson, Stanley. 1980. *A Piece of the Pie: Blacks and White Immigrants since 1880.* Berkeley and Los Angeles: University of California Press.

Lopata, Helena Znaniecka. 1976. *Polish Americans: Status Competition in the Ethnic Group.* Englewood Cliffs, NJ: Prentice-Hall.

Maloney, Thomas N. 1994. "Wage Compression and Wage Inequality between Black and White Males in the United States, 1940–1960." *Journal of Economic History* 54:358–81.

Marston, Elizabeth. 1931. "Shop Mathematics versus Algebra." *Chicago Schools Journal* 13:428–30.

Massey, Douglas, and Nancy Denton. 1993. *American Apartheid: Segregation and the Making of the Underclass.* Cambridge, MA: Harvard University Press.

Mayor's Committee on Race Relations. 1944. *City Planning in Race Relations: Proceedings of the Mayor's Conference on Race Relations.* Chicago.

McCoy, William T. 1929. "Individual Differences in Junior High Schools." *Chicago Schools Journal* 12:89–96.

McDermott, R. P. 1977. "Social Relations as Contexts for Learning in Schools." *Harvard Educational Review* 47:198–213.

McGreevy, John T. 1996. *Parish Boundaries: The Catholic Encounter with Race in the Twentieth-Century Urban North.* Chicago: University of Chicago Press.

Merrill, Letitia Fyffe. 1923. "A Report concerning the Plans of 596 Children on Leaving the Eighth Grade." *Chicago Schools Journal* 5:154–60.

Metz, Mary Haywood. 1978. *Classrooms and Corridors: The Crisis of Authority in Desegregated Secondary Schools.* Berkeley and Los Angeles: University of California Press.

Meyer, John W., and Brian Rowan. 1977. "Institutionalized Organizations: Formal Structure as Myth and Ceremony." *American Journal of Sociology* 83:340–63.

Mirel, Jeffrey. 1993. *The Rise and Fall of an Urban School System: Detroit, 1907–1981.* Ann Arbor: University of Michigan Press.

Model, Suzanne. 1993. "The Ethnic Niche and the Structure of Opportunity: Immigrants and Minorities in New York City." In *The "Underclass" Debate: Views from History,* ed. Michael B. Katz, 161–93 (Princeton, NJ: Princeton University Press, 1993).

Morawska, Ewa. 1985. *For Bread with Butter: Life-Worlds of East Central Europeans in Johnstown, Pennsylvania, 1890–1940.* Cambridge: Cambridge University Press.

Morse, Frank L. 1926. "Reducing Failures at Harrison Technical High School." *Chicago Schools Journal* 9:125–29.

Mortenson, Peter A. 1922. "Report of the Superintendent of Schools." *Chicago Schools Journal* 5:61–70.

Mrazek, Albie Frances. 1938. "Development of Commercial Education in the Chicago Public Schools." Master's thesis, University of Chicago.

Mullen, Frances A., and William Itkin. 1961. "The Value of Special Classes for the Mentally Handicapped." *Chicago Schools Journal* 42:353–63.

Nathan, Meyer Oscar. 1940. "Occupational Training and Employment of Commercial Graduates of Hirsch High School." Master's thesis, University of Chicago.

Nelli, Humbert S. 1970. *Italians in Chicago 1880–1930: A Study in Ethnic Mobility.* New York: Oxford University Press.

Nelson, Raymond Edward. 1929. "A Study of an Isolated Industrial Community: Based on Personal Documents Secured by the Participant Observer Method." Master's thesis, University of Chicago.

Noguera, Pedro. 2003. *City Schools and the American Dream: Reclaiming the Promise of Public Education.* New York: Teachers College Press.

Ogbu, John U. 1974. *The Next Generation: An Ethnography of Education in an Urban Neighborhood.* New York: Academic Press.

Pacyga, Dominic A. 1991. *Polish Immigrants and Industrial Chicago: Workers on the South Side, 1880–1922.* Columbus: Ohio State University Press.

Palmore, Erdman. 1954. "The Introduction of Negroes into Four White Industrial Departments." Master's thesis, University of Chicago.

Pardee, Ruth Evans. 1937. "A Study of the Functions of Associations in a Small Negro Community in Chicago." Master's thesis, University of Chicago.

Parot, Joseph John. 1981. *Polish Catholics in Chicago, 1850–1920: A Religious History.* De Kalb: Northern Illinois University Press.

Peebles, James Clinton. 1948. "A History of Armour Institute of Technology." Manuscript.

Peterson, Paul E. 1985. *The Politics of School Reform, 1870–1940.* Chicago: University of Chicago Press.

Phillips, Meredith, and Tiffany Chin. 2004. "School Inequality: What Do We Know?" In *Social Inequality,* ed. Kathryn M. Neckerman, 467–519. New York: Russell Sage Foundation.

Portes, Alejandro, and Min Zhou. 1993. "The New Second Generation: Segmented Assimilation and Its Variants." *Annals of the American Academy of Political and Social Sciences* 530:74–96.

Prinsen, George E. 1926. "Failure Prevention at Mayfair Branch." *Chicago Schools Journal* 9:55–58.

Pupa, Andrew N. 1953. "A Manual for High School Principals on College Entrance Procedures." Ed.D. diss., Columbia University.

Rape, Arthur O. 1924. "What Mental Tests Mean to the Class-Room Teacher." *Chicago Schools Journal* 7:18–19.

Rast, Carlisle L. 1960. "Building a Program for the Heterogeneous High School." *Chicago Schools Journal* 42:1–10.

Rast, Joel. 1999. *Remaking Chicago: The Political Origins of Urban Industrial Change*. DeKalb: Northern Illinois University Press.

Ravitch, Diane. 2000. *Left Back: A Century of Failed School Reforms*. New York: Simon and Schuster.

Replogle, Frederick Allen. 1936. "A Study of the Problems Encountered by Senior High School Students in the Selection of a Vocation." Ph.D. diss., University of Chicago.

Richards, Helen. 1924. "Some Evidence of the Reliability of Mental Tests as Prognostic Measures." *Chicago Schools Journal* 6:364–73.

Rosen, Joseph. 1961. "The Story of a School That 'Changed' Successfully: Devotion, Human Warmth Solve School Problems." *Chicago Schools Journal* 42:216–28.

Royster, Richard Stanhope. 1928. "An Investigation of the Vocational Experience and Status of One Hundred Graduates of the Pullman Free School of Manual Training." Master's thesis, University of Chicago.

Rury, John L. 1999. "Race, Space, and the Politics of Chicago's Public Schools: Benjamin Willis and the Tragedy of Urban Education." *History of Education Quarterly* 39, no. 2:117–42.

Ryan, Nellie F. 1939. "Getting Down to Cases." *Chicago Schools Journal* 20:123–28.

Sanders, James W. 1977. *The Education of an Urban Minority: Catholics in Chicago, 1833–1965*. New York: Oxford University Press.

Schiavo, Giovanni E. 1928. *The Italians in Chicago: A Study in Americanization*. Chicago: Italian American Publications.

Schwartz, Charlotte F. Green. 1947. "The Vocational Ambitions of Two Groups of Negro Girls." Master's thesis, University of Chicago.

Shack, William A. 1957. "Social Change in an Isolated Negro Community." Master's thesis, University of Chicago.

Shaw, Stephanie J. 1996. *What a Woman Ought to Be and Do: Black Professional Workers during the Jim Crow Era*. Chicago: University of Chicago Press.

Slayton, Robert A. 1986. *Back of the Yards: The Making of a Local Democracy.* Chicago: University of Chicago Press.

Sleezer, Margaret. 1933. "Change in Methods of Teaching." *Chicago Schools Journal* 15:55–58.

Smith, Timothy L. 1972. "Native Blacks and Foreign Whites: Varying Responses to Educational Opportunity in America, 1880–1950." *Perspectives in American History* 6:309–35.

Spear, Allan H. 1967. *Black Chicago: The Making of a Negro Ghetto.* Chicago: University of Chicago Press.

Spero, Sterling D., and Abram L. Harris. [1931] 1968. *The Black Worker: The Negro and the Labor Movement.* New York: Atheneum.

Strayer, George D., Fred Engelhardt, John K. Norton, Lester Dix, and Newton H. Hegel. 1932. *Report of the Survey of the Schools of Chicago, Illinois.* Vol. 1. New York: Teachers College Press.

Strayer, George D., Paul R. Mort, W. W. Wright, W. B. Featherstone, Milo H. Stewart, D. H. Eikenberry, E. S. Evenden, and F. B. O'Rear. 1932. *Report of the Survey of the Schools of Chicago, Illinois.* Vol. 2. New York: Teachers College Press.

Strayer, George D., Jesse H. Newlon, Herbert B. Bruner, L. Thomas Hopkins, Paul R. Hanna, Lester Dix, J. R. McGaughy, Edwin H. Reeder, Jean Betzner, Jesse F. Williams, Frederick W. Maroney, and L. A. Wilson. 1932. *Report of the Survey of the Schools of Chicago, Illinois.* Vol. 3. New York: Teachers College Press.

Sugrue, Thomas J. 1996. *The Origins of the Urban Crisis: Race and Inequality in Postwar Detroit.* Princeton, NJ: Princeton University Press.

Suloway, Irwin J. 1956. "Chicago's High School Curriculums, 1856–1956." *Chicago Schools Journal* 38:93–98.

Summers, Lillian A., and Adele C. Walden. 1949. "Adjusting Disabled Readers." *Chicago Schools Journal* 30:145–49.

Tobin, Lillian M. 1926–27. "Classification in 6-A and After." *Chicago Schools Journal* 9:131–33.

Tropea, Joseph L. 1987. "Bureaucratic Order and Special Children: Urban Schools, 1890s–1940s." *History of Education Quarterly* 27:29–53.

Tyack, David B., and Larry Cuban. 1995. *Tinkering toward Utopia: A Century of Public School Reform.* Cambridge, MA: Harvard University Press.

Wagenschein, Miriam. 1950. "'Reality Shock': A Study of Beginning Elementary School Teachers." Master's thesis, University of Chicago.

Washington, Forrester B. 1919. "Reconstruction and the Colored Woman." *Life and Labor* 9: 3–7.

Washington Intercollegiate Club of Chicago. 1927. *1927 Intercollegian Wonder Book; or, 1779—The Negro in Chicago—1927.* Chicago: Washington Intercollegiate Club of Chicago.

Wavrinek, Anna J. 1922. "The Failing Pupil." *Chicago Schools Journal* 4:294–97.

Weck, Frederick W. 1925. "The Elimination of Waste in Education." *Chicago Schools Journal* 7:177–81.

Whatley, Warren C. 1990. "Getting a Foot in the Door: 'Learning,' State Dependence, and the Racial Integration of Firms." *Journal of Economic History* 50:43–66.

White, Shane, and Graham White. 1998. *Stylin': African American Expressive Culture from Its Beginnings to the Zoot Suit.* Ithaca, NY: Cornell University Press.

Wight, Ambrose B. 1923. "What the Bureau of Standards and Statistics Expects to Accomplish through Instructional Research Activities." *Chicago Schools Journal* 6:121–24.

Wild, Beulah Temple. 1929. "Special Divisions of the Chicago School System: A Study of the Rooms for Truants and Incorrigibles in the Chicago Schools." Master's thesis, University of Chicago.

Wilson, William Julius. 1987. *The Truly Disadvantaged: The Inner City, the Underclass, and Public Policy.* Chicago: University of Chicago Press.

Wirth, Louis, and Margaret Fuerz, eds. 1938. *Local Community Fact Book 1938.* Chicago: Chicago Recreation Commission.

Wright, Richard R. Jr. 1901. "The Industrial Condition of Negroes in Chicago." B.D. thesis, University of Chicago.

Wrigley, Julia. 1982. *Class Politics and Public Schools: Chicago, 1900–1950.* New Brunswick, NJ: Rutgers University Press.

Yair, Gad. 2000. "Educational Battlefields in America: The Tug-of-War over Students' Engagement with Instruction." *Sociology of Education* 73:247–69.

Zand, Helen Stankiewicz. 1987. *Polish Folkways in America: Community and Family.* Ed. by Eugene Edward Obidinski. Lanham, MA: University Press of America.

Zunz, Olivier. 1982. *The Changing Face of Inequality: Urbanization, Industrial Development, and Immigrants in Detroit, 1880–1920.* Chicago: University of Chicago Press.

Index